JOHN SOMMERS-FLANAGAN
RITA SOMMERS-FLANAGAN

Tough Kids, Cool Counseling:
User-Friendly Approaches
With Challenging Youth

AMERICAN
COUNSELING
ASSOCIATION

5999 Stevenson Avenue
Alexandria, VA 22304-3300

Tough Kids, Cool Counseling

10 9 8 7 6 5 4

American Counseling Association
5999 Stevenson Avenue
Alexandria, VA 22304

Director of Acquisitions
Carolyn Baker

Director of Publishing Systems
Michael Comlish

Cover design by Jennifer Sterling, Spot Color

Library of Congress Cataloging-in-Publication Data
Sommers-Flanagan, John, 1957-
    Tough kids, cool counseling: user friendly approaches
    with challenging youths / John Sommers-Flanagan,
    Rita Sommers-Flanagan.
       p.   cm.
    Includes bibliographical references and index.
    ISBN 1-55620-172-9 (alk. paper)
      1. Problem Youth—Counseling of.
  I. Sommers-Flanagan, Rita 1953-
  II. Title.
RJ506.P63S66   1997
362.74'86—dc21   97-5512
                                            CIP

CONTENTS

PREFACE

All too frequently, efforts to counsel young people are met with resistance. This is particularly true when children or teenagers are brought to therapy because of behavior patterns that bother or irritate adults. Counseling becomes problematic when adults are more motivated to change a young client's behavior than is the client. Specifically, the problem involves how to work most effectively with young clients who do *not* think they have problems and do *not* want to engage in counseling.

In part, this book is about successfully circumventing youthful resistance to therapy. More importantly, it is about helping counselors and therapists relate to young clients, ultimately helping them to say "*Yes,* I want and value your assistance." We believe many, if not most, "resistant" young clients desperately want and need adult attention and assistance. In this sense, young clients are not so much resistant as they are different. This book focuses on how counselors can capture the interest, attention, and motivation of young clients, who are often much different than their counselors.

Overall, we refer to our approach to working with young clients as "user-friendly." Similar to user-friendly computer programs, the strategies we describe in this book are designed to facilitate access to a useful resource; in this case we are in the business of facilitating access to counseling, rather than access to computer technology.

As a part of our user-friendly orientation, we want to clearly acknowledge our debt to existing therapy procedures and approaches. We draw from behavioral, cognitive, family systems, solution-oriented, psychodynamic, gestalt, and hypnotherapeutic treatment approaches. What we describe in the following chapters is not new; instead, we offer user-friendly methods for applying traditional treatment approaches to challenging young clients.

We hope this book will be useful to mental health care workers from many professional backgrounds. While we recognize the differences in background, training, and mission among helping professionals (e.g., counselors, psychologists, social workers, psychiatrists, family therapists), we also believe these professions share enormous common ground. Because of our belief in this common ground, throughout the book we use "therapist" and "therapy" interchangeably with "counselor" and "counseling." We apologize to those who might think a distinction is warranted between these terms, but at present we believe the conceptualizations, techniques, and goals of therapy are quite similar in most cases to those same aspects of counseling. Thus, we use the terms interchangeably, even though we recognize that there are sometimes differences in the activities which they represent.

This book was written in accordance with ethical principles in counseling and psychology. We are committed to nonsexist language and have used a variety of strategies to balance our use of male and female pronouns. Additionally, in most cases, client material is sufficiently disguised to render identification of clients impossible. Otherwise, client permission has been sought and obtained.

TREATMENT PLANNING

As the astute reader will note, the title of this book uses generic terms which label certain youth as "tough" and "challenging." We chose these terms because they are descriptive of the internal reaction of the professional, not because they are particularly diagnostic of young people. On occasion, almost any child or adolescent can present as tough or challenging to an adult charged with teaching, caring for, guiding, counseling, or raising her or him. Therefore, even if the youth in question do not meet specific diagnostic criteria from DSM-IV (for instance, oppositional defiant or conduct disorder; American Psychiatric Association, 1994), this book will provide useful strategies for professionals.

This book is less about diagnosis and treatment planning and more about developing positive working relationships with young clients. Good treatment plans are based on careful analyses of the presenting problem(s), the environment(s) in which the problems occur, and the time, setting, and resources available to bring about some sort of solution or growth or positive development that will help resolve the problem. We contend that the *relationship* between the referred youth and the professional, which serves as a foundation for both assessment and counseling, is as central in determining outcome as accurate diagnosis and clear treatment planning. Obviously, from our perspective the initial treatment planning objective in virtually every child or adolescent counseling case is to establish an adequate working relationship. Without adequate rapport and relationship, young clients simply will not implement counseling techniques and treatment plans.

Due to our relationship-oriented bias, the strategies described in this book are primarily designed to enhance the therapeutic or counseling relationship between counselor and young client. Use of these strategies does not correspond with a certain diagnosis; rather, the needs of the professional relationship should dictate their use. Effective mental health providers constantly assess the quality of the client—counselor relationship and adjust interactions, pace, and strategies accordingly.

To address issues pertaining to counseling challenging or difficult young clients, this book is divided into three parts. Part One, titled "User-FriendlyFoundations," includes two chapters focusing on how to understand and emotionally connect with young clients. In Chapter 1 we address a central premise of the book: that counseling with young people is analogous to cross-cultural counseling. There are many physical, social, and psychological aspects of childhood and adolescence which counselors must consider when working with young people. In Chapter 2 we describe user-friendly strategies for establishing rapport, gathering information, and conducting informal assessments with young clients. The emphasis is on managing first impressions, collaborative approaches for identifying treatment goals, and specific informal assessment techniques (e.g., evaluating attachment, self-esteem, and self-concept using casual or informal methods).

Part Two (Chapters 3–6) is titled "User-Friendly Strategies." These chapters are extremely technique-oriented. They include numerous techniques applicable to challenging young clients in a variety of situations. Techniques in Chapter 3 focus broadly on how counselors can quickly modify client emotional states. Chapter 4 describes a number of user-friendly treatment techniques designed to change maladaptive cognitions, behaviors, and interpersonal relationships. In Chapter 5, we explain the use of both indirect and directive storytelling, providing examples of various types of stories that counselors can effectively implement. Additionally, Chapter 5 includes an example of a structured hypnotic procedure which therapists may apply in either an individual or group format. Chapter 6 focuses exclusively on approaches to parent education and training. Due to the importance of acknowledging and addressing the many factors that influence child and adolescent development, we place parent education and training approaches within the context of ecological theory. Several methods of influencing parents are described and discussed.

Part Three, consisting of Chapters 7 through 9, is titled "Special Topics in Treating Young Clients". In Chapters 7 through 9 we address special topics including suicide assessment and management, how to determine whether young clients should be referred for medication evaluations, and issues related to therapy termination. Each of these topics: suicide, medications, and termination, are frequently present and problematic for counselors working with challenging young clients.

Finally, to the readers of these book, we wish you luck and success in your adventures in counseling young people.

ACKNOWLEDGMENTS

We wish to thank Carolyn Baker, Director of Acquisitions of American Counseling Association Publications, for her insightful editing and congenial manner. Carolyn's balanced style makes it easy to write for ACA; it has been a pleasure to work with her. Brett Steenbarger and David Scherer provided efficient, insightful, and invaluable professional reviews of the manuscript. Their thoughts, reactions, and suggestions are peppered throughout the book—our gratitude to them is immense.

To our daughters, Chelsea and Rylee, who endured sharing the computer and lugging the luggage, we say thanks and we promise appropriate compensation. And to JSF, I, RSF, say, "Way to go, Elmo. You sure we got enough references?" And to RSF, JSF says, "How about another title change?"

ABOUT THE AUTHORS

JOHN SOMMERS-FLANAGAN, Ph.D. is a clinical psychologist and executive director of Families First, a parent education program in Missoula, Montana. John received his Ph.D. in 1986 after completing his predoctoral internship at the S.U.N.Y. Health Science Center at Syracuse, New York (where he had the pleasure of working with Brett Steenbarger, Roger Greenberg, Michael Gordon, and others). He maintains an active private practice, is a consultant for Vocational Resources, Inc., Big Brothers and Big Sisters of Missoula, and Community Care, Inc., and is an adjunct assistant professor in counselor education and social work at the University of Montana. John has numerous professional publications and conducts workshops locally, regionally, and nationally.

RITA SOMMERS-FLANAGAN, Ph.D. is an associate professor and director of counselor education at the University of Montana. Rita obtained her Ph.D. in clinical psychology from the University of Montana in 1989. She completed her internship at the Morrison Center for Children and Families in Portland, Oregon. Rita is active in a number of University and community organizations, including service as a consultant for the Missoula Vet Center and for Seasons, a community-based family-systems grieving program. Rita was awarded a teaching exchange in Belize, Central America in Spring, 1996. She has conducted research and/or published in the areas of ethics, gender issues, childhood depression, and multicultural counseling.

PART I

User-Friendly Foundations

1

Adventures in Child and Adolescent Counseling

On Tuesday morning at eight o'clock a stranger walked into the Grass Valley office of the Overland Stagecoach Company. "When does the next stage leave for La Grande?" he asked. "I have to catch the five o'clock train."

Pete Parker, the ticket agent, laughed in his face. "You're outta luck Mister. There ain't NO next stage to La Grande. There ain't no next stage nowhere. Not today, not tomorrow. Might not be one for another week. Ain't you heard? There's avalanches in the pass, road agents on the road. ...On top of that the river's rising and the bridge is most likely out. If you wanna go to La Grande, you're gonna hafta fly. Ain't that right, boys?" (from Charlie Drives the Stage; Kimmel, 1989, p. 2)

ADVENTURES IN COUNSELING
YOUNG CLIENTS

When counseling young people, therapists should be prepared for an adventure. Sometimes connecting with young clients is like negotiating through avalanches, dodging road agents, and crossing rickety bridges. Providing counseling or psychotherapy to young clients is an adventure; depending on your perspective, it can be fraught with peril or imbued with excitement.

The challenges of counseling young clients originate in the cultural differences between adults and young people. In many very important ways, work with young people is *multicultural* work. Most adults we know do not watch Music Television and they do not get up at 3:00 AM to stand in line for Pearl Jam tickets. Most adults do not play Pogs, collect "X-men" cards, engage in burping contests, burn the drag, get chased on the playground by leering boys, or get harassed at the bus stop by neighborhood bullies. As they balance their checkbooks, pay their mortgages, sip their coffee, answer their voice mail, and attend marriage enhancement seminars, there is no doubt that most social workers, counselors, and therapists have daily experiences very different from those of their young clients, clients who are busily bumming cigarettes, skipping classes, and reading comic books.

Given that adults and young people are simultaneously engaging in divergent cultural practices, or even living in two different worlds and certainly facing very different developmental tasks, it is not surprising that counseling children is very different from counseling adults. Unusual things happen when children hang around your office. Children are sometimes not conscious or careful about where they put their hands and fingers. Although neither of us have had adult clients "accidently" poke us in the eye, scratch themselves carelessly in private places, or suddenly begin picking their nose, our child clients regularly do so. Similarly, our adult clients rarely lose control of bodily functions during the therapy hour, but children will lose control of their bowels, dash out of the room for imminent bathroom breaks, and launch their "lunch" onto the carpet in the midst of group therapy sessions.

Adolescent clients provide their own, developmentally unique adventures. For example, whereas adults rarely refuse to talk during therapy, it is not unusual for teenagers to give their therapist the silent treatment. Many teenagers have very different views on interpersonal boundaries as well. They may spontaneously begin asking about your intimate sexual experiences, comment on the size of your rear end, suddenly start rummaging through your desk drawers, or impulsively ask if you might be available to drive them on a 500-mile trip over the weekend.

It is an understatement to say that therapy with children and adolescents often requires a departure from traditional "talk therapy" or contemporary behavior modification. For many, if not most young clients, adult-oriented approaches to counseling do not provide an appropriate fit. Counseling young people requires that therapists be prepared for, and take advantage of, a wide range of behaviors; young clients can be constructive and cooperative one moment and obstructionistic and sullen the next. Young clients are predictably unpredictable. This is particularly true with the population of young clients on whom we focus in this book.

Who Are the "Challenging" Young Clients?

A number of years ago we began offering classes, seminars, and workshops on how to work effectively with "difficult" or "treat-ment-resistant" young clients. Our purpose in these workshops was to teach therapists specific techniques we had found useful for working with "resistant" young people. We believed that young clients found certain therapeutic interactions more interesting and engaging than others and subsequently, our difficult young clients became gener-ally more compliant and cooperative. Essentially, we were teaching therapists to make therapy more friendly or accessible to young people. We called this therapeutic approach "user-friendly." Our underlying rationale was that if counselors can learn about, under-stand, and appreciate child and adolescent culture then they will interact (or interface) in a user-friendly, cross-culturally effective manner with young clients. Obviously, therapists facilitate coun-seling and psychotherapy with young people when they learn lan-guage and norms associated with youth culture and become comfortable in the adult–youth intercultural exchanges that occur when relating well with young people.

Over the past several years our views on working with young clients have continued to shift. This shift has occurred partly due to continued therapeutic work with difficult young clients, but also as a function of feedback from professional colleagues. In particular, our view of what we previously defined as "treatment-resistant behavior" has changed. We have begun to understand that, in the words of one of our colleagues, it may be counselors who are youth-resistant as much as it is youth who are treatment-resistant (B. Steenbarger, personal communication, October 13, 1996). After all, often upon leaving our offices they quickly and efficiently connect and interact with their peers. Further, young people are frequently very suggestible and influenced by one another and by certain types of adults. Consequently, it appears that although many young clients behave in ways that might be viewed by adult therapists as resistant (e.g., trying to sleep during a counseling session), this apparently resistant behavior is, in many instances, an artifact of cultural differences between adults and children (Newman, 1994). As in all multicultural counseling, the responsibility for making the connection and doing therapeutic work falls on the professional, not on the client (Patterson, 1996).

Generally, young clients who present therapists (and most other adults in their environment) with great challenges are those who display behaviors associated with inattentiveness, impulsivity, defiance, opposition to authority (or an anti-establishment attitude), and irritability. Further, this type of young person frequently has academic or learning problems and typically comes to therapy or to see the school counselor only when strongly encouraged or even forced by their parents, teachers, principals, or probation officers. Often, these same people have labeled the youth as delinquent or predelinquent, and many referred young clients meet diagnostic criteria for attention-deficit/hyperactivity disorder, oppositional defiant disorder, or conduct disorder (American Psychiatric Association, 1994). In other words, some of the most challenging young clients are either reluctant about or opposed to receiving psychological treatment, frequently have symptoms of disruptive behavior disorders (as defined by the 4th edition of the Diagnostic and Statistical Manual of Mental Disorders DSM-IV), and/or frequently are experiencing depressive symptoms (e.g., sadness or irritability) as well as academic problems or learning disorders. Not surprisingly, young clients who fit into this general group also sometimes display signs and symptoms consistent with attachment problems (Ainsworth, 1989; Rutter, 1979).

The overall purpose of this book is to provide a wide variety of mental health professionals with interesting and effective cognitive, behavioral, emotional, and interpersonal change strategies and techniques for working with young clients who initially present as resistant to therapy. The point is to help counselors and psychotherapists become more user-friendly in their work with young clients. User-friendly counseling strategies are specifically aimed at making counseling more accessible, palatable, sensible, and even enticing to young clients who are initially unenthused about participating in any kind of therapeutic endeavor. User-friendly techniques help counselors more effectively and more consistently meet the challenges of working with difficult young people.

Empirical Foundations

Unfortunately, in the child/adolescent counseling and psychotherapy field there has been little systematic research establishing the efficacy of specific techniques with specific treatment populations (Hibbs & Jensen, 1996). This is particularly true with regard to treatment techniques for children and adolescents who are generally disagreeable and specifically opposed to seeing a therapist (Selekman, 1993; Sommers-Flanagan & Sommers-Flanagan, 1996a). Quite frankly, we have found a number of existing treatment approaches to be of minimal value in reaching undermotivated young clients. Many young clients hold anti-establishment attitudes, are rebellious, and express anger about being dragged by their parents (or teacher or probation officer) to see a counselor. In some ways, their anger is justified, and certainly their rebelliousness has a developmentally appropriate quality. Much like minority groups, young people are ignored or oppressed and the dominant culture (adults) pay attention to them primarily after they become bothersome and much like minority groups, many young people are angry, resentful, and opposed to what they view as adult coercion (Sidman, 1989).

In response to working with young people who are accustomed to opposing authority we have developed stylistic strategies and specific assessment and therapy techniques designed to hook difficult young clients into participating in potentially therapeutic interactions. Although originally designed to facilitate treatment processes, we are hopeful that these approaches also will eventually show themselves to positively affect treatment outcomes as well. In many cases, the techniques in this book are designed simply to enhance the therapeutic relationship, assuming that more positive therapy relationships will translate into greater youth cooperation with more traditional and empirically validated procedures (Hibbs & Jensen, 1996; Wright & Davis, 1994).

Ongoing study and observations of difficult young clients and existing therapy approaches which have shown empirical promise form the inspiration and basis for our work (Hibbs & Jensen, 1996; Weisz, Donenberg, Han, & Weiss, in press). We believe that certain truths about difficult young people are essential to embrace prior to attempting to work with them therapeutically. Consequently, we begin this text with a review of developmental issues that can make conducting therapy with young clients different from, and perhaps more difficult than, conducting similar therapy with adults. Working with young, angry clients who initially oppose and resist therapeutic contact can be an enormously challenging journey, but we believe that with adequate preparation and the right attitude it is a worthwhile and gratifying adventure.

DEVELOPMENTAL MISCONCEPTIONS

Children are not like us. They are beings apart: Impenetrable, unapproachable. They inhabit not our world but a world we have lost and can never recover. We do not remember childhood—we imagine it. We search for it, in vain, through layers of obscuring dust, and recover some bedraggled shreds of what we think it was. And all the while the inhabitants of this world are among us, like Aborigines, like Minoans, people from elsewhere, safe in their own time-capsule. (from Moon Tiger, Lively, 1989, p. 4)

One of our favorite erroneous statements, first coined by zoologist Ernst Haeckel (1874) and oft repeated, is: "Ontogeny recapitulates phylogeny" (quoted in Mahoney, 1991). This claim, also known as the "Law of Recapitulation," refers to the belief that each developing organism repeats every stage of its species' evolutionary history during its individual developmental process. Perhaps the Law of Recapitulation has maintained its tenacious hold in scientific writings due to semantic elegance. Or perhaps the idea it suggests is just so astonishing—it is one of those die-hard conversation stoppers evoking intriguing images of the fetus progressing from a one-celled amoeba through acquiring gills, gaining and losing a tail, and so on. Despite its popularity, ontogeny simply does not recapitulate phylogeny; it has been thoroughly disproven and is no longer used to explain biological development (Garstang, 1922; Lickliter & Berry, 1990).

We believe there is a similar erroneous belief present in many adult humans. If stated, a generic version of this belief would go something like this: "Been there, done that." From conception to the present state of the individual, there is an erroneous belief that we can understand a younger human being's experience simply because we were young once, too. We have heard many statements from adults that spring from this belief, including, but not limited to, the following:

"This is my child. She's just like me when I was her age."
"My dad spanked me and I turned out just fine."
"I know what it is like to give in to peer pressure; I used drugs when I was a teenager too."
"Big brothers are supposed to pick on their little sisters; my big brother picked on me."
"The best solution to the sexual pressures kids feel today is abstinence. We need to go back to having values of self-restraint and monogamy, just like the good old days."

Implied in these statements is the belief that adults, having experienced their own childhoods and adolescences, have accumulated information and knowledge which makes them experts on how to grow up well. The unfortunate truth is that no matter how strongly adults believe that they "know what's best," most children and adolescents would beg to differ. In fact, if you are moved to field test this claim and happen to have a willful teenager in the family or neighborhood, directly tell the teen how he or she should behave, adding a phrase like, "I'm telling you this for your own good," or, "I know more about this than you do." In our experience, the response, either spoken or communicated in posture and facial expression, will be something like," Yeah, sure. Like you know what's best for me. You're clueless. You don't know how I feel or what I think. Where do you get off telling me how I should act?"

Perhaps what is most interesting about the type of interaction that occurs when adults try to tell strong-willed young people how they should act is that both the adult *and* the youth have strong evidence to support their perspectives; this makes fertile ground for conflict and opposition. Specifically, adults are often correct in their belief that they know what is best for young people. How often have you heard adult friends say something like, "I wish I could go back and live that part of my life over again, knowing what I know now."

It is a basic truism that age and experience tend to increase wisdom and good judgment (Lerner, 1990). At some level it would be so much nicer, not to mention safer, if we could directly guide and possibly even control our children's and our young clients' crucial decisions and behaviors. Think of all the teenage pregnancies, automobile accidents, sexual assaults, and damaging drug use that could be averted.

On the other hand, despite the logical and rational strength behind the "father (or mother or counselor) knows best" argument, the child or teenager's response carries equal validity. After all, from the child's perspective, most adults really are clueless regarding what it is like to be a youth struggling with contemporary issues. In essence, statements that young clients often make (e.g., "You don't know how I feel or what I think") are true. Adults will find themselves making little progress if they try to convince children otherwise. In addition, adults who try to coerce young people into compliance and cooperation often activate the very (oppositional and negativistic) developmental urges they are trying to suppress.

Although every human adult has passed through a series of similar physical, emotional, and psychological developmental phases beginning prenatally and continuing through life, there is ample evidence that our memories of ourselves passing through those stages are anything but complete and accurate (Loftus, 1992; Neisser, 1991). In addition, each of us experienced childhood in a particular place and at a particular time in human history, with a unique family position in a family that has now grown up. Our peers and our culture surrounded us. Our individual talents, drives, deficits, and temperament influenced our environments, even as they influenced us. In short, then was then and now is now; diversity, cultural and otherwise, is ubiquitous. You are you. The child is someone else. Having been a child not only does *not* make you an expert on humans who are currently children, but also, it sometimes even works against you.

"Okay," you may say. "I'll grant you that I may not know all there is to know about being a teenager right now, but how could my having been a teenager work against me?" While this is not a therapist self-help book, we do encourage you to explore that question. It is the rare person who claims a perfect childhood. In fact, we would recommend that such a person find a different field than social work, counseling, or psychology because to claim a perfect childhood is, in our humble opinion, an indicator of a person either vastly out of touch with being human or in deep denial (or both). Neither make for the empathy, acceptance, compassion, and insight that we feel are necessary to conduct effective therapy. Our basic point is to be careful with your projections!

Before reading our ideas, stop and consider for yourself how having been the kind of child *you* were, with the kind of childhood *you* had, could work against your understanding the world of a child in the here and now. You might even want to jot down a few ideas or imagine your childhood for a little while. Becoming effective in working with difficult youth requires ongoing internal work and awareness on your part. Why? Although our reasoning on that question follows, we encourage you to generate your own thoughts on this matter as well.

Your Assumption of Similarity May Be Incorrect

The first reason having been a child can work against you is the assumption that you know what a child is experiencing because you can remember experiencing something similar to what the child is describing. You may think you know what it means to Kelsey that her dad is upset at her for her math grade because your mom was often upset with you because of your science grade. You think you know what Jason feels like as an overweight, uncoordinated kid who never gets picked to play games because in fourth grade, you were picked last once too. Or you were fat or skinny or had an eating disorder too. Sometimes, you might be right and you might have special insight into how a particular child is feeling and thinking. However, other times—often times—you will be wrong and the child may be offended when an adult whom she views as having little commonality acts too familiar.

So why is this any different from adults working with adults? Aren't we susceptible to the same error with adults? To a degree, yes, of course. We must always be vigilant in monitoring assumptions based on projections of our own experiences and feelings onto others. Sam's experience of stage fright may be very different than yours, and you could make the error of assuming you know just how Sam feels. But Sam is an adult, like you. It is easier, in the span of a few sentences, for Sam to go on describing his experience and for you to compare and say internally "This guy's experience is much different than mine." Because he is operating in the adult world *with* you, a natural compare-and-contrast thinking process happens which can correct an inaccurate assumption on your part, and if that doesn't happen, it is likely that Sam can simply inform you that your assumption is wrong.

Children, however, are living in a different set of circumstances than you are. Someone tells them when to get up, when to go to bed, what they can eat, what they can wear—even when they can go to the bathroom. In workshops we conduct, we tell participants that they will need to raise their hand and signal if they would like to go to the bathroom before they will be excused. A murmur of disbelief and protest goes through the crowd. Then laughter. So easily, we forget the details of our lives as children. We think we remember, and we may remember, but sometimes our projective assumptions are incorrect. Therefore, projective assumptions of understanding are more likely to be in error and are much less likely to be corrected either by the compare-and-contrast process in adult–adult conversations or by the child. Even when the child does find a way to say "No, you do not know what I am experiencing," we may be tempted find a way to interpret this protest as oppositional behavior... or lack of insight... or difficulties with attachment.

Your Own Psychological Pain May Interfere With Objectivity

This brings us to the second reason why our own childhood can make it hard to work with young clients. Listening to the struggles of kids in the here and now is a threatening process. We have successfully "forgotten" much of the pain of our own childhoods. The pain we have not forgotten, we usually avoid thinking about. The danger in listening to a child's painful story is that either we will put up thick defenses against the memories of our own pain and come off as a cool, aloof expert, or we will overidentify with the child (often in error, as we have discussed) and wallow in our own newly reopened anger, sadness, fright, rejection, or longing. Either way, we risk failing as a counselor. We must be able to come alongside the pain, share it with empathy, carry a portion of it, and still be able to clear the way forward. We cannot avoid feeling and touching the pain, but also we cannot allow it to overwhelm us. It is especially difficult to have a balanced perspective when dealing with children's emotional pain.

As a very important counterpoint to all we have just said, it is essential to note that our experiences of having been children can also be central to our success in establishing a therapeutic relationship and conducting successful therapy with young clients. For this to be the case, the following all are necessary:

1. We must seek to remember our childhoods honestly in all their pain and glory; if there is unfinished business in our past, at the very least, we must bring it to awareness. Ideally,

we should work to bring healing and closure to troubling memories and experiences.

2. We must allow for the possibility of errors in our memory and never insist that because we remember things a certain way, that is the way it was and is.

3. We must allow for the possibility that our childhood has very little similarity to the childhoods of young clients. Children of any given peer group and time period constitute their own subculture. It is difficult for baby boomers to fully join and understand "generation X-ers."

4. Even when our experiences are similar to those of a young client, we must understand that our clients may not see it that way. As adults, counselors look so much different than young clients that it takes creative imagination for them to envision us as having had problems similar to theirs.

5. Prior to self-disclosing to a child/adolescent client, it is important to closely scrutinize motives associated with intended disclosures. This is especially important because limited self-disclosure can be an effective therapeutic strategy when working with young people. However, it is crucial for counselors to have insight into the possible motives which sometimes underlie self-disclosure as a therapeutic technique (Sommers-Flanagan & Sommers-Flanagan, 1993).

You May Try To Parent (Rather Than Counsel) Young Clients

A final danger in working with children is the urge to be a parent rather than a therapist. This has less to do with having been a child and more to do with the fact that our species requires a long period of parenting activities to keep little ones alive and developing. We are probably biologically predisposed to some sort of parenting activity in the presence of small people—especially small people in distress (Ainsworth, 1979; Rutter, 1979). It is important to be very clear that our role in the young client's life is that of therapist—not parent. With many challenging young clients, this is good news, but once in a while, even with very irritating adolescents, therapists will catch themselves having acted or reacted in a most parental fashion. Ongoing peer supervision, establishing solid boundaries, and keeping therapy goals clearly in mind all mitigate against this potential pitfall.

DEVELOPMENTAL CONSIDERATIONS

One way to minimize our tendency to view young people as miniature adults is to remind ourselves of the ways in which children and adolescents systematically differ from adults. The remainder of this chapter highlights a few therapeutically relevant, basic developmental differences between children and adults. We do not thoroughly explain any particular developmental model, but it is important to note that theories of human development have matured from early linear or stage models to more comprehensive transformational or transactional models (Bronfenbrenner, 1986; Minuchin & Fishman, 1981; D. Scherer, personal communication, October 24, 1996). These contemporary models emphasize the reciprocal, interactive course of development as children and adolescents affect and are affected by their social environment and family ecology. The following developmental concerns and differences are essential to remember as the counselor becomes part of the child's social environment.

The Role of Play

"I'm grown up now," he said. "But I do remember when I was very, very small and first came to see you. I remember the toys, the doll house and the sand and the men and women and children in the world I built. I remember the bells and the time to go and the truck. I remember the water and the paint and the dishes. I remember our office and our books and our recording machine. I remember all the people. And I remember how you played with me" (From Dibs: In Search of Self, Axline, 1964, p. 211).

For children, play is serious work. There is no doubting the role of play in child development. Children play to resolve conflicts, to stimulate cognitive development, and to test their skills and limits and the skills and limits of those around them. Children who do not play generally have serious cognitive, emotional, and behavioral disturbances (Rutter & Rutter, 1993).

It is crucial for therapists to integrate play and playfulness into therapy with young clients. There are many ways to integrate play into therapy. Although discussion of formal play therapy techniques within this book is limited, we recognize the importance of play in normal development. For us, integrating play and playfulness into child/adolescent therapy is not a question of whether, but rather a question of how much.

Although integrating play into therapy with younger children is relatively simple and straightforward, being playful with adolescents or teenagers is more complex and perhaps more challenging. Consequently, we discuss how to be playful with older children and adolescents throughout this text, but we focus on this dimension especially when discussing methods of getting acquainted and developing rapport with young clients (see Chapter 2).

Social Development

In terms of social development, childhood and adolescence are generally characterized by an odd combination of social conformity *and* social deviance. That is, there is strong pressure for generational conformity during childhood and adolescence, but at the same time, there is also pressure to deviate from accepted adult norms and sometimes even pressure to deviate in certain ways from peer-based norms. Over the years quite an extensive literature and general discussion regarding social or peer pressure has developed (Dupre, Miller, Gold, & Rospenda, 1995; Fridrich & Flannery, 1995); there is most certainly strong pressure on children and teenagers, both through stereotypical media presentations and within school or neighborhood social subsystems, to conform to a particular standard of "cool" behavior (Sommers-Flanagan, Sommers-Flanagan, & Davis, 1993). These standards include, but are not limited to whether it is acceptable to dress in particular clothing; engage in sexual relationships; participate in fights, assaults, etcetera; experiment with drugs; perform well in school; and befriend members of other groups, cultures, or the other sex.

For younger children, social standards often include judgments about whether it is "cool" to talk with boys (or girls), play particular games or sports, and watch various television shows. With regard to the latter issue, we had an opportunity to observe one of our daughters a few years ago as she discussed with a fellow first grader the social appropriateness of watching the television show *Barney*, the purple dinosaur. Apparently the social rules were very clear: It was acceptable to watch *Barney* as a kindergartner, but completely immature to watch *Barney* as a first grader.

From an adult perspective, child and adolescent social standards can become rather tiresome. Many adults and parents try to directly coach youth into "not caring" about their peers' harsh judgments. It is generally easier for someone outside of a particular social system to disregard its norms. Unfortunately, young people, especially teenagers who are becoming increasingly self-conscious, are exceptionally sensitive and perceptive when it comes to discerning social norms and judgments. As we have seen from experimentation in social psychology, increased self-awareness and self-consciousness can be excruciatingly painful (Baumeister & Scher, 1988; Carver & Scheier, 1981; Raymond, Dowrick, & Kleinke, 1993). Avoiding the pain of negative social judgments and their accompanying (and sometimes even more harsh) self-judgments provides young clients with a motivational source that is hard for generally uncool adults and parents to overcome. Counselors must strive to remain as aware as possible regarding young clients' social norms and perspectives and associated motivational factors. Although many young clients will deny it, peer pressure is a powerful, and often negative, social force in their lives.

Fortunately, maintaining peer approval and deviating from adult standards are not the only factors that influence adolescent identity development. Perhaps the most significant factor of all, children's tendencies to select adults with whom they identify and after whom they model their behavior is a powerful force that shapes identity development and child/adolescent behavior (Bandura, Ross, & Ross, 1963; Bienert & Schneider, 1993). Effective counselors (similar to effective parents) somehow become attractive and respected enough for children and teens to select them as positive role models. The following behaviors and qualities can help motivated adults attain this most-coveted position of positive role model.

1. Demonstrate integrity. That is, follow through on promises, carefully consider and reflect on client questions, and behave in ways that show young clients that you are thoughtful, considerate, and consistent.

2. Be interested in youth and youth activities. As noted above, children and teenagers are very sensitive to social cues. They will know if you are genuinely interested in them or not. This requires an attitude of openness toward and interest in a wide range of youth behaviors and thoughts.

3. Respect them and their opinions. This does not mean that you *agree* with their behaviors or opinions, but it does mean suspending quick judgments and criticisms. Most young people referred for counseling already have experienced their share of adult criticism.

4. Emphasize the importance of personal qualities such as competence, self-awareness, and personal growth. It is virtually impossible for adults *not* to have value-laden expectations regarding how young persons should think and behave. Consequently, when transmitting such values, espouse values that will facilitate positive self-development and constructive social behavior. The message should communicate something like, "I want you to be able to make constructive decisions in your life. I know we have different values, that we come from different generations, and that we may not always agree on how you should behave, but I am mostly interested in helping you obtain skills for analyzing and evaluating your own behavior in a healthy and constructive manner."

5. Maintain a sense of humor. It is crucial for adults to appreciate child and adolescent humor—to laugh *with* young people. Whether this involves suffering through redundant and tiresome "knock-knock" jokes or laughing with a client who thinks it is incredibly funny that a classmate "farted" in class (see Chapter 5), making an effort to see humor from the young person's perspective can be both difficult and worthwhile. And

as a final note: This does not work in reverse. Young clients are *not* and will not be responsible for finding your humor funny. If your jokes are not funny, it is your problem, not theirs.

During adolescence, some young people begin to rebel not only against parental or authority figures, but also against their own peer group. Essentially, as Erikson's psychosocial theory suggests, in the process of establishing an identity teenagers begin rejecting some of the social and authority pressures that have been placed on them for so long (Erikson, 1968). In a search for identity and individuation, many teens pierce their bodies, tattoo their skin, dye their hair, and simply refuse to conform to conventional standards (JSF worked with one boy who, at 17, refused to wash his hair for 2 months because he believed that shampoos were damaging to his delicate hair).

If counselors assume a strong position of authority, they run the risk of further activating an already active adolescent drive for self-definition (Church, 1994; Sommers-Flanagan & Sommers-Flanagan, 1995a). In the case of the boy who would not wash his hair, it was tempting to emphasize the basic importance of health and hygiene and argue directly for at least occasional hair washing. It would have been a rational position—a position very similar to the approach previously utilized by frustrated group home staff who had failed to persuade this independent young man of the merits of clean hair.

Instead, JSF explored the issue empathically, respecting his age, his right to make adult choices, the delicate quality of his hair, and noting that JSF himself was certainly not an expert on hair care but that such experts undoubtedly existed. The result was an eventual agreement that he would consult with a hair professional. Finally, after consulting with a hair professional, he was able to purchase and began using specially designed shampoo that did not damage his "sensitive hair." This outcome was clearly facilitated by taking a position that was basically respectful of his perspective. In the end, he was proud of his special shampoo and of how he had battled with the group home staff for the right to deal with his hair in his own way.

Cognitive Competencies and Limitations

Cognitive competencies and limitations are defined as thinking skills and abilities that enable or limit children and adolescents in their efforts to function effectively in the world. These competencies and limitations include, but are not limited to cognitive developmental dynamics; calendar time, temporal order, and time duration; and thinking styles.

Cognitive developmental dynamics. Over the years, Piaget's stage theory of cognitive development has served as a standard from which virtually all theories of cognitive development are derived and measured (Piaget, 1965, 1975). As we might expect from a theory formulated over six decades ago, many in the field have strongly criticized, reevaluated, and in some cases, disproven some of Piaget's specific views of cognitive development (Baillargeon, 1987; Lempers, Flavell, & Flavell, 1977; Vygotsky, 1987). Nonetheless, Piaget's concepts of cognitive adaptation, assimilation, accommodation, and the basic nature of his cognitive stages of development remain remarkably useful in understanding child and adolescent cognitive development.

Piaget's concepts are so robust that Allen Ivey, a prominent force in counseling, used concepts and terminology from Piaget's developmental theory as the foundation for his "Developmental Counseling and Therapy" approach (Ivey, 1986, 1991). Ivey (1991) stated that developmental counseling and therapy: "... is a new interpretation of Piaget that illustrates how cognitive and affective development are manifested in the counseling and therapy session" (p. 4). Specifically, Ivey (1991) identified adults as generally fitting into sensorimotor, concrete operational, formal operational, and dialectical/systemic (postformal) categories in terms of their emotional, cognitive, and behavioral development.

In the spirit of Piaget's and Ivey's developmental formulations, the behavioral qualities of certain difficult young people can be understood as a manifestation of their cognitive developmental style. We emphasize *style* because recent and current research on development in general and cognitive stage theory in particular suggest that developmental changes occur in a gradual and interactive way, rather than in a linear and discrete manner (Baillargeon, 1987; Brofenbrenner, 1977, 1986). The following case example illustrates how Piaget's and Ivey's developmental concepts can be applied in formulating counseling approaches which may be effective with challenging youth. Abe, an 11-year-old American Indian boy, was referred for counseling because of repeating patterns of impulsive and overactive behavior. When he arrived for his first session he was quickly drawn to his counselor's book shelf (which contained a variety of sports cards that were displayed, in part, to facilitate rapport and relationship building between the counselor and young clients). After examining the bookshelf Abe moved to the desk and briefly explored several drawers, while tossing Pogs onto the floor and inquiring "Why do you have all this stuff?" By the end of the hour, Abe had fingered virtually every item in his counselor's office and he had either spontaneously used or queried regarding the use and origin of most items. In addition to being grossly impulsive and overactive, Abe was clearly a boy who was profoundly curious regarding his environment.

In attempting to understand the meaning and function of Abe's first session behavior, it was tempting to hypothesize regarding psychodynamics that may have contributed to Abe's intense curiosity and inquisitiveness. Certainly, his environmental scanning and scrutiny might have reflected a concern with safety, potential danger, and compensating efforts to establish control. It was also tempting, especially given the movement toward quick treatment and diagnosis associated with a managed care environment, to prematurely categorize and label Abe as a boy suffering from attention-deficit/hyperactivity disorder (ADHD) and to refer for medication treatment (American Psychiatric Association, 1994; Fox, 1995).

However, in addition to understanding Abe's behavior in terms of psychodynamics and psychodiagnostics, it was equally useful to view it in terms of cognitive dynamics. Specifically, from a Piagetian perspective, Abe could be viewed as a boy who had many qualities consistent with children at the sensorimotor stage of development. It is during this developmental stage (usually dominant from birth to about 2 years of age) that children engage in intense exploration of their environment. Infants in the sensorimotor stage of development gradually acquire, by physically manipulating objects and producing consequent effects, a basic grasp of the concept of cause and effect.

Therefore, rather than formulating a case plan based solely on psychodynamics or diagnostic formulations, developmentally oriented counselors could implement treatment procedures designed to facilitate Abe's ability to effectively utilize symbolic or representational thinking. Abe would likely benefit from discovering that his thinking skills could sometimes replace his physical exploration skills as a means for learning about his environment. Further, in designing treatment strategies with Abe, attention should be paid to how he could adapt or accommodate (rather than assimilate) new cognitive strategies into his behavioral repertoire. Finally, it is important to note that Abe's behavior also could be conceptualized as being derived, in part, from his social–cultural context (Brofenbrenner, 1986). Consequently, an assessment of how Abe's social and family ecology influenced his behavior patterns was essential.

Calendar time, temporal order, and time duration. Young children commonly have little ability to accurately understand and discuss time concepts. Until about age 8, children are usually incapable or inconsistent in their ability to understand and articulate calendar time and temporal order (Kovacs & Paulaukus, 1984). This means that counseling processes or techniques that emphasize calendar time or temporal order must include concrete manifestations of these concepts for children to comprehend or carry out therapeutic activities. Consequently, counselors may benefit from logging in sessions and discussing number of sessions remaining in counseling on a visually appealing calendar designed for use with individual clients. Further, cognitive-behavioral strategies that rely on three-step, four-step, etcetera, procedures may prove unwieldy for children under 8 or 9 years old. Appropriate modifications must be made for such treatment techniques to stand a chance of working with younger clients.

It is very important for counselors to systematically modify their expectations when working with children and adolescents. Take, for example, the 11- or 12-year-old child who resists counselor questions about how long it has been since he or she visited with his or her noncustodial parent. All too frequently children who resist such questions or whose responses are grossly inaccurate are quickly presumed to have an attitude problem. Of course, instead of presuming a problem with attitude, counselors should know and recall that children younger than 12 years old usually have difficulty estimating the duration of time that has passed since the occurrence of an event. As a result, what appears on the surface as evidence of resistance may instead be evidence of specific developmental limitations with regard to understanding and differentiating the passage of linear time.

Thinking styles. The identification and elimination of distorted, maladaptive, or irrational thinking styles is well established as a cornerstone of cognitive therapy (Beck, Rush, Shaw, & Emery, 1979; Ellis, 1988). This is true with regard to cognitive therapy with both adults and young people (Wilkes, Belsher, Rush, & Frank, 1994). Consequently, counselors should be familiar with the maladaptive thinking styles commonly found among young clients. These include egocentricity or personalization, polarized or black/white thinking, magnification and minimization, mindreading, and emotional reasoning (Belsher & Wilkes, 1994; Burns, 1989).

Egocentrism. Elkind (1984) identified a number of thought processes which underlie behavioral patterns during adolescence. It is important for counselors to be aware of these normal thinking and behavior patterns, which are likely to emerge (and may become problematic) during adolescence. Elkind (1984) identified criticism of authority figures, argumentativeness, self-consciousness, self-centeredness, indecisiveness, and apparent hypocrisy as attributes characteristic of adolescents. These attributes emerge, in part, because of the adolescent's acquisition of formal operational thinking abilities (in combination with a generally pervasive egocentrism).

Polarized or black/white thinking. Children and adolescents frequently employ black/white or polarized thinking to understand their environments and personal experiences and to make behavioral choices. This tendency to view events as good or bad (i.e., "That was awesome" or "It sucked"), right or wrong, best or worst, etcetera, is not unlike the cognitive styles of many adults. Teenagers often vacillate between thinking of themselves as great or as horrible persons, as cool or as losers. Similarly, polarized thinking often is associated with magnification–minimization (e.g., for several years, our teenage daughter enthusiastically reported to us that nearly every movie she viewed was "the best ever!!").

With younger children, polarized thinking may translate into quick assumptions that the first idea about how to respond to a situation is the best idea (Shure, 1992). Alternatively, without support and encouragement, young clients often can identify only one or two behavioral options. For example, when asked how he might handle being teased at the bus stop, one young client reported, "I can ignore them." Subsequently, when pressed for a second behavioral alternative, he stated, "I could kill them." This example illustrates how polarized thinking styles can influence behavioral choices.

Mindreading. Mindreading is a maladaptive cognitive process that has been usefully identified and remediated in a number of areas, including couples counseling (Bornstein & Bornstein, 1986; Gottman, 1979). Mindreaders are usually very sensitive and use subtle interpersonal cues to ascertain what another person is thinking. A limited amount of mindreading is relatively natural and will not excessively interfere with normal functioning. For example, young children may come home and tell their parents, "My teacher doesn't like me," but such statements and accompanying beliefs are often not strong convictions, so they change the next day when the teacher smiles at the child and calls on the child when he or she volunteers an answer. Obviously, mindreading becomes problematic when children develop extreme and strongly held convictions about what others think in the absence of concrete evidence.

Most commonly, young people use mindreading to formulate beliefs about what authority figures are thinking about them and what their peers are thinking about them. As with most cognitive approaches, it is important to teach young clients to reality test their telepathic or intuitive powers. However, somewhat in contrast to teaching adults about mindreading, teaching children and teenagers about mindreading should be a more playful, fun, and interactive activity.

Emotional reasoning. Adolescents are classic emotional reasoners. For emotional reasoners, if something "feels" bad, it must be bad, while things that feel good must be good. Although examining one's feelings as one potential source of decision-making is certainly useful, emotional reasoners base decisions solely on feelings, without careful examination of many factors that might be contributing to their feelings. When working with adolescents, therapists should validate adolescents' feelings as an important source of decision-making information, but also assist these often impulsive young clients to explore other information salient to effective decision making.

Emotional Competencies and Limitations

Children as young as 2 years old often have a vocabulary describing basic emotions. By age 5, most children can differentiate emotions experienced by others. However, without clear external cues, children younger than 10 are prone to confuse emotions such as sadness, anger, and fear. Of course, as most counselors know from working with adults, clients of any age vary considerably in their abilities to identify, bind, and express affect appropriately. Often, pictures and sounds may be required therapeutic props in the service of facilitating emotional communication with children.

Depression is a very common complicating factor associated with treating young clients, particularly teenagers. Despite the fact that the DSM-IV defines child/adolescent depression as virtually identical to adult depression, such is not always the case. For example, young clients are more likely to exhibit and focus on other coexisting problems such as headaches, stomachaches, social difficulties, school problems, learning disorders, and a wide range of disruptive and/or predelinquent behaviors (Achenbach, 1991a; Harrington, 1993). Additionally, many young teenagers who are experiencing depression will liberally use substances "because it is fun!" and express apathy when confronted with potential health risks (e.g., "I don't care"). It is important for therapists to recognize the methods young clients use to express their uncomfortable or depressive emotional states. Because depression and mood problems are often central to child and adolescent disorders, Chapter 3 of this book is specifically devoted to methods for modifying emotional states of young clients.

Initiative, Identity, and Independence

Henry David Thoreau once wrote:

> Age is no better, hardly so well, qualified for an instructor as youth, for it has not profited so much as it has lost. One may almost doubt if the wisest man has learned any thing of absolute value by living. Practically, the old have no very important advice to give the young, their own experience has been so partial, and their lives have been such miserable failures, for private reasons, as they must believe; and it may be that they have some faith left which belies that experience, and they are only less young than they were. I have lived some thirty years on this planet, and I have yet to hear the first syllable of valuable or even earnest advice from my seniors. (1962, p. 111)

If you work with strong-willed young clients, you will recognize in Thoreau's words the kind of rugged individualism and valuing of independent self-discovery commonly associated with adolescence. Most adult readers of Thoreau are not likely to conclude that he was being "adolescent" when making the preceding statement; instead, they likely recognize that Thoreau's statements are placed in a historical–cultural context and should be viewed as a justifiable reaction to the ubiquitous cultural uniformity of his time. Of course, current adolescents might claim their reactions to authority figures (including therapists) as similarly justifiable. In essence, Thoreau's statement articulates the brash "I'll figure it out myself" attitude commonly associated with adolescent development. Or perhaps more accurately, it represents a temperamental style associated with individuals of any age, but usually most pronounced during toddlerhood and adolescence (Brazelton, 1989; Steinberg & Levine, 1990).

When working with brash and independent-minded young clients, therapists must sometimes accept extreme statements as a communication about the importance young clients place on independent self-discovery. For example, if we take Thoreau's extreme statement seriously, we must conclude that Thoreau learned absolutely nothing of value during his period of living with one of his mentors, Ralph Waldo Emerson. Although this conclusion is possible, it is unlikely. The important issue here involves how it feels to the therapist or parent, who, like Emerson, not only receives no credit for contributing to Thoreau's development, but is also aggressively rejected. For therapists and parents to handle such rejection well, it is crucial to view it impersonally: this rejection is a powerful individuation and identity-forming process, sometimes having little to do with the authority figures toward which it is directed.

One of the most important roles of therapist (or parent) is to serve as a secure base which children and adolescents can view as supportive and comforting, yet not excessively restrictive or controlling. Mahoney (1991) paraphrases Bowlby's (1988) position on this issue:

> The primary responsibilities of the psychotherapist are to provide a secure base that is safe, emotionally supportive, and respectful of the client's current experience. The main task of therapy is exploration, with the intent to understand and appraise old, unconscious stereotypes of self and world and to experiment with feeling, thinking, and acting in novel ways, (Mahoney, 1991, p. 168)

On the other hand, we believe that young clients need to experience limits and to sometimes be made fully aware of the therapist's (or parent's) protective impulses. A secure base is *not* simply a place where young children come for emotional refueling (Mahler, 1972) and experience permissive acceptance. It is also a place of protection and safety that sometimes limits, controls, and even transcends youthful decisions.

For example, when working with self-destructive adolescents, therapists should take authoritative positions advocating health and denouncing self-destructive behavior patterns. Further, therapists may need to bolster parental authority by supporting parents in their efforts to set reasonable behavioral limits and to enforce reasonable and logical consequences with acting-out teenagers. We will discuss further in Chapter 2 how therapists should describe their therapeutic alliance with young clients; the alliance (or secure base) is aligned with health and well-being and therefore supports healthy and constructive behaviors, while seeking to limit self-destructive behaviors (e.g., smoking, drug use, unsafe sexual practices, self-mutilation, and suicide).

Overall, therapists promote initiative, identity, and independence within their young clients to facilitate healthy development. However, therapists should not provide unlimited support for complete independence because young clients may interpret such unlimited support by therapists, similar to unlimited permissiveness by parents, in any one of a number of negative ways. For example, some young clients have reported that when they are completely left to their own judgment they believe that their parents (or therapists) no longer care and they experience abandonment.

GENDER ISSUES AND CULTURAL DIVERSITY

Gender Issues

Most of us are born with a definitive set of primary sexual features which define us as either male or female. With sonograms and amniocentesis, parents can even determine their offspring's sex before birth. Additionally, as amply demonstrated by sex role research, once parents know whether they will have a little boy or little girl, they begin to act accordingly within the teachings and customs of their culture (Deaux, 1993). There are girl colors and boy colors, girl clothes and boy clothes, girl adjectives and boy adjectives, girl diapers and boy diapers. And later, there will be girl sports and boy sports, girl accessories and boy accessories, girl advertisements and boy advertisements, girl problems and boy problems. Some of these boy–girl differences are probably legitimate, while others are social and cultural fabrications (Pipher, 1994; Tavris, 1992).

This book will not delve deeply into the nature versus nurture debate on how boys become boys and girls become girls. However, it is essential for therapists to realize that children receive enormous socialization pressure to conform to their cultural (and subcultural) standards for male and female behavior, body type, attitudes, and emotional life (Tavris, 1992). This pressure can have serious implications for therapeutic insight and work with young people.

Cultural Diversity

While in some ways childhood is a culture unto itself, the members of that culture are heavily influenced by their ethnic socialization (Canino & Spurlock, 1994). Many observations we have made in this chapter hold true across most cultures. Some do not. Similarly, traditional theories of counseling and psychotherapy are based on middle-class European and European-American cultures. Not surprisingly, therapy techniques derived from Euro-American theories may not be appropriate or effective when working with clients of divergent ethnic backgrounds, lower or higher socioeconomic classes, or nonwestern cultures (Wohl, 1989). Consequently, it is incumbent on mental health professionals to sensitize themselves to basic principles of multicultural counseling. We strongly recommend advanced coursework and continuing education in this area (Pedersen & Ivey, 1993).

It is inappropriate and perhaps damaging for mental health professionals to assume commonality when working with a child or adolescent from another culture. However, it can be helpful to search for common ground (after all, despite cultural diversity, we belong to the same species). In our experience, children do not want to be the primary source of cultural information for their counselor. They are willing to share facets of their culture, but for the most part children want to be understood by their counselor. This may necessitate outside reading or consultation by the counselor and gentle experimentation with regard to the guidelines, strategies, and techniques in this book.

When working with young clients with divergent ethnic backgrounds, sensitivity to cultural differences in affective, attitudinal, and behavioral cultural differences is important. Specifically, Rotheram and Phinney (1986) and Whiting and Whiting (1975) have identified the following "ethnic patterns" along which individuals from different cultural backgrounds are likely to exhibit consistent differences:

1. Interdependence versus independence.
2. Active achievement versus passive acceptance.
3. Authoritarianism versus equalitarianism.
4. Expressive/overt/personal versus restrained/formal/impersonal communication style.
5. Nurturant versus dominant childrearing style.
6. Reprimanding and assaulting versus sociable and intimate childrearing style.

In addition to this list, culture influences the expression of humor, the assumption of proper male and female behaviors, roles, and aspirations, nonverbal behavior, and the assessment of normality and abnormality (Patterson, 1996; Pedersen, 1990, 1991; Sue, 1991). We believe that effective counselors strive to know and understand differences between themselves and their clients at all levels, whether differences stem from age, gender training, or cultural background. Effective counselors utilize strategies that facilitate growth, healing, and healthy development without violating the cultural values of individual clients.

To achieve this goal, counselors must add to their knowledge-base regarding particular cultures through reading, personal contact, classes, and supervision; they must constantly examine attitudes, countertransference reactions, and judgments arising in their work with ethnically diverse clients; they must work toward an open, authentic relationship wherein both differences and commonalities inherent in the human condition are valued; and they must maintain personal checklists to remind themselves of principles for working with culturally diverse youth and for working with the culture of youth (see Table 1.1).

Table 1.1. Checklist for Working with Difficult Youths

_____ 1. Be playful and stimulating

_____ 2. Develop and maintain a therapeutic alliance

_____ 3. Be curious and attentive to young clients' social perspectives and competencies

_____ 4. Develop and maintain your child/adolescent sense of humor and sense of interpersonal distance

_____ 5. Pay attention to cognitive competencies and limitations

_____ 6. Pay attention to emotional competencies and limitations

_____ 7. Facilitate self-discovery through interdependence

_____ 8. Be a secure base

_____ 9. Attend to socialized, damaging assumptions regarding male/female roles and differences

_____ 10. Attend to different ethnic values in many areas, including interdependence, achievement, childrearing, nonverbal behavior, and sex roles

CONCLUDING COMMENTS

We designed this chapter to orient counselors toward working sensitively and effectively with difficult or challenging young clients. We proposed that by becoming sensitive to the culture of childhood/adolescence, counselors could become more "user-friendly" in their therapeutic strategies. If counselors become more user-friendly, the therapeutic relationship between young clients and their therapists will be strengthened and children and adolescents will participate more fully in potentially therapeutic activities.

For therapists to become user friendly they must gather knowledge and experience regarding many developmental perspectives and issues. In addition, they must take into account the influences of external environmental and familial factors on the development and functioning of the individual child and his or her family (Bronfenbrenner, 1986). This chapter focused on developmental issues including (a) the role of play; (b) social development; (c) cognitive competencies and limitations; (d) emotional competencies and limitations; and (e) initiative, identity, and independence as pathways to self-discovery. Finally, we emphasized attending to gender and cultural differences when working with challenging young clients.

2

Establishing Rapport, Gathering Information, and Informal Assessment

Of course the reason that all the children in our town like Mrs. Piggle-Wiggle is because Mrs. Piggle-Wiggle likes them. Mrs. Piggle-Wiggle likes children, she enjoys talking to them and best of all they do not irritate her. (from Mrs. Piggle-Wiggle, *MacDonald, 1947, p. 1)*

Establishing rapport and developing a therapeutic alliance constitute crucial aspects of therapeutic success in any context and from virtually all theoretical perspectives (Frank, 1979; Greenson, 1967; Safran, 1993). Unfortunately, many young people do not come to therapy willingly (Weiner, 1992). Instead, they are often pressured or coerced to attend therapy by one or both parents, by teachers, principals, probation officers, and others. In extreme cases, children who are exceptionally resistant to treatment may refuse to cooperate with or even to speak to their therapists. For example, JSF worked with a 15-year-old client who indicated a few minutes into his therapy session that the only words he would speak for the rest of the hour were "F--- off," so for the next 40 minutes, the client's contributions to the session consisted exclusively of profanity or silence!

Obviously, when young clients are angry about and opposed to attending counseling sessions, the processes of gathering information and establishing a therapeutic alliance become major challenges (Rogers & Meador, 1984; Sommers-Flanagan & Sommers-Flanagan, 1995b). As a consequence, some therapists have suggested that adolescents constitute the most difficult of all treatment populations (Meeks, 1980; Mishne, 1986). Because adolescents and some young children are often not interested in treatment or in obtaining help to change problem behaviors, therapists and counselors carry the burden of establishing an initial rapport that will hopefully develop into a productive therapeutic alliance (Meeks, 1980). Counselors can carry this burden more easily if they follow Mrs. Piggle-Wiggle's lead: Children and teenagers will quickly perceive whether their counselors like them and enjoy talking with them, or instead, are irritated by their attitudes and behaviors. Put simply, if a young client does not believe that their counselor or therapist likes and respects him or her, there is less chance that he or she will listen to the therapist, utilize the therapist's recommendations, choose to continue with counseling, benefit from its process, or like or respect the counselor in return (Lambert, 1989; Rogers, 1957; Stern, 1993).

This chapter describes strategies for impression management, gathering information, and getting acquainted with difficult young clients in a manner that facilitates establishing and maintaining a therapeutic alliance. Additionally, we review several informal assessment procedures toward the end of this chapter. Assessment, technical intervention, and rapport building are interactive in any therapy, but with young people it is good practice to develop specific assessment and intervention techniques and strategies directly aimed at increasing rapport and enhancing the therapeutic relationship.

ESTABLISHING RAPPORT

Often, interesting techniques can overcome the youth's initial resistance to forming a therapy relationship and to engaging in therapeutic procedures. In fact, with young clients, interesting techniques may enhance the therapeutic alliance regardless of the particular technique's impact on symptom reduction. Our point is that simply *doing something interesting together* with young clients often enhances the counseling relationship. Of course, we recommend that the something the professional and client do together be safe, appropriate, and potentially therapeutic within the context of any theoretical orientation.

First Impressions

When working with difficult young clients, we have found that unless the first impression is neutral to positive, it may also be the last impression. Counselors need to be friendly, active, interesting, attractive, and upbeat when greeting young clients in the waiting room.

When possible, we recommend orienting to young clients at the outset of counseling. Frequently, contact with parents initially occurs over the telephone when gathering referral information. Whatever the case, it is important to know the child's name before initially meeting him or her in the waiting room. Although it may be tempting to engage in adult talk with parents upon meeting them in the waiting room, doing so can make rapport building with young clients more difficult. Consequently, although greeting parents is important, we recommend orienting first toward young clients when initially meeting them in the waiting room. The therapist's underlying message should be that he or she has been looking forward to meeting the young person.

Depending upon the youth's age, the therapist may make statements focusing on the child's appearance, clothing, and demeanor, such as: "So you must be Michael. Do you like to be called Michael or Mike or something else?" or, "That's a pretty cool hat. Are you a Chicago Bulls fan?" or, "You've probably been looking forward to coming here for this appointment today," or, "I bet you had to drag your parents down here for counseling?" Of course, the latter two comments assume that the youth has given verbal or nonverbal clues that she or he did *not* want to come to therapy; it is a sarcastic form of empathy that will sometimes ease an awkward or hostile situation and reduce initial client reluctance or resistance (Newman, 1994). Although we refer to this procedure as sarcastic empathy, it is crucial for therapists to be sarcastic *with* young clients, rather than *at* them.

Office Management and Personal Attire

Physical surroundings can quickly turn young clients on or off. Consequently, when working with young clients, we suggest placing a few "cool" items in clear view. Depending upon age, items such as X-Men cards, sports cards, Pogs, fantasy books, playing cards, drawing pads, clay, or hats can be useful to have available in an office. Also, soothing items such as puppets or stuffed animals can increase young clients' comfort levels. Teenagers sometimes may comment negatively about such items because they are normally associated with younger children, but their comments may be a facade designed to cover needs for comfort and dependence (Brems, 1993). Overall, the office should reflect an active but not overly busy therapeutic style.

Rather than overtly drawing attention to objects of interest within the office, it is best to simply let young clients notice particular items on their own. Additionally, client responses to items can serve as an assessment tool. For example, some adolescents will be attracted to soothing objects such as stuffed animals, whereas others will avoid and make fun of them. Some clients will not be able to keep their hands off of certain items. In fact, some materials may need to be placed in drawers or boxes if they become too distracting, whereas others, such as clay or a doodle pad, can give the client something to "mess around with" while talking and this may consequently reduce anxiety.

Young clients in general and adolescents in particular tend to respond better to therapists who, even in their choice of dress, indicate that they can connect with adolescents on their own level. One of the most successful female therapists we know attracts and maintains relationships with a significant number of difficult adolescent girl clients, at least in part because she dresses "way cool." The reader may wonder how we would know this bit of information. Teens seen in counseling often compare notes. They talk with each other about their respective "shrinks" and will often offer their own therapist progress reports on their friends seeing other therapists. Listening to these assessments can be most informative.

In contrast, some clothing choices may be "uncool." For example, traditional, conservative attire (shirt and tie) may be viewed by adolescents with oppositional and conduct-disordered traits as signs that the therapist is a rigid authority figure. Delinquent adolescents may have strong transference reactions to authority figures; such reactions can impair or inhibit initial rapport (Spiegal, 1989). Generally, more casual attire is recommended when working with young clients. This is not to say that therapist and client cannot overcome other styles and learn valuable lessons in the process, but when working with youth it is often useful to eliminate a few obstacles to rapport development whenever possible.

It is also important for the therapist to feel as comfortable as possible moving around the room, sitting or lying down on the floor, or engaging in other spontaneous therapeutic activities. As a part of a therapist wardrobe with children and teenagers, JSF keeps an extra pair of beat up high-top basketball shoes in his closet to be worn when working with young boys who infer high status from expensive but well-worn sneakers.

These same general principles apply to school counselors as well. We know of at least one highly regarded school counselor who dons her high-tops and shoots hoops with her seventh and eighth grade "tough-guy" clients. Reputation can be an important aspect of counseling acceptability in the school setting (Holmgren, 1996; Miller, 1995). While individuals need to present themselves and their work in a way that feels authentic to them personally and professionally, we believe that keeping an eye to youth-friendly accessories and settings is very important.

Discussing Confidentiality and Informed Consent

Many young people (especially teenagers) are extremely sensitive to personal privacy. Therefore, it is especially important to begin discussing confidentiality at the *beginning* of the first session. Also, teenagers sometimes may believe that their therapist is working as an undercover agent for their parent(s); they may fear that what they say in private will be reported back to their parent(s). Consequently, although clients should read and sign written informed consent forms prior to an initial session, therapists also should discuss confidentiality immediately after child and parent(s) are comfortably seated in the office and have finished basic paperwork (Gustafson, McNamara, & Jensen, 1994; Handelsman & Glavin, 1988; Plotkin, 1981). We recommend an approach similar to the following:

> You both may have read about confidentiality on the registration forms, or you may have heard the word before, but I want to discuss it with you now anyway. Confidentiality is like privacy. That means what you say in here is private and personal and will not leave this office. Of course, I have a secretary and files, but my secretary also will keep information private and my files are locked and secure.
>
> What I am saying is: I won't talk about what either of you say to me outside of here, except in a few rare situations where I am legally or ethically required to speak with someone outside of this office. For example, if either of you is a danger to yourself, or to anyone else, I will not keep that information private. Also, if I find out about child abuse or neglect that has happened or is happening, I will not keep that information private either, but I will work with you, if I can, in the reporting process. Any questions about confidentiality (privacy) here?
>
> Now (*look at the child/adolescent*), one of the trickiest situations is whether I should tell your mom and dad about what we talk about in here. Let me tell you how I like to work and see if it's okay with you. (*Look back at parents*) I believe your son (daughter) needs to trust me. So, I would like you to agree that information I give to you about my private conversations

with him (her) be limited to general progress reports. In other words, aside from general progress reports, I will not inform you of details of what your child tells me. Of course, there are some exceptions to this, such as if your child is planning or doing something that might be very dangerous or self-destructive. In those cases, I will tell your child (*turn and look to child*) that he (she) is planning something I feel very uncomfortable with and then we will have everyone (*turn back to parents*) come in for an appointment so we can all talk directly about whatever dangerous thing has come up. Is this arrangement okay with all of you?

It is very important for teenagers to see and hear their therapist explain about how privacy will be maintained and protected. Further, most parents appreciate their children's need to talk privately with someone outside of the home and family. In rare cases where parents insist on being constantly apprised of therapeutic details, a family therapy or family systems intervention is probably most appropriate.

School and agency mental health professionals must also be very clear regarding the constraints of the position they hold and the system they work for. Young clients often assume their life is an open book. Simply assuring them of confidentiality and carefully explaining its limits will enhance their sense of being a respected participant in the relationship.

Confidentiality laws regarding working with minors vary from state to state. We strongly advise all mental health professionals to review their paperwork and practices with regard to the regulations in each particular setting and state.

Teenagers may respond better to a modified version of the previous confidentiality disclosure. Counselors can provide more relevant and sometimes humorous examples. For example, when turning to the teenager, you may make the following statement:

So if you're planning on doing something dangerous or destructive, such as dissecting your science teacher, it's likely that we'll need to have a meeting with your parents or school officials to talk that over, and it's the law that I would need to warn your science teacher. But day to day stuff that you're trying to sort out, stuff that's bugging you, even if it's stuff about your parents or teachers or whoever—we can keep that private.

Of course, setting confidentiality limits such as those mentioned may be controversial, but all therapists must determine (preferably beforehand) if, when, and how they might inform parents if they become aware of a teenager's dangerous behavior (Gustafson et al., 1994). Many mental health professionals who work with young clients in private practice or within a school or agency develop written descriptions of the points discussed above and have both parents and young clients sign, indicating their understanding and willingness to cooperate.

Handling Referral Information

Often, challenging young people are referred to a counselor by distraught teachers, family members, or others with whom they have interacted in less than cordial ways. We believe that it is the responsibility of the professional to share this information with the client in most circumstances. Keeping referral source secrets can seriously harm the working relationship with the youth.

For example, a school counselor may be contacted by a concerned teacher who, undetected, observed a student throwing up in the bathroom after lunch. At the teacher's request, the counselor may invite the student to stop by for a visit. We believe that it would be a mistake to fail to mention the reason for concern. In some cases, the source of referral information may need to be kept anonymous, but in the vast majority of situations, the counselor should tactfully, compassionately, and honestly convey the information itself.

Wishes and Goals

Managed care and ethical mandates for counselor/therapist competence require that counselors utilize clear procedures for problem identification and goal setting with all clients (American Counseling Association, 1995; American Psychological Association, 1992; American School Counselor Association, 1992; Fox, 1995; Stern, 1993). This procedure is straightforward with parents, but more difficult with children; parents usually come to therapy with a list of goals for their child to accomplish, whereas their child comes to therapy with no particular goals at all. After discussing confidentiality and informed consent, therapists should begin to examine why parent(s) and/or children have sought therapy. Initially, the counselor should ask young clients about personal goals for therapy. Subsequently, the counselor should obtain the parents' list of concerns and problems. We recommend exploring therapy goals in this order because children or adolescents probably have not formulated their list of goals and may be influenced by what their parents say. The opposite is less likely; parents will proceed with listing their goals regardless of what their child has said previously.

Unfortunately, children are sometimes brought to a counselor's office without knowing or understanding the purpose of counseling. When practicing with children, it is not unusual for them to, when asked why they have come (or been brought) to counseling, give responses such as the following:

"My mom wants to talk with you because I've been bad."
"I don't know."
"Because I hate my teacher and won't do my homework."
"Because my parents are stupid and think I have a problem."

Additionally, some young clients will simply remain quiet when asked about the reasons they have come for counseling; in such cases it may be that they are unable to understand the question, unable to formulate and/or articulate a response, unwilling (or afraid) to talk about their true thoughts and feeling with their parents in the room, unwilling (or afraid) to talk openly about their true thoughts and feelings with a virtual stranger, and/or unaware of or strongly resistant to admitting any personal problems.

In contrast to younger children, adolescents are often aware of at least some of the reasons for counseling, but they are more likely to externalize blame (e.g., "I'm normal, it's my parents who have the problem"). Additionally, adolescents sometimes express personal opinions of being philosophically opposed to counseling ("I don't believe in counseling" or "I don't believe our family needs to talk with some stranger to solve our problems").

Obtaining a child-focused problem list from parents or teachers presents counselors with a very practical difficulty. That is, how can counseling be effective if the "identified patient" is unable or unwilling to identify their personal problems and goals? The Wishes and Goals procedure is designed to engage children and adolescents in problem identification and goal-setting activities required at the beginning of counseling. Further, because it encourages interaction between parent(s) and children, it can facilitate the identification of parent problems and goals and thereby increase the likelihood for therapeutic change opportunities within the entire family system (Szapocznik, Kurtines, Santisteban, & Rio, 1990).

Structuring problem identification and goal setting. The therapist should make a statement similar to the following:

> I'm very interested in the reasons why you have come for counseling. In my experience, I have found that parents (*look at parents*) usually have clear goals in mind for counseling, but kids (or teenagers) may not have clear goals for counseling. So, first I want to ask you (*look at the child*) what you would like to have happen in counseling and in a few minutes I will ask your mom and dad the same question. So (child), if you came to counseling for a while and, for whatever reason, your life got better, what would change; what would get better?

Some children/adolescents understand this question clearly and respond directly. However, several potential problems and dynamics may occur. First, the child may not understand the question. Second, the child may be resistant or reluctant about responding to the question due to family dynamics. Third, the child may focus immediately on his or her perceptions of the parents' problems.

Fourth, the parents may begin making encouraging comments to their child, some of which may even include tips on how to respond to the counselor's question. Whatever the case, two rules follow: (a) if the child/adolescent does not answer the question satisfactorily, clarify the question in terms of wishes (see below) and (b) for assessment purposes make mental (or written) notes regarding family dynamics.

Introducing the wish. The introduction of wishing as an approach to obtaining treatment goals from young clients is useful because it involves using a language that young people are more likely to accept (Sommers-Flanagan & Sommers-Flanagan, 1995a). It also demonstrates the counselor's tenacity or persistence with regard to obtaining goals from young clients.

> Let me put the question another way. If you had three wishes, or if you had a magic lamp in the movie Aladdin, and you could wish to change something about yourself, your parents, or your school, what would you wish?

This question structures goal setting into three categories: self-change, family change, and school change. Thus, the child/adolescent has a chance to identify personal goals in any or all three of these categories. Depending upon the child and on the parents' influence, there may still be resistance to identifying a goal in one or more of these areas. In such cases, you may amplify the question:

> You don't have any wishes to make your life better? Wow! My life isn't perfect so maybe I should wish to change places with you? How about your parents? Isn't there one little thing that you might change about them if you could? (*Pause for answers*) How about yourself? Isn't there anything... even something small, that you might change about yourself?

Nervous or shy children/adolescents may continue to resist this questioning process. If so, give young clients the chance to pass on immediately responding to the wishing question.

Would you like to pass on this question for now? I can ask your parents first and then, if you come up with any wishes of your own, you can bring them up any time.

The purpose of this questioning procedure is to get young clients, in a somewhat playful, provocative, and perhaps humorous way, to admit that their lives are not perfect. Once a young client has admitted that life is not perfect, the counselor can establish an opening for identifying goals and establishing a therapy rationale. Further, this questioning procedure can provide helpful diagnostic information. Usually, clients with disruptive behavior disorders (i.e., ADHD, oppositional defiant disorder [ODD], or conduct disorder [CD]) will acknowledge that the school and parents have problems, but will admit few, if any, personal problems. In contrast, clients who are primarily experiencing internalizing disorders (e.g., anxiety, depression) will be more likely to identify their own personal problems.

Obtaining parents' goals. After a young client admits at least one way in which life is not perfect (or after he or she has passed on responding to the wishes question), and the therapist has reframed this imperfection (or wish) into something closely resembling a therapy goal, then shift the focus to the parent(s). Although parents will have observed the therapist trying to establish rapport and set goals with their child, direct interaction and attention to parental concerns is crucial to eventual treatment compliance (e.g., parents may not support therapy or provide reliable transportation to therapy unless they view their concerns as being addressed). Also, it is helpful for children and adolescents to watch the therapist become serious and thoughtful when discussing important topics and problems with parents.

When addressing parents, therapists should take detailed notes; it is very important that parents know you are taking their concerns seriously. However, it is equally, if not more important to limit the number of negative and critical comments parents make about their children, especially during the first session. Consequently, we usually allow parents to identify up to three primary concerns they have about their child's behavior. The purpose of limiting negative comments from parents is to protect young clients from feeling devastated or overwhelmed by their parents' criticism. If parents indicate that they have more than three concerns, additional concerns should be written out or discussed in a later session. In some cases, after there is initial rapport between therapist and child, the therapist can conduct a separate meeting with parents (with the young client's permission) to address parental concerns more directly and more completely. Similarly, we sometimes ask young clients if it is okay for their parents to make us a list of parental concerns. After we have informed everyone of how important it is for us to have all of the information about a particular individual or family and after we establish an initial trust relationship, we find little resistance to these information-gathering strategies.

Managing tension. During the wish-making procedure, tension may rise, especially if we ask children/adolescents to make wishes about how they would like to see their parents change. Despite this tension, we have found child/adolescent wishes about their parents to be a crucial part of the assessment process. Additionally, it is reassuring to most young clients to hear the counselor say things like: "I guess your parents aren't perfect either." And, as noted above, focusing on parental behaviors at the outset of counseling may provide a foundation for working on changing parental behaviors throughout counseling. Finally, as suggested previously, parent–child interactions during this goal-setting procedure are sometimes revealing regarding family dynamics. For example, we have observed children who clearly appear afraid to comment on their parents' behavior (and their parents do not reassure them) and we have seen children who are rather vicious as they wish for their parents to change.

For the purposes of developing a therapeutic alliance, it is important for young clients to identify at least one goal they might accomplish through therapy. If, after help, encouragement, and humor, and after passing on their initial opportunity to wish for life change, they are still unable or unwilling to identify a personal therapeutic goal, prognosis for therapeutic success is probably poor. As a consequence, we recommend pressing young clients (especially teenagers) to identify at least one therapy goal.

Discussing Assessment and Therapy Procedures

After the counselor has explained confidentiality and the clients have shared background information and identified initial therapy goals, a brief review or explanation of assessment and therapy procedures is appropriate. Depending on the situation, therapists may choose to send parents into the waiting room with an assignment or questionnaire (e.g., a developmental history questionnaire and a problem behavior checklist). On the other hand, if a direct interview with parents is necessary, the counselor can give young clients drawing assignments or questionnaires to complete in the waiting room. In most cases it is useful to spend individual time with an adolescent and then to have parents return for 5 to 10 minutes at the end of the hour to review therapy procedures (e.g., appointment frequency, who will be attending appointments, and a description of specific treatment approaches such as anger management, treatment of depressed mood, etc.).

INFORMAL ASSESSMENT: USER-FRIENDLY INFORMATION-GATHERING PROCEDURES

The purpose of formal assessment or evaluation procedures is to obtain information pertaining to client functioning that may be used to facilitate counseling (Peterson & Nisenholz, 1987). Although many mental health professionals utilize traditional, formal assessment procedures (e.g., intellectual testing, questionnaires, etc.), many do not because they view assessment as either of low utility or as potentially interfering with the counseling process (Gaylin, 1989; Goldman, 1972). Unfortunately, young clients often express criticism and/or sarcasm when asked to participate in traditional assessment (e.g., "That test was lame"). We designed the following procedures to help counselors gather information, and at the same time capture client interest and cooperation. Additionally, because these techniques can facilitate rapport and trust, they usually have a positive effect on validity of subsequent traditional, self-report assessments (Shirk & Harter, 1996).

This section describes several qualitative or user-friendly approaches to information gathering and assessment with children and adolescents. These approaches glean important information and facilitate client talk in a friendly and nonoffensive manner. Assessment approaches include: siding with young clients, the "what's good (bad) about you?" question, draw-a-person interpretations, offering rewards, inferring attachment issues, and traditional assessment and feedback. Using these qualitative information-gathering procedures early in treatment can increase youth cooperation with counseling and provide the therapist with important assessment information.

Siding With The Young Client

One of the first challenges facing child/adolescent therapists is how to gain the trust and respect of young clients. It would be nice if young clients arrived in our offices eager to trust us, respect us, and follow our sage advice. Unfortunately, this is rarely the case. Instead, difficult young clients who are experiencing distress generally distrust therapists and eschew advice from parents, teachers, and therapists (Meeks, 1980). This is particularly true for difficult adolescents. More often than not, when faced with personal problems, such adolescents seek out the advice of peers. Unfortunately, advice from fellow teenagers is frequently of poor quality. The problem is how to get oppositional and impulsive adolescents to seek out and follow advice from a reasonable adult. Our initial solution is to "side with the adolescent."

Young clients are more likely to listen to and follow the advice of adults *after* they believe the adult is on their side. Obviously, the concept of siding with adolescents and validating clients' feelings is not new (Meeks, 1980). Counselors can use the following procedures to build trust through empathy and feeling validation (Sommers-Flanagan & Sommers-Flanagan, 1993).

Define the conflict/problem and separate the parties. As noted above, initial meetings with young clients and their parents usually include some form of goal setting or problem identification process. Although our procedure focuses on goals (which are intrinsically more positive than problems), parents may, at some point during the initial session, begin bombarding the therapist with descriptions of their child's numerous "problems." If this occurs, therapists may observe parent(s) complaining about a long list of their child's problems, such as: avoidance of homework, lying, curfew violations, backtalk, disruptive school behavior, illegal behavior, merciless teasing or picking on younger siblings, lack of values, drug/alcohol use, generally poor attitude, etcetera. It may be extremely difficult or impossible to quickly shift a parent's attitude toward his or her child from negative and pessimistic to positive and optimistic. Consequently, if a parent begins to belittle his or her child (e.g., by assigning blame exclusively to the child, by listing the child's faults) or if the child begins to become very defensive (e.g., by using the silent treatment, eye rolls, or excessive profanity), it may be necessary to initiate conflict diffusion strategies by separating the parties. In such cases, the therapist should briefly listen to both sides of the conflict, clarify or define the nature of the conflict, comment on the adolescent's affective state (i.e., angry, disagreeable, depressed, etc.), comment on the state of the conflict (i.e., stuck, stalemated, etc.), and politely dismiss the parent from the room:

> Well, I can see that both you and your son are kind of stuck on this issue (e.g., curfew) and neither of you feel good about it. How about if I meet with your son for a while and then we'll have you come back in toward the end of the hour to discuss things further?

When given the opportunity to escape the conflict, virtually every parent we have ever worked with cooperatively (and gladly) leaves the room (although in some cases a parent may launch a final insult toward their child as they exit).

The purposes of separating parent and child are to diffuse or deescalate the conflict, to prevent the parent from further damaging the child's self-esteem, to prevent continued building of child retaliatory impulses, to enhance child–therapist rapport, trust, and alliance by working directly on an important family conflict, and to assess the child's ability to discuss the conflict constructively without the parent(s) present.

Discuss the problem individually with the young client. When meeting individually with a young client about an in-session parent–child conflict, it is important to not only use typical Rogerian empathic listening techniques (e.g., "You feel angry when your dad criticizes you"), but also to actively engage in feeling validation (e.g., "I can see that it *really* is hard to deal with your dad being so critical of you," or "Does it always get so negative when you and your mom are trying to solve a problem?"). We also sometimes use quick and empathic phrases like "Ouch" or sarcastic empathy like "Well, *that* was pretty pleasant."

Siding with young clients is a strategy that needs to be implemented cautiously. This is especially true with teenagers who may decide to quote their therapist the next time they get in an argument with parents, teachers, or any relevant authority figure. Several principles should be followed. First, therapists should empathize with and validate the child's feelings, but *not* the child's behavior (which may or may not have been appropriate). Second, if using strong negative language, therapists should be careful to primarily use the child's negative language, rather than providing children with innovative and possibly profane language alternatives. Third, utilize strong negative language or expressions only briefly and discuss why you used the language before reuniting parent and child at the end of the session.

Many therapists avoid strong validation of young clients' feelings and negative labeling of authority figures because of fear that the adolescent may take such statements back to school or home and adults will be offended. Additionally, psychoanalytically trained therapists may worry about encouraging splitting defenses so frequently employed by adolescents (e.g., when adolescents play one adult against another to get their way; Kernberg & Chazan, 1991). However, unless the adolescent feels a connection to the therapist within her or his perceptual and communication framework, he or she will not be able or willing to modify the perception of the situation to a more adaptive level. The point is that young clients sometimes can begin to see the irrational or inappropriate nature of their position only *after* a listening adult has heard and validated their thoughts and feelings. Meeks (1980) describes a similar attitude that psychotherapists should hold toward their adolescents' behavior:

> The important point is that even the most repulsive and self-defeating behaviors are comprehensible. The patient needs to know that we believe deeply that there are good reasons for everything he does, even when what he does is not good for others or for himself. (p. 33)

For example, a 12-year-old boy came to therapy after having threatened to sue his teacher for being "sexist." The boy dogmatically held on to his right to sue the teacher until after the therapist listened closely and agreed with the boy that his teacher sounded "sexist." After mutually complaining about how some people in the world are sexist for several minutes and using the boy's language (e.g., some people in the world are such "assholes"), the therapist stated: "It sounds like everything you did was pretty justified—except when you threatened to sue your teacher... in a way, that was kinda dumb 'cause it just ended up getting you in more trouble and now the teacher is really gonna be watching you closely."

At this point the boy simply responded with "Yeah, that was pretty dumb." Then he and the therapist set to work on how he could recover from his interpersonal mistake (i.e., the boy ended up agreeing—without coercion—to write a letter of apology to the teacher).

Parent–child reunification. After siding with a young client and engaging in productive problem solving, reuniting parent and child can be extremely enjoyable. It can demonstrate to parents that change and conflict resolution are possible. It also can provide important assessment information regarding how well parents and children can recover from interpersonal conflict. Some parents and children will continue in conflict or will renew conflict immediately upon reunification. We discuss parent–child reunification after strategic separation further in Chapter 4.

What's Good (Bad) About You?

A relationship-building assessment procedure that can provide a rich interpersonal interaction between young clients and counselors is titled the "What's good about you?" question and answer game (D. Dana, personal communication, May 21, 1993). The procedure also provides useful information regarding child/adolescent self-esteem. Initially, introduce it as a "game" with specific rules:

> I want to play a game with you. I'm going to ask you the same question 10 times. The only rule is that you cannot answer the question with the same answer twice. In other words, I'll ask you the same question 10 times, but you have to give me 10 different answers.

When playing this game counselors simply ask their young client, "What's good about you?" (while writing down the client's responses), following each response with "Thank you" and a smile. If the client responds with "I don't know" the therapist simply writes down the response the first time, but if the client uses "I don't know" (or any response) a second time, the counselor reminds the client, in a light and possibly humorous manner, that he or she can use answers only one time.

The "What's good about you?" game provides interesting insights into client self-perceptions and self-esteem. For example, some youth have difficulty clearly stating a talent, skill, or positive personal attribute. They sometimes identify possessions such as "I have a nice bike" or "I have some good friends" instead of taking personal ownership of an attribute: "I am a good bike rider," or "My friendly personality helps me make friends." Similarly, they may describe a role they have (e.g., "I am a good son"), rather than identify personal attributes that make them good at the particular role (e.g., "I am thoughtful with my parents and so I am a good son"). Obviously, the ability to clearly state one's positive personal attributes is considered as evidence supporting more adequate self-esteem.

Counselors can obtain interpersonal assessment data also through the "What's good about you?" procedure. For example, we have had some assertive or aggressive children request or even insist that they be allowed to switch roles and ask us the "What's good about you?" questions. We have always complied with these requests, as it provides us with a modeling opportunity and the clients with an empowerment experience. Additionally, the manner in which young clients respond to this interpersonal request can be revealing. In our experience, youth who meet the diagnostic criteria for CD (or who are angry with adults) sometimes ridicule or mock the procedure, while most other children and adolescents cooperate and seem to enjoy the process.

An optional follow-up to the "What's good about you?" procedure is the "What's bad about you?" query. Although asking young clients "What's bad about you?" is more negative and perhaps controversial, it can yield interesting information. We ask this negative question only five times. Perhaps our most interesting observations are that young clients frequently are quicker at coming up with negative attributes than they are at coming up with positive attributes, and they sometimes identify as negative some of the same traits that were included on their positive attribute list.

Counselors should be careful not to end a session while focusing on negative or "bad" attributes. Consequently, refocusing on the adolescent's positive attributes is important after completing the "What's bad about you?" activity. Also, sometimes identifying ways in which a "bad" trait might, in fact, be a helpful or positive trait in certain circumstances can alleviate some of the stress associated with focusing on negative attributes.

During both "What's good about you?" and "What's bad about you?" counselors should observe how clients describe their positive and negative traits. For example, adolescents frequently use qualifiers when describing their positive traits (e.g., "I'm a good basketball player, sometimes"), and when describing negative traits, adolescents may quote someone else (i.e., an adult authority figure) and they may make an excessively strong statement (e.g., "My teachers say that I'm *never* able to pay attention in school").

Draw-A-Person Interpretations

Counselors can use the traditional Draw-A-Person procedure (Machover, 1949) with young clients in a provocative and interactive manner that captures client interest, enhances counselor credibility, and elicits projective information. Initially, utilize standard instructions:

> On your piece of paper I would like you to draw a whole person. It can be any kind of person you want to draw, just make sure that it is a whole person and not a stick figure or a cartoon figure. (Tharinger & Stark, 1990, p. 368)

Of course, some young clients hate to draw and resist the procedure. If resistance is manifest, provide standard encouragement: "Just do the best you can. You're not expected to be an artist." After the client produces the drawing or drawings (you also may use an opposite sex human figure and/or kinetic family drawing), ask clients to sign and date the drawings before handing the drawings over to the counselor.

Interpretation phase. Upon receiving the drawings, the interpretation phase of this activity commences:

> Do you know why psychologists (counselors, social workers) have clients draw pictures? (*Some adolescents shrug or act disinterested.*) Well, I can tell all kinds of interesting things about you, just by what and how you drew these pictures. Want me to tell you some things about yourself based on these pictures? (*Some adolescents continue to act uninterested and say something like, "Whatever."*)

At this point the counselor has to be willing to engage in a little speculative, free-spirited interpretation. Keep in mind that a few

Barnum statements may be acceptable (i.e., Barnum statements are generalities like: "you are a complex person" or "you like to take short-cuts... or the easy way out sometimes" or "sometimes it is very hard for you to express your anger to people who are most important to you right when you're feeling it"; Barnum statements are supposed to apply to almost everyone; Furnham, 1989). Additionally, it may be appropriate to weave into interpretations some of your early observations of the client, some of which are not necessarily based on the Draw-A-Person activity. Finally, knowledge of human figure drawing interpretation is a requirement (Holmes & Wiederhold, 1982; Koppitz, 1968; Machover, 1949; Reynolds, 1978; Sims, Dana, & Bolton, 1983). In most cases, if counselors use this procedure early in therapy we recommend using it as an individualized therapeutic procedure. In other words, after making a tentative statement pertaining to a potential client attribute, the therapist checks with his or her client to see if the statement seemed accurate or inaccurate:

> The usual interpretation of the way you drew this picture... the light and shaded coloring of the person and the fact that you erased several parts of the figure several times... most people think that might mean you worry a bit about doing things just right. Does that seem to fit? Are you the kind of person who is sometimes unsure, sometimes worrying if you are doing the right thing?

Counselors also can use Draw-A-Person interpretations at points in therapy when clients are resistant or stuck. After several psychotherapy sessions, a 14-year-old boy suddenly stopped talking openly and became resistant. Subsequently, he was given the following instructional set: "I'll bet if you just draw a person on this piece of paper, I'll be able to tell you all kinds of things about yourself." He eagerly took the challenge and produced a large version of the drawing in Figure 2.1. I (JSF) gave him the following interpretation:

> The person in your picture is on the left of the page. That means you're kind of stuck in the past. It means there are some

things from your past that you're having trouble getting over. The toilet is in the middle and it's stuck. All clogged up. Water is usually associated with emotions and so it looks to me like your emotions are all stuck up inside of you. And some of them stink. And you're trying to loosen them up, but it doesn't look like you're having much luck. Now that plunger, I can't tell, is it stiff like a pretzel, or is it flexible like cooked spaghetti? ("*It's flexible like cooked spaghetti.*") Oh, so it's like your efforts to loosen the emotions up... it's like they're hopeless... you don't even have good tools for dealing with all those stinky emotions.

Figure 2.1. Sample Draw-A-Person.

The boy's response to this interpretation was predictably strong. Based on observations of his behavior over the past several weeks, it had become fairly obvious that he was "stuffing" his emotions about his parents' divorce and after the initial general interpretation, the counselor went further and made the link to the boy's life experiences. The boy resisted the interpretation to some extent, stating: "You can't tell all that from this picture." But, less than a minute after the interpretation, he became animated, grabbed another piece of paper and stated: "I'm gonna make another picture... this time you won't be able to figure it out." The procedure achieved its goal, to re-engage the boy in the counseling relationship and elicit additional assessment information.

A word of caution regarding Draw-A-Person procedures. Much of the research pertaining to the Draw-A-Person technique as a specific assessment strategy is highly critical. Specifically, as an assessment technique, human figure drawings in general, and Draw-A-Person strategies in particular, have little reliability and validity. Draw-A-Person interpretations are typically criticized because they are often utilized (i.e., misused) by individuals with inadequate training in providing such interpretations (Smith & Dumont, 1995). Further, therapists are prone to projecting their own issues and/or assumptions onto their clients when providing interpretations. Finally, we must agree with much of the scientific literature in this area by emphasizing that counselors should never base conclusions regarding an individual's personality or likely behavioral repertoire exclusively on human figure drawings; at best, drawings are a generative technique used to suggest hypotheses and/or to support assessment data obtained through other, more reliable and valid acceptable procedures.

Despite limitations of human figure drawings as an assessment tool, we remain confident that they provide supplementary assessment information that can be interesting and stimulating to both therapist and client. We believe that human figure drawings are, as is the case with most assessment tools, most valuable when used in an individualized and interactive manner which respects clients' perspectives and their acceptance or rejection of the hypotheses generated by the assessment procedures.

Offering Rewards

With disruptive, behavior-disordered youths, impulsivity and lack of behavioral compliance is a common identified problem. As an assessment tool, offering rewards allows therapists to evaluate how clients might respond to behavioral incentives. The question is whether or not anticipation of a specific reinforcer(s) can motivate a young client to reduce his or her impulsivity and increase his or her behavioral compliance.

To utilize this procedure, after the parents leave the room ask the youth what would happen if you paid him or her to take a break from engaging in a problem behavior (e.g., hitting a little brother or sister, leaving the house without seeking permission, forgetting homework at school or refusing to complete homework). For example, "If I were to pay you $10.00 (or give a $10.00 gift certificate) next week for completing all homework assignments and always checking with your parents before leaving the house, do you think you could do it?" Note that counselors can conduct this procedure in an "as if" mode or as an actual reward offer.

The purposes of the offering rewards assessment procedure are at least fourfold. First, it helps determine the client's perception of his or her self-control skills. Some clients will be overconfident in their ability to modify their behavior, while others will be underconfident. Obviously, it is important for counselors to know how realistic young clients are when they describe their personal potential and ambitions.

Second, offering rewards can provide diagnostic information. Specifically, children/adolescents diagnosed with ADHD get excited about the money possibility, but often quickly fail the homework assignment; sometimes they even fail the homework assignment before leaving the office (Barkley, 1990). In contrast, children/adolescents diagnosed with ODD often comply with the counselor's request and simply earn the money (i.e., if they want to). Finally, children/adolescents diagnosed with CD often try to negotiate or manipulate for additional reinforcers (e.g., more money) or for payment in advance (Rutter & Rutter, 1993).

Third, this procedure introduces and then models the importance of informing parents of therapeutic homework (even if the child thinks the parent will not approve of the homework) and of the importance of having an objective monitor of homework success. Although the counselor initially discusses this activity privately with the youth, toward the end of the session the counselor tells the youth, "Now we need to tell your parents (or teacher) about our arrangement; after all, we need someone besides you to keep track of your success."

Fourth, therapists can educate parents and/or teachers as to the potential usefulness of contingency programs. Sometimes parents are against using what they call "bribery" to obtain behavioral compliance. If parents object (or perhaps before they object), you can explain that bribery is defined as "paying someone to do something illegal" (defining bribery is discussed further in Chapter 4; Gordon, 1991). Additionally, counselors can discuss with parents the fact that positive reinforcement is a much more efficient behavior modifier than punishment and they can emphasize this by inquiring about positive reinforcers parents receive in their daily lives.

Finally, caution regarding this procedure is warranted. Aside from possible parental objection, counselors must take care to inform young clients that this is only a one-time incentive. Otherwise, the client may expect payments of some sort every week. Additionally, ADHD clients may not pay attention to the rules of the homework assignment, so you should clearly write them out and ADHD clients should repeat the rules of the assignment back to the counselor. Finally, counselors should consider an effort reward for children with ADHD who do not have the ability to sustain attention and effort for a reward that is distant in time (i.e., 1 or 2 weeks away).

In school settings, where the counselor may have daily access to the youth, it is still wise to have parents or teachers monitor the desired behavioral change. Involving an "objective" third party, usually one affected by the behavior, can provide additional assessment information.

Inferring Attachment Issues

Recently, therapists have become more oriented to attachment problems in children and adolescents (Bradford & Lyddon, 1994). Consequently, there are now formal measures of attachment which counselors can administer to clients at the beginning of or during counseling. However, rather than relying upon questionnaire administration, this approach focuses on therapist ratings of client attachment behaviors based on Bartholomew's (1990) reformulation of Hazan and Shaver's (1987) and Bowlby's (1977) attachment models. Specifically, therapists can categorize their young clients' attachment behaviors into one of Bartholomew's (1990) four attachment styles.

Secure prototype. The client appears comfortable and open interacting with the therapist. He or she is capable of being emotionally close to the therapist. There are no significant problems with separation from parents or with separation from the therapist when the session ends.

Preoccupied prototype. The client seems to want to be exceptionally close to the therapist. There is an apparent desire (spoken or unspoken) for more and more time with the therapist. Sometimes it seems as if these children/adolescents would gladly go home and live with their therapist after only a few minutes of counseling.

Fearful prototype. The client seems to want to be emotionally close but is fearful of being hurt. This often occurs with children in foster care because they have had numerous experiences of being close to adults and then being emotionally hurt because of a placement change. These clients are most likely to put the therapist through tests of trust (Fong & Cox, 1983).

Dismissing prototype. These clients appear disinterested in emotional closeness. They like to feel self-sufficient. It is important to distinguish this prototype from the fearful prototype because those with the fearful prototype may act disinterested to protect themselves from emotional hurt. Dismissing clients may be more prone to violence and other emotionally distancing behaviors than are clients of the other three types.

It is important to remember that although attachment styles may have implications for psychopathology, they are not diagnostic entities representative of particular forms of pathology. Instead, these categories may help therapists understand more deeply early childhood dynamics that have led to the ways in which an individual child/adolescent chooses to interact with adults. Also, we should note that although we described the preceding attachment styles in a categorical manner, individual clients most likely display attachment behaviors falling along a continuum within the secure, preoccupied, fearful, and dismissing prototypes.

Traditional Assessment and Feedback

In many situations, we highly recommend using traditional assessment procedures with children and adolescents. Traditional assessment procedures include questionnaires, parent/teacher rating scales, projective tests, intellectual testing, and more. When using such procedures, we recommend adopting a policy of openness and honesty. Therapists should inform children and adolescents of the purpose of particular assessment devices and they should offer feedback regarding young clients' scores. This is because young clients in general and adolescents in particular are likely to feel anxious and distrustful of adults who are trying to evaluate them. We commonly make a statement similar to the following:

As a part of therapy I have people, like yourself, fill out a questionnaire. In your case, I would like you to complete the MMPI-A. The MMPI-A is a test that has been given to thousands of teenagers. It is horribly long and probably boring to most young people who take it. It may sound weird, but I've taken it myself, several times. The reason I take it and the reason I'm having you take it, is because it can provide us with useful information about certain personality traits we have. You know, sometimes people can have too much of a certain trait or quality, or a healthy amount, or even too little of a particular quality. After you have taken the test, I'll have it scored and we will look at the results together and I will explain what the different scores mean. Maybe at the end of counseling you can take the test again and we can see if there have been any important changes.

Obviously, we would not use the Minnesota Multiphasic Personality Inventory—Adolescent Version (MMPI-A; Archer, 1992; Butcher et al., 1992) unless there was a specific purpose for its administration. The reason why we have explained its use in the preceding example is because many clinicians are reluctant to give clients feedback regarding MMPI-A scores. Certainly, because the MMPI-A is a test designed to measure pathology, it can be difficult to provide positive feedback to clients who obtain elevated scale scores. On the other hand, just as therapists should avoid taking notes during a session that they would not want their clients to read, therapists should also avoid administering tests to their clients if they are nervous about providing oral or written feedback regarding the client's test results. We recommend showing clients their test profiles and explaining the meaning and interpretation of each clinical scale of the MMPI-A. For example, we provide sample verbal or written descriptions of clinical elevations on MMPI-A Scales 1 (hypochondriasis) and 6 (paranoia) below.

Scale #1 of the MMPI-A is called the hypochondriasis scale. That's a pretty long and weird word. The scale primarily includes test items related to physical health and physical discomfort. As you probably know, some people are healthier than others and some people worry about their health more than others. People who score high, such as yourself, usually either have some physical health problems or they are worried about having physical health problems in the future. Also people with scores like yours are more likely than the average person to feel physically sick or physically uncomfortable when they are under stress. Does this description sound at all like you?

Note that the preceding feedback statement is straightforward and basically nonpathologizing. Also, whenever giving feedback, we ask clients if the descriptions or interpretations seem to fit for them.

Scale #6 of the MMPI-A is called the paranoia scale. Now just because the scale is called paranoia, doesn't mean that people who have high scores are paranoid. In fact, really the scale is a measure of sensitivity. People with high scores are more likely than the average person to be sensitive to how other people act and what they might be up to. In other words, sensitive people notice little things that other people do that an average person might not even notice. As you can see, your Scale 6 is a little higher than average. Therefore, I'd guess that you are a keen observer and you notice how other people's actions might relate to you. An example might be noticing that other people are laughing and then wondering if maybe they are laughing at you. Also, higher scores on Scale 6 are associated with intelligence. So your high score here might mean that on your good days you are intelligent and sensitive but on your bad days, days when you're experiencing lots of stress, you can become touchy and suspicious of others. Does any of this seem to fit how you see yourself?

Perhaps more important than the specific scores obtained by young clients who complete psychological or personality questionnaires is the manner in which the tests are administered and feedback is provided. Openness with young clients regarding the purpose of formal assessment procedures and assessment results can facilitate the development of trust. Because assessment procedures, depending on *how* they are used, can either interfere with or facilitate the development of trust, we recommend that therapists select specific procedures carefully and that they present procedures to clients in an open and honest manner. If therapist–client trust decreases after using an assessment procedure, in the long run it may have been better to avoid using such a procedure at all.

CONCLUDING COMMENTS

We have reviewed several procedures for building rapport, gathering information, and conducting informal or user-friendly assessments with difficult youth. The underlying goal of these procedures is to facilitate information gathering, while at the same time establishing and maintaining a therapeutic alliance. It is also true that the procedures described above often have therapeutic intent; that is, we designed them, in part, to encourage personal insight and behavior change. These procedures may help therapists be more efficient in establishing a productive working relationship with young clients; efficiency is of paramount importance in the managed care era (Fox, 1995; Stern, 1993). Additionally, we have found that using these assessment procedures generally enhances client cooperation with all aspects of counseling, even administration of more traditional assessment approaches.

PART **II**

User-Friendly Strategies

3

Rapid Emotional Change Techniques:
Teaching Young Clients Mood Management Skills

> *For the first time Ramona looked into her very own mirror in her very own room. She saw a stranger, a girl with red eyes and a puffy, tearstained face, who did not look at all the way Ramona pictured herself. Ramona thought of herself as the kind of girl everyone should like, but this girl....*
>
> *Ramona scowled, and the girl scowled back. Ramona managed a small smile. So did the girl. Ramona felt better. She wanted the girl in the mirror to like her. (from* Ramona the Brave, Cleary, *1975, pp. 95–96)*

Most children and adolescents who are referred for therapy could easily be labeled Grumpy Grizzlies or some similarly descriptive and endearing term. In many cases, the bad mood has been distressing to the youth, but in virtually all cases, it has been distressing to parents, teachers, and others as well. Many difficult-to-treat child-hood disorders (e.g., depression, ADHD, ODD, and CD) include a pervasive irritability as an associated or primary characteristic. This irritability usually causes considerable distress in family members (Achenbach, 1991a, 1991b; Petersen et al., 1993). These children and adolescents are generally miserable and it often seems that they are dedicated to making others miserable as well.

Research has shown that the presence of depressed or irritable mood, whether based on adolescents' or parents' reports, is the most significant single symptom separating clinically referred from nonreferred youth (Achenbach, 1991a, 1991b). Although this may be due partially to the comorbidity of depressed mood with a number of specific disorders (e.g., eating disorders, disruptive behavior disorders, and anxiety disorders; Kashani, Reid, & Rosenberg, 1989; Rohde, Lewinsohn, & Seeley, 1991), it also points to the significance of negative mood as an indicator of psychological disturbance. And certainly, negative mood caused by any one of a number of factors has the potential to adversely effect interpersonal relationships, eating behavior, school performance, cognitions, and so on (Beck et al., 1979; Petersen et al., 1993; Sommers-Flanagan & Sommers-Flanagan, 1995c).

If most young clients are referred for counseling or therapy due to negative moods, then treatment focusing on changing or modi-fying mood states should stand a good chance of being viewed in a positive manner by therapy recipients and their parents. Unfor-tunately, many cognitive-behavioral strategies for mood manage-ment require high levels of client motivation, interest, and cooperation (Spivack, Platt, & Shure, 1976; Zarb, 1992). It is unlikely that young people who are experiencing high levels of irritability, sadness, or anger, especially if they are also exhibiting comorbid symptoms of disruptive behavior and distrust of adults, will have the level of cooperation and therapeutic involvement necessary for implementation of most cognitive-behavioral mood modification strategies (Gorin, 1993; Loeber, Lahey, & Thomas, 1991; Sommers-Flanagan & Sommers-Flanagan, 1995c).

In addition to lack of motivation, there are (as always) issues of control in working with adolescents and mood. Young clients have their own bad mood and they usually do not want anyone messing with it. Of course, as discussed in Chapter 2 (see Goal Setting), a very important task facing therapists who work with young clients is convincing them that counseling may be useful or helpful to them (Edwards, 1996). Therefore, a major problem at the outset of counseling with difficult young clients involves how to get them to participate in potentially therapeutic activities when they are in a lousy mood and do not really feel like doing anything healthy or trusting any adults.

This chapter focuses on techniques that have a good chance of rapidly changing young clients' bleak or nasty moods. The goals of the rapid emotional change techniques are fivefold:

1. To increase client involvement and interest in counseling by improving in-session mood.
2. To teach clients effective techniques for modifying negative and undesirable mood states.
3. To further facilitate and maintain the therapeutic alliance by introducing interesting and constructive mood-changing techniques within therapy sessions.
4. To assist parents (and teachers) in recognizing the centrality of mood in improving behavioral compliance.
5. To demonstrate ways parents can help their children with mood modification.

We strongly recommend using rapid emotional change techniques early and throughout the therapeutic process. They are easy rapport builders and status quo busters—and liberal amounts of each are needed to work effectively with youth. Once you get the feel of them, you will probably be able to expand on these or invent your own using therapeutic improvisation strategies (Selekman, 1993).

RAPID MOOD-CHANGING TECHNIQUES

Food and Mood

While initiating a series of therapy groups for prepubertal children diagnosed with ADHD, we decided to follow a standard policy we first encountered at an inner-city child and family treatment center (i.e., the Morrison Center in Portland, Oregon, where RSF did her clinical internship). We decided to serve snacks at the beginning of each group. This procedure reflects a combination of kindness and self-preservation because the groups we were facilitating began immediately after school. The idea of conducting group therapy with a half-dozen hungry children diagnosed as having ADHD and immediately after they had been let out of school struck us as potentially masochistic. Consequently, we did not initially conceive the decision to serve treats at the outset of every group as a technique as much as it was simply common-sense practice with hungry children.

Not long after the group started it became apparent that for virtually every child, the snack or treat time was a major highlight of the group. Although the treat contents were usually ordinary (a muffin and apple juice was our most common selection), group participants were consistently enthusiastic about receiving food at the beginning of group. We also found that children were not simply interested in eating the food. Until a rotating system was developed, group participants argued over which child had the "honor" of assisting with preparing and serving snacks. Also, at the end of each group session, some children begged to take extra treats home with them. Throughout group sessions, serving, eating, and cleaning up food became a central activity, and some of the most productive, insightful, and revealing conversations occurred during snack time. We set up a ritual of having everyone share their week's highlights and lowlights during snack time if they so desired. The combination of food, open-ended questioning, and general camaraderie facilitated wide-ranging discussions of the children's thoughts, feelings, experiences, and values. Occasional sarcastic comments aside, our food and weekly discussion ritual helped reestablish rapport, increase social bonding, and settle children down in preparation for subsequent group activities.

Although the children's preoccupation with food was initially puzzling (these were not undernourished kids), we came to believe that the most direct and accurate interpretation of what we were observing was this: For children (and perhaps for adults), sharing food—eating food together—has a basic, positive effect on mood and rapport. For millennia, religious and political figures have recognized the significance and power of the shared meal or breaking bread together. Eating and drinking are elemental aspects of being human—and as a shared activity, they work to break down barriers, warm up relationships, and open the doors to deeper sharing. This brings us to our first rule about facilitating a positive mood in difficult children: *Keep an adequate supply of reasonably healthy food and drink at your office.*

Case example. We have observed the rule of "food availability" confirmed repeatedly, even with very difficult children and adolescents. For example, in my (JSF) first session with Bobby, a 17-year-old boy who had been incarcerated because of building (and planning to use) explosive devices, he informed me without the slightest bit of ambiguity that he would never trust me and that he would never talk with me about "anything worth shit." So we started therapy by talking (primarily) about "trivial" topics such as food and drink and Bobby's tastes and preferences. Bobby loved coffee. He loved to stay out late—very late—with his friends and talk philosophy over coffee.

At the beginning of my second session with Bobby, I brought up the idea of us drinking some hot beverages together: "I know you like coffee, but I don't usually have any drinks with caffeine around here. What I do have is this variety pack of herbal teas that I recently bought... do you want to try some?" Bobby said "Sure, why not" and without the least bit of fanfare, therapy crept forward. Bobby discovered 10 flavored "honey sticks" in the herbal tea package and he systematically used them week after week. I faithfully saved them for him, putting them away where they would not accidentally be used by other office mates. We talked about his mother while he sipped apple spice tea with a cinnamon-flavored honey stick. Bobby had picked the combination, hovering over the tea box and sniffing the ingredients like a connoisseur: "I think apple spice and cinnamon honey are a good match, what do you think?" Of course, I applauded his eminently good taste. Later, we talked of how his mother and stepfather were not a good match and how "especially" he and his stepfather had been a "very bad match."

Bobby was quite eclectic in his tea selections, whereas I always selected licorice spice. He taunted me to take a risk, "to get a life" in his words, whereas I suggested he get focused and decide what he wanted from life. For Bobby and me, the metaphors offered by drinking hot tea together almost literally spilled into therapy— making our work together much more palatable to Bobby simply because we had a shared, basic ritual.

As suggested previously, the main point here has little to do with drinking herbal tea and everything to do with finding a mechanism through which Bobby could begin to trust and talk with me. Bobby had been caught by the authorities while in the process of building a bomb, and Bobby was indeed, emotionally explosive and filled with primitive affective impulses. At the outset of our relationship, he expressed absolutely no desire to talk with any adult in the world about his feelings or his life. Toward the end, Bobby became increasingly open with me and we were able to conduct experiments regarding how open he could be with other adult authority figures. One session, while Bobby was ranting on and on about how he wanted to have a weekend pass (away from the group home facility) I pushed him to call his probation officer and discuss his wishes directly. Much to his surprise and despite high anxiety, he was successful in convincing his probation officer of his readiness to have a weekend pass. Because we had a relationship, I was able to implement a series of directive cognitive-behavioral social problem-solving approaches. As some of them yielded successful outcomes, Bobby began to generalize his trust for me to other important adults in his life. He was able to take social risks with authority figures and face the possibility of rejection.

Undoubtedly, there are many explanations for why food, hot chocolate, tea, or chewing gum might have a positive effect on therapy process with young clients. Behaviorists would claim that, in the therapy situations we described above, food functioned as a very effective positive reinforcer. Wolpe (1958) would likely formulate the preceding case as a cure that came about as a function of systematic desensitization (*aka* reciprocal inhibition). On the other hand, psychoanalysts might suggest that feeding young clients facilitates a transference cure by fostering oral dependence on the therapist. Whatever the explanation, food tends to improve rapport and mood and subsequently increases openness; improved communication follows.

A few cautions about using food with young clients are worth noting. First, we only keep relatively healthy snacks available (e.g., sugarless gum, juice, herbal tea, granola bars). Second, we do not always offer something to eat, but with adults and children alike, we usually offer something to drink at the beginning of each session. Third, occasionally kids will overstep boundaries and ask for more and more food and sometimes they begin to expect treats, or even to criticize their counselor for the types of treats available—but of course, such behavior simply provides the astute professional with more material for exploration and interpretation. Perhaps children who act out with respect to food lack social inhibition—or are not eating well—or are impulsive—or are hungry for attention. Whatever the case, the presence of food items provides opportunity for discussion, feedback, and behavior change.

Also, along these same lines, I (RSF) have had young clients who began bringing in food or drink to share with me. In every case, clients offering food to me constituted a clear step forward in our relationship; as I accepted the offering and we shared the treat together, rapport was enhanced. Of course, it is important to not only accept the gift, but also to explore the trust being built and the relationship progress signaled by the food offering. As an example, one of my clients, Katy, a young molestation survivor whom I had seen for a number of months and who had very limited financial resources, proudly brought me a can of Coke one day.

"This is for you," she said shyly and handed the ice-cold can to me. I hesitated for a split-second, caught in guilt. I knew what 60 cents meant to this young woman. I was taken aback too, at the switch in roles. I usually offered *her* something to drink. That thought was what saved me. I took the soda, popped it open, and said "Hey, thanks. Guess you decided to be the hostess today, huh?" I smiled as I said it and waited.

"Well, not exactly," she said. "But I, I just want you to know how much it has meant to me to be able to talk through all this court crap. I feel so out of control, and you help me feel like, well, like I can get a life again." This was quite a move forward for Katy—envisioning a future beyond the miserable mangling she was enduring from the legal system. As with any trauma survivor, viewing the future had been a constant therapy goal. Bringing the Coke was an act of faith—there *would* be a future and she was pressing forward into being an active, contributing member of that future.

Three-Step, Push-Button Emotional Change Technique

Alfred Adler (1969) developed the push-button technique to demonstrate that thinking different thoughts can effectively change mood states. The purpose of Adler's technique was to help clients experience an increased sense of control over their emotions, thereby facilitating a sense of encouragement within clients. The push-button technique is easily adaptable to work with young clients. When we implement this technique, we do so in a playful manner, with counselor and client exploring together how to have more control over emotions. In essence, this is an emotional education technique; the primary goal is to teach young clients that, rather than being at the mercy of their feelings, they may learn some strategies and techniques that provide them with increased personal control over their feelings.

Depending upon the child's age, therapists can introduce this strategy as a "magic trick" for changing emotions or simply as "way to get out of a bad mood when you want to." The following example illustrates the Adlerian approach expanded to three distinct steps.

Case example. Sam, a 13-year-old European American boy, was referred because of his tendency to become suddenly stubborn, rigid, and disagreeable when interacting with authority figures. Sam arrived for his appointment accompanied by his mother. It quickly became obvious that Sam and his mother were in conflict. Sam was sullen, antagonistic, and difficult to talk with for several minutes at the outset of the session. Consequently, the Three-Step, Push-Button Emotional Change Technique (TSPB) was initiated:

Preparation/Explanation.

> *JSF:* I can see you're in a bad mood today. I have this... well, it's kind of a magic trick and I thought maybe you'd be interested. Want to hear about it?
>
> *S:* (*Shrugs*).
>
> *JSF:* It's a trick that helps people get themselves out of a bad mood *if* they want to. First, I need to tell you what I know about bad moods. Bad moods are weird because even though they don't really feel good, lots of times people don't want to change and get out of a bad mood and into a better mood. Do you know what I mean? Its like you kind of want to stay in a bad mood; you don't want anybody forcing you to change out of a bad mood.
>
> *S:* (*Nods in agreement.*)
>
> *JSF:* And you know what, I've noticed when I'm in a bad mood, I really hate it when someone comes up to me and says: "Cheer up!" or "Smile!"
>
> *S:* Yeah, I hate that too.
>
> *JSF:* In fact, sometimes the best thing to do is just really be in that bad mood—be those bad feelings. Sometimes it feels great to get right into the middle of those feelings and be them.
>
> *S:* Uh, I'm not sure what you're talking about.
>
> *JSF:* Well, to get in control of your own feelings, it is important to admit they are there. Kind of get acquainted with them. Get them out and look at them. So, the first step of this emotional change trick is to express your bad feelings. See, by getting them out and expressing them, you are the one in control. If you don't express your feelings, especially icky ones, you could get stuck in a bad mood even longer than you want.

As you can see from this dialogue, preparation for the TSPB technique involves emotional validation of how it feels to be in a bad mood, information about bad moods and how people can resist changing their moods or even get stuck in them, hopeful information about how people can learn to change their moods, and more emotional validation about how it feels when people prematurely try to "cheer up" someone.

Step 1.

Most young people have only very basic ideas about how they might go about expressing their negative feelings. Consequently, Step 1 of the TSPB technique involves helping clients identify various emotional expression techniques and then helping them to try these out. We recommend brainstorming with young clients about specific methods for expressing feelings. The client and therapist should work together (perhaps with a chalk/grease board or large drawing pad), generating a list of expressive strategies that might include: scribbling on a note pad or drawing an angry picture, punching a large pillow, writing a nasty note to someone (but not necessarily delivering it), grimacing and making various angry faces into a mirror, and using words, perhaps even yelling if appropriate, to express specific feelings.

The expressive procedures listed above are easier for young clients to learn and understand when therapists actively model affective expression or assist clients in their affective expression. It is especially important for therapists to model expressing emotions in cases where clients are inhibited or unsure about how to express themselves. Again, we recommend engaging in affective expression jointly with clients. We have had particular success making facial grimaces into a mirror. (Young clients often become entertained when engaging in this task with their therapist.) The optimal time for shifting to Step 2 in the TSPB technique is when clients have just begun to show a slight change in overall demeanor and affect. (Often this occurs as a result of the therapist joining the client in expressing anger or sadness or general nastiness.)

Note: If a young client is unresponsive to Step 1 of the TSPB technique, the therapist/counselor should *not* move on to Step 2. Instead, an alternative mood-changing strategy should be considered (e.g., perhaps food and mood or the personal note). Be careful to simply reflect what you see. "Seems like you aren't feeling like expressing those yucky feelings right now. Hey, that's okay. I can show you this trick some other day. Want some gum?"

Step 2.

> *JSF:* Did you know you can change your mood just by thinking
> different thoughts? No kidding. Thinking certain things is
> like pushing a button in your brain and the things you think
> of start making you feel certain ways. Let's try it. Tell me the
> funniest thing that happened to you this week.
> *S:* Yesterday in math, my friend Todd farted (*client smiles and laughs*).
> *JSF:* Really! I bet people really laughed. In fact, I can see it makes
> you laugh just thinking about it. I had a friend when I was in
> school who used to do that all the time too.

Frequently, as in the preceding example, the content of what
young people consider funny may not seem particularly funny to
adults (one of those central cultural differences). Nonetheless, it is
crucial for therapists to make efforts at being interested and entertained—welcoming the challenge to empathically see the situation
from the 13-year-old perspective. It is also important to stay with
and build on the mood shift, asking for additional humorous thoughts,
favorite jokes, or recent events. With clients who respond well, counselors can pursue further experimentation with various affective states
(e.g., "Tell me about a sad [or proud, or surprising] experience").

In some cases, young clients may be unable to generate a funny
story or a funny memory. This may be an indicator of depression, as
depressed clients often report greater difficulty recalling positive
or happy events (Forgas, 1991). Consequently, it may be necessary
for the therapist to take the lead in generating a funny statement.

> *S:* I can't think of anything funny.
> *JSF:* Really? Well, keep trying… I'll try too (*therapist and client
> sit together in silence for about 20 seconds, trying to come up with a
> positive thought or memory*).
> *JSF:* Got anything yet?
> *S:* Nope.
> *JSF:* Okay, I think I've got one. Actually, this is a joke: How do
> you spell shop?
> *S:* Huh?

JSF: How do you spell the word, shop?

S: S-H-O-P.

JSF: Right. What do you do at a green light?

S: Stop.

JSF: Boy, good thing you don't have a driver's license.

S: What?

JSF: Well... I asked "What do you do at a green light?" and you said "Stop." Remember, you stop at red lights and go at green lights!

S: Oh man. That's lame (*smiling sheepishly*).

Telling a joke or a funny story can help young, depressed clients generate a story of their own. However, we have two additional comments for therapists who might choose to use a "teasing" riddle (illustrated above). First, therapists should use teasing riddles only when there is a strong therapeutic relationship established; otherwise, the client may interpret teasing negatively. Second, because preteen and teen clients often love to tease, therapists must be prepared to be teased back (i.e., young clients frequently generate a "comeback" teasing riddle in response to a therapist's teasing riddle).

Finally, therapists need to be sensitive to young clients who remain unable to generate a positive thought or story, even after having heard an example or two from the therapist. If a young client is unable to generate a funny thought, it is important for the therapist to remain positive and encouraging.

JSF: Well, you know what, there are some days when I can't think of any funny stories either. I'm sure you'll be able to tell me something funny next time. Today I was able to think of some funny stuff... next time we can both give it a try again.

It may be that depressed young clients will need to borrow from the therapist's positive thoughts and affect during some sessions because they are not able to generate their own positive thoughts and feelings. If so, the TSPB technique should be discontinued for that particular session. The process of TSPB requires completion of each step before continuing on to the next step.

Step 3.

Step 3 of this procedure involves teaching young clients about the contagion quality of mood states and it reinforces the new good mood. The purposes of teaching clients about contagious moods are twofold. First, it provides them with further general education about their emotional life. Second, it gives them an opportunity to obtain an empowerment experience; if they complete the assignment associated with this activity, they may be able to have a positive effect on another person's mood:

> *JSF:* I want to tell you one more interesting thing about moods. They're contagious. Do you know what contagious means… it means that you can catch them from being around other people who are in bad moods or good moods. Like when you got here. I noticed your mom was in a pretty bad mood too. It made me wonder, did you catch the bad mood from her or did she catch it from you? Anyway, now you seem to be in a much better mood. And so I was wondering, do you think you can make your mom "catch" your good mood?
>
> *S:* Oh yeah. I know my mom pretty well. All I have to do is tell her I love her and she'll get all mushy and stuff.
>
> *JSF:* So, do you love her?
>
> *S:* Yeah, I guess so. She really bugs me sometimes though, you know what I mean?
>
> *JSF:* I think so. Sometimes it seems especially easy for people who love each other to bug each other. And parents can be especially good at bugging their kids. Not on purpose, but they bug you anyway.
>
> *S:* You can say that again. She's a total bugging expert.
>
> *JSF:* But you did say you love her, right?
>
> *S:* Yeah.
>
> *JSF:* So if you told her "I love you mom," it would be the truth, right?
>
> *S:* Yeah.
>
> *JSF:* And you think that would put her in a better mood too, right?

S: No duh, man. She'd love it.

JSF: So, now that you're in a better mood, maybe you should just tell her you love her and spread the good mood. You could even tell her something like: "You know mom, you really bug me sometimes, but I love you."

S: Okay. I could do that.

It is obvious in this case example that Sam knows at least one way to have a positive influence on his mother's mood, but he is reluctant to use the "I love you" approach. Eventually, in this case, it would be useful for Sam to explore alternative methods for having a positive effect on his mother's mood.

Although some observers of this type of therapy interaction may think the therapist is just teaching Sam emotional manipulation techniques, we believe that viewpoint makes a strong negative assumption about Sam and his family. Instead, our position is that successful families (and successful marriages) include liberal doses of positive interaction (Gottman & Krokoff, 1989). Consequently, unless we detect that Sam is an exceptionally manipulative boy (i.e., with a CD), we feel fine about reminding him of ways to share positive (and truthful) feelings with his mother. In fact, difficulty expressing positive and affectionate feelings is a deficit commonly associated with stereotypic male communication patterns (Tannen, 1990).

Young clients sometimes need assistance planning how to "spread the good mood." To spread a good mood to someone else requires a certain amount of empathic perspective taking. In our experience, youth are more able to generate empathic responses and to initiate positive interactions with their parents (or siblings, teachers, etc.) after they have achieved an improved mood state and the concomitant increased sense of self-control. This is consistent with social–psychological literature suggesting that positive moods increase the likelihood of prosocial or altruistic behavior (Isen, 1987). Because of developmental issues associated with being young, it is sometimes helpful to introduce the idea of changing other people's moods as a challenge (Erikson, 1968). "I wonder if you have the idea down well enough to actually try and change your mom's mood."

Recently, a 14-year-old boy thought a few minutes, then brought his mom into the office and said "Now Mom, I want you to think of how you would feel if I agree to clear the table *and* wash the dishes without you reminding me for a week." Mom looked a bit surprised, but admitted she felt good at the thought, whereupon I (JSF) gave the boy a thumbs up signal and said "Well done." The boy then also offered to accept a fine as punishment if he forgot or argued about this set of chores.

Step 4.

At this point, readers should beware that when working with difficult young clients, things are not always as they seem. Consequently, although we are describing a Three-Step technique, you may notice that we have now moved to Step 4.

When using the TSPB procedure, we have found it useful to request that our young clients teach the TSPB procedure to another person after they have learned it in therapy. For example, one girl successfully taught her younger brother the method when he was in a negative mood during a family hike. By teaching the technique to her brother, she achieved an especially empowering experience; she began to view herself as having increased control over her and her family's emotional states. This procedure is consistent with principles of a systems approach to working with difficult youth: One-Person Family Therapy (Szapocznik, Kurtines, Santisteban, & Rio, 1990). Of course, some family systems are very resistant to changing family affect and, in such cases, more direct family therapy interventions may be appropriate (Henggeler, Melton, & Smith, 1992; Kazdin, 1988; Selekman, 1993).

Passing Personal Notes

A simple method for re-engaging an angry or "checked out" child/adolescent in counseling is the note-passing technique (Sommers-Flanagan & Sommers-Flanagan, 1996a). This technique is generally indicated when a young client suddenly appears sullen and angry; the client has become quiet and nonresponsive to therapist inquiry. In some cases, counselors may have clues as to why their clients have become so quiet. However, in other cases the young client's silence may be a mystery. Whatever the case, note passing is used to communicate sensitively to clients through an alternative format, to reduce ostensible pressure on young clients to be verbally productive, to express empathy for an emotional state wherein the client does not "feel like" talking openly, and to surprise the client (and thereby modify affect) by being supportive and affectionate rather than critical in response to the client's silence (similar to a corrective emotional experience; Alexander & French, 1946).

Children, teenagers, and even some college students are notorious for passing notes in class. Most often the notes are brief and focus on gossip or things that are bothering the note writer at the moment. Generally speaking, among teenagers, passing notes is cool.

To utilize this technique the counselor simply needs a notebook and pencil or pen. When the client appears angry and sullen and efforts to interact verbally result in continued withdrawal and silence, the counselor should pick up the notebook and begin writing. This activity often attracts the youth's attention. In our experience, young clients frequently assume we are writing something negative about them. One 12-year-old boy immediately questioned: "Are you writing a note to the group home?" as he expected he would be reprimanded for becoming silent in therapy. I (JSF) responded: "Nope, I'm just writing a note to you."

When using this technique, the counselor should hold the notebook so that the client cannot see the content of the writing; part of the effect of this technique rests on the client's surprise at receiving a personal note and on surprise at the content of the note. Of course, the note should be individualized and personal (see Box 3.1).

The personal note is person-centered, similar to Carl Rogers' (Rogers & Meador, 1984) verbal responses to the "silent young man." Additionally, it is useful to include a humorous or light closing and an interest in hearing back from the client. Finally, counselors should write only what young clients will feel comfortable taking home (e.g., critical comments about teachers or family members, even if such comments are in the service of empathy and emotional validation, may have negative repercussions).

Box 3.1. Note-Passing Sample

Dear Tiffany:

You're really quiet today, but that's okay. I'm writing this note because I want you to know that it's alright not to talk sometimes. Sometimes it just feels better to be quiet. But if I have somehow done something to make you mad… maybe I've said something to upset you, then I'm sorry. I didn't mean to bug you or upset you. Or maybe somebody or something else upset you and you just don't feel like talking with me about it. Whatever is going on, I want you to know you can talk with me about it when you want to.

Your Very Own Counselor,

Rita S-F

P.S. Write back if you want to.

Our observations suggest that the reaction of individual clients to this procedure is uniformly positive. Often clients act surprised when told: "I wrote you a note." One client asked to take it into the bathroom to read. Other clients have asked: "Can I keep it?" To which the standard response is, "Of course, I wrote it to you." Another client refused the note during the session, but accepted it later from her mother (i.e., it was sealed and given to the mother to deliver at home). Sometimes young clients have initiated a note-writing exchange after receiving a note from one of us.

One possible explanation for why this approach reopens communication is that it moves young people out of a negative mood state; it is hard for clients to maintain a negative mood state when they are also experiencing an alternative mood state of surprise or pleasure. Research suggests that it is common for young people who have behave aggresively to expect hostility or overt coercion from others during times of stress or threat (Dodge & Frame, 1983; Dodge & Somberg, 1987). Therefore, when instead of hostility or demands for verbal interaction, young clients receive the unexpected (i.e., a kind and nondemanding note), it is difficult for an angry and resistant stance to be maintained. Also, in many cases young people we see in therapy have *never* received a personal handwritten note from an adult (especially from an adult male). Overall, it seems that a sincere and nonthreatening effort by a counselor to enhance emotional intimacy and establish a personal connection does not go unnoticed.

The Hand Pushing Game

Many young clients are not particularly interested in sitting still and talking with a therapist. It is not an activity they would choose to do on their own accord. Instead, given a choice, young clients would frequently prefer playing games, going on walks, going out for ice cream, going for a drive, or even just hanging out on the street corner over simply sitting and talking. Additionally, many young people are active learners. That is, they learn best through experience and demonstration. Passive learning (or passive teaching) techniques (such as the lecture) are notoriously poorly received by youth in general and by troubled youth in particular. The last two techniques in this chapter integrate active learning experiences into the therapeutic process.

The Hand Pushing game is based on the premise that adolescents sometimes automatically oppose the wishes or directives of their parents, teachers, and various authority figures based on the source rather than on the content of the wish or directive. This oppositional characteristic is somewhat natural for even very young children, but it can become increasingly problematic as teenagers begin emancipation processes (Church, 1994; Erikson, 1968; Houser, Daniels, D'Andrea, & Konstam, 1993). The emancipation and identity problems during adolescence essentially entail an adolescent's effort to achieve identity by opposing authority. This Hand Pushing game gives young clients a physical experience of how futile and ineffective it can be to define oneself by simply vigorously pushing back against any perceived authority or barrier.

The therapist may introduce the Hand Pushing activity as a game "designed to demonstrate why resisting everything your parents or teachers ask of you is not an effective strategy." Alternatively, the game can simply be initiated in a more spontaneous manner by the therapist: "Stand up, I want to show you a game." Regardless of *how* the game is initiated, it is helpful to initiate it when the client has been talking about or acting out his or her identity and emancipation issues.

To begin the game, ask the adolescent to stand up and face the therapist. Tell him or her to place toes 6 to 10 inches away from your toes and to hold both hands, palms out, directly in front of their shoulders. The therapist stands in a mirroring position so that if both client and therapist extend their hands/arms a few inches, their hands/palms touch one another's. As they stand face-to-face, the therapist states:

> In this game we push forward against each other's hands to try to make the other one lose balance and move. Whoever moves one or both of her feet loses the game. You can't hold on to each other's hands and you can only make contact on the hands. You can put your hands up or draw them away, and so can I.

Care should be taken to make sure that a soft chair or couch is directly behind the client. This is because, upon learning that this game involves pushing, some young people quickly begin pushing the therapist's hands with great effort and, if the therapist weighs more than the client (or has better balance), the client can knock him or herself over backwards by virtue of his or her own forceful pushing.

Young clients generally respond positively to this physical game, perhaps because it constitutes a break from talking seriously, but perhaps because of other factors. After playing a series of hand pushing games, the following game playing strategies or principles should be discussed: (a) the winner is not usually the person who pushes the hardest; (b) instead, the winner is usually the person who is most grounded and balanced; (c) it is easy to lose, or even knock oneself down, by consistently employing an aggressive strategy; and (d) by dodging the other person's efforts at pushing and by giving way to forceful pushing, one person may not win the game, but by being centered and avoiding major power struggles, that person can manage to *never* lose the game.

The Hand Pushing game is fertile ground for analogies, such as how important it is to determine where you stand, who you are, what you want, and how you want to proceed, rather than simply reacting to others in a competitive and/or oppositional manner. Alternatively, if one does not identify his or her own goals, identity, and achievement strategies, he or she may simply react to or oppose all authority figures; this results in the adolescent being defined by his or her opposition to the system, rather than by the process of self-definition.

It also may be useful to have adolescents play the Hand Pushing game with their parents. Obviously, in cases in which there is significant anger and hostility between parent and child, the therapist should emphasize caution; some parents and children have experienced, or are on the verge of experiencing physical intimidation or abuse. The Hand Pushing game should not be employed with families with any history of physical abuse because of the possibility of re-enacting abusive scenarios and/or retraumatizing the abuse victim. However, with less disturbed parent–child dyads, the Hand Pushing game can help clients explore ways in which adolescents and parents struggle with separation–individuation issues (Church, 1994; Houser et al., 1993). Most adolescents enjoy this game, acknowledge its lessons, and are able to play it with their parents so that they can demonstrate the lessons to them as well.

Note: It is important for therapists to practice the Hand Pushing game prior to using it with young clients. We recommend it for after-dinner bonding with family members or as a diversion during professional consultation groups.

Arm Wrestling

Many children and adolescents referred for therapy are socially and emotionally awkward and unskilled (Goldstein, 1988; Spivack & Shure, 1982; Tisdelle & St. Lawrence, 1988). They are also frequently unable to communicate personal thoughts and feelings in a clear and constructive manner (Goldstein, 1988; Ladd, 1984). In particular, young people diagnosed with ADHD may be limited in their verbal, social, and emotional skills; in contrast, they are often very physical or motorically oriented in their interpersonal interactions and learning styles (Barkley, 1990). As is the case with the Hand Pushing game, physically or motorically oriented clients can benefit from therapeutic interactions that utilize a physical modality followed by subsequent discussion of thoughts and feelings stimulated by the interaction.

The arm wrestling procedure involves meeting the client at his or her developmental level (i.e., physical interaction), followed by coaching and modeling him or her through a verbal expression of thoughts and feelings generated by the physical interaction.

Case example. An 11-year-old girl with a history of physically aggressive altercations and previous psychotherapy trials attended an intake session. Despite her high intelligence level and advanced verbal skills, she clearly opposed the process of "sitting around and talking." Rather than beginning a power struggle over talking early in the first session, the therapist laid down on the floor and stated: "Let's arm wrestle!" The client's response was mixed. She got down to the floor, but stated (in a somewhat positive manner): "You're weird!" After the client lost the first arm wrestling match the therapist commented, "You're sure strong for your age. I guess it gives me an advantage because I weigh about 80 pounds more than you? How about if you use both hands this time?"

Subsequently, the girl used both hands, managing an arm wrestling victory. While she chattered on about her victory, the therapist helped her focus on how it felt to lose the first match and guided the conversation toward other losses and failures the girl had experienced. When the therapist reached out to give the girl a firm handshake at the end of the session, she looked him in the eye and asserted: "I've been in counseling before, but they just sat there. You are really weird." The therapist was thus reassured that the beginnings of a therapeutic alliance had been established. Being "weird" in this case was a positive assessment, as demonstrated by the client during subsequent sessions.

At one point, she began sobbing upon discovering that she had come at the wrong appointment time and therefore would not have an opportunity to talk (and arm wrestle) with the therapist on that particular day. Despite her rough and tough exterior, she was clearly capable of attachment and affection toward the therapist; this helped the child make significant interpersonal gains. At the time of this writing her case was inactive, but, if at some point she returns to therapy, she will likely get down on the floor quickly for an arm wrestling rematch.

Arm wrestling is traditionally more of a male-oriented activity. In the preceding demonstration, it was used effectively with a young female client, but obviously therapists must be selective regarding which clients this sometimes provocative technique should be applied with. Specifically, we have found that preadolescent girls or "tough tomboyish" adolescent girls are more receptive and playful with this type of technique than are other types of girls. In contrast, adolescent girls or girls with stronger stereotypically feminine attributes are less-than-ideal candidates for this approach.

CONCLUDING COMMENTS

We described and reviewed several techniques for producing rapid emotional change in young clients. These techniques are especially suited for difficult children/adolescents. They primarily consist of technical innovations designed to articulate generally accepted cognitive-behavioral and psychotherapeutic techniques (Kazdin, 1988). In the demanding environments faced by school counselors and agency mental health professionals, such techniques can make a difference in functioning and illustrate important adaptive options to challenging young referrals. In addition, the onset of national health care reform, health maintenance organizations, etcetera requires that mental health professionals provide intensive, rapid-acting, and high-quality interventions for children and adolescents (Donovan, Steinberg, & Sabin, 1994; Stern, 1993). The techniques described in this chapter may help increase the pace with children and adolescents while still maintaining treatment coherence, quality, and integrity.

4

Behavioral, Cognitive, and Interpersonal Change Strategies

He now said the words Omri had been dreading most.

"It's true and I can prove it!" And his hand went to his pocket.

Omri did the only thing possible. He jumped at him and knocked him over. He sat on his chest and pinned his hands to the ground.

"You dare—you dare—you dare—" he ground out between clenched teeth before Mr. Johnson managed to drag him off.

"Get out of the room!" he roared.

"I won't!" Omri choked out. He'd be crying himself in a minute, he felt so desperate.

"OUT!"

Omri felt his collar seized. He was almost hiked off his feet. The next thing he knew, he was outside the door and hearing the key turning.

Without stopping to think, Omri hurled himself against the door, kicking and banging with his fists.

> *"Don't show him, Patrick, don't show him! Patrick, don't, I'll kill you if you show him!" he screamed at the top of his lungs.*
>
> *Footsteps came running. Through his tears and a sort of red haze, Omri saw Mrs. Hunt, the headmaster's elderly secretary, bearing down on him. He got in a couple more good kicks and shouts before she got hold of him and, with both arms around his waist, carried him, shrieking and struggling, bodily into her own little office.*
>
> *The minute she put him down he tried to bolt, but she hung on.*
>
> *"Omri! Omri! Stop it, calm down, whatever's come over you, you naughty boy!"* (from The Indian in the Cupboard, *Banks, 1980, p. 137)*

Motivation is as mysterious as it is powerful. In the preceding excerpt, Omri is powerfully motivated but his behavior is puzzling to the outside observer. Omri has a clear, all-encompassing goal. He wants to prevent his friend Patrick from showing the school's headmaster a miniature live cowboy and Indian. Although Omri does not succeed in accomplishing his goal, his effort is commendable, even heroic. He is so motivated that he disregards everything else; his heart, soul, and body are filled with determination.

Many times we have listened to parents as they scratch their heads and puzzle about their children's displaced motivational energy. Parents say things like: "If only she would put as much effort into cleaning her room as she puts into taking care of her hair, her room would be immaculate." Perhaps even more frustrating to parents is this: "If only he would put as much effort into *doing* his homework as he does into *avoiding* his homework, he'd be a straight A student."

In these cases, parents are wishing they could redirect their children's motivation. These parents do not necessarily want to control their children, they just want to channel some of their children's energy and motivation into more constructive activities.

This chapter focuses primarily on behavioral and cognitive techniques for redirecting children's motivation toward potentially growthful and constructive therapeutic activities. Although redirecting children's motivation is challenging and difficult, it is absolutely required for therapeutic success. Additionally, several techniques in this chapter have an interpersonal focus; they are techniques designed to shift interpersonal attitudes and behaviors.

NEVER UNDERESTIMATE THE POWER
OF CONTINGENCIES

More often than not, young clients' behavior can be understood in terms of contingencies. In fact, when therapists or parents are trying to persuade young clients to make behavioral changes, the young person often will make their awareness of behavioral contingencies clear with a single word: *why.*

Children and teenagers are notorious for asking "why?"; they ask *why* they have to take out the garbage, *why* they have to be home by midnight, *why* they can't go out and drink some beers with their friends, and *why* they can't experiment with drugs. It is important for parents and therapists to be sensitive to children's questions about why they should or should not engage in particular behaviors. This is because "why" questions are questions about contingency and motivation. In other words, when young clients ask why, they are trying to understand: "What's the payoff?" And, like adults, they are interested, to at least some degree, in obtaining some form of external reinforcement in return for their cooperative behaviors.

Depending on their own values and upbringing, parents may insist that children should not be bribed to get good grades, to complete their chores, or to comply with curfew. They will sometimes insist that children of this generation are spoiled and too dependent on external rewards. In many ways, these parents are right; children are bombarded with messages about acquisition and materialism. However, complete avoidance or denial of the role of external motivation and rewards is impossible. The process by which external motivation becomes internal motivation is an important area of psychological research (Lepper, Greene, & Nisbett, 1973). Very generally, findings to date indicate that modest external rewards that convey performance information to children can contribute to the development of intrinsic motivation (Deci & Ryan, 1980). In contrast, if rewards are used to control children's behavior, children may work hard to obtain the reward, but not develop an intrinsic interest in the target behavior (Ryan, 1983). Obviously, intrinsic motivation and/or self-reinforcement systems are crucial to the development of self-discipline. Consequently, as therapists, we preach moderate reinforcement strategies designed to provide performance feedback to young clients instead of large-scale reinforcements designed to control child behavior. However, before focusing on reinforcement, we suggest using a behavioral assessment technique: Analyze the existing contingencies.

Parents and children usually focus on different sets of behavioral contingencies. Parents focus on long-term contingencies (e.g., "Doing your homework will help you get good grades and getting good grades is important to getting into college"). In contrast, children and teenagers focus on short-term contingencies (e.g., "I need some money for the movie tonight"). Therapists may need to help parents refrain from lecturing about the great benefits of long-term contingencies because these lectures ordinarily fall on closed ears. Instead, to be developmentally attuned to oppositional young clients requires that parents and therapists be sensitive to short-term contingencies. In a sense, therapists function as developmental translators; they help parents understand the motivational language of their children.

Defining Bribery

Many parents mistakenly confuse positive reinforcement with bribery. They discount potential benefits of positive reinforcement by stating things like: "Oh, we've tried bribery." Or if the therapist uses an incentive to encourage a teenager to effectively communicate within a session, parents sometimes say: "You just bribed her to get her to do that. She won't do it without being bribed." In most cases, when we use specific contingency programs or positive reinforcement techniques with young clients, we explain to parents the difference between bribery and positive reinforcement.

Before we talk about using positive reinforcement techniques with Jennifer, I want to explain the difference between positive reinforcement and bribery. Do you know the definition of bribery? (*Short pause, usually parents just look at you.*) The definition of bribery is to pay someone to do something illegal. So if we come up with a plan to pay Jennifer something, whether it's fruit snacks, a trip to the mall, or a new CD, for consistently completing her homework, we are not bribing her... because *there is nothing illegal about Jennifer doing her homework.*

All of us, especially adults, are responding to positive reinforcement every day. That's why most of us go to work, either because we get paid for it or because we enjoy it. And if we enjoy it, it is because there is something about going to work that we perceive as positively reinforcing. So if our goal is to have Jennifer consistently complete her homework, we have to figure out how to make doing homework more rewarding to her.

In addition to defining bribery, parents usually benefit from hearing how important it is *not* to provide their children with excessively large or excessively frequent reinforcers designed to control behavior. Therefore, we usually inform them of research showing that providing children with excessive reinforcement to control behavior can undermine development of intrinsic motivation (Ryan, 1983).

Therapeutic Wagering

Wagering with teenagers may be therapeutic because of issues associated with adolescent development; generally, adolescents use various challenges as a means of forming and solidifying their identity or sense of self (Erikson, 1968). Young clients often view therapeutic wagers as a challenge. In other words, winning a bet or proving an adult authority figure wrong can be developmentally stimulating for young clients. Of course, winning a bet also simply may be a profitable contingency for young clients. Whichever is the case, a small wager or bet between therapist and client can enhance motivation (Sommers-Flanagan & Sommers-Flanagan, 1995b).

Wagering on communication. One of our favorite applications of wagering or positive reinforcement with young clients is in the area of communication. Frequently, by the time of referral, communication between parent(s) and child is characterized by interpersonal conflict and cross-complaints (Gottman & Krokoff, 1989). Additionally, often both parents and child are so angry that they have little motivation or interest in making attempts to communicate effectively. We have found that the wagering technique can remotivate young clients to apply specific communication skills with their parents. In particular, we provide young clients with reinforcement for using paraphrases, feeling reflections, "I" statements, and problem-solving language.

The simple form of wagering on communication involves an initial statement such as, "I'd be willing to bet that when your parents come back in this room, you won't be able to sit and listen to them without losing your cool." In virtually every case in which we have used this statement, the client, usually a teenager, takes the bait (or bet) and becomes motivated to prove that he or she can sit and listen and keep cool. Subsequently, the task involves defining relevant criteria such as what is meant by sitting and listening, what is meant by losing one's cool, and what is to be wagered.

After the wager has been initiated, we proceed to define sitting and listening as including eye contact, appropriate body posture, minimal encouragers (e.g., head nodding and uh huhs), and verbal tracking or short paraphrases (Ivey, 1991; Sommers-Flanagan & Sommers-Flanagan, 1993). Counselors can review and write down each of these signs of effective listening for the client's convenience. If a client balks at this process, a simple statement such as, "I'm just trying to give you every chance possible to win the bet," or "I want to be fair by making sure we both are using the same definition for sitting and listening." Similarly, keeping one's cool is defined in positive terms as keeping one's voice low and controlled and waiting for the other party to finish speaking before speaking oneself.

Prior to recalling parents to therapy, it is important for therapists to initiate practice communication. Of course, this involves role-playing wherein therapist and client anticipate what parents might say and rehearse positive communication skills. We might note at this point that there is nothing particularly unusual about this procedure aside from using the wager to motivate young clients and consequently squeeze in some serious communication skills training before reuniting parent(s) and child.

Successful communication is the most important outcome in this procedure. If the therapist believes that it is impossible or unlikely for the child to win the bet, then the wager should be modified (e.g., "I want you to have a fair chance at winning this bet, so let's allow one interruption and you only have to listen for 5 minutes and then we stop and you win"). In other words, for the technique to succeed, the child must win the bet and receive at least three forms of payoff. First, the child receives positive social reinforcement from parents and therapist for using effective communication skills. Second, he or she receives positive self-reinforcement in the form of good feelings and a sense of self-efficacy associated with successful communication. Third, he or she receives whatever reinforcer was previously agreed upon with the therapist in the wager.

Parent cooperation is essential for this technique to succeed. Consequently, depending upon the expected level of parent cooperation, parents may need to be informed of the planned communication task and planned positive reinforcer. If they are hesitant in expressing positive reinforcement after their child's demonstration of effective communication skills, parents may need to be prompted (e.g., "Did you know that Jennifer could sit and listen to you so well without interrupting?"). Also, before the communication interactions, therapists should act excited about winning the wager, and after losing the wager therapists should complain about having to pay off the client (e.g., "I can't believe you won the bet. Oh no, now I have to pay you off!").

Finally, this technique is also useful for evaluating family and client communication skills. Specifically, it can help determine if communication problems are a result of skill deficits or of low motivation.

Wagering on cognitions. Traditional aggression control procedures recommend that aggressive adolescents identify alternative social cognitions about particular situations likely to trigger an aggressive response (Feindler & Ecton, 1986). Dodge's (Dodge & Frame, 1983; Dodge & Somberg, 1987) research on delinquent adolescents' cognitive distortions suggests that aggressive young people often interpret incidental interactions with others as signs of hostility. For example, another youth may accidently bump into an adolescent client at school and the adolescent client may interpret the "bump" as an intentional effort to hurt or demean him or her. These interpretations of hostility can often lead to aggressive interactions. The problem is exacerbated when, as commonly occurs, other adolescents reject the hostile youth and thereby deny him or her the opportunity for corrective social interactions.

If young clients are able to modify their typical interpretations of hostility, they may be able to prevent, manage, or control aggressive urges. Unfortunately, often teenagers have little or no intrinsic motivation when it comes to modifying social cognitions. After all, many clients say, "what's the point?; I know Preston is out to get me... there's no other explanation." By using the wager technique, therapists may be able to enhance client motivation to identify alternative, and hopefully less paranoid, social interpretations. To use this procedure, we simply make a statement similar to the following: "I bet you can't think of any other explanations for why Preston bumped you in the hall."

In some cases, just initiating "the bet" using the preceding statement will activate motivation within a young client. Other clients may need more concrete betting contingencies. For example, they may want to know "how much" the bet is, or "What do I get if I can come up with other explanations for Preston bumping me?" In either case, it is helpful for therapists to have small rewards immediately available. Alternatively, some young clients will want to negotiate their specific reward before generating alternative social cognitions. For those young clients who quickly seek to negotiate special rewards, therapists should be warned that some such clients will be excellent negotiators; it is important to begin negotiations with skillful young clients with preset limits in terms of what you are willing to provide as positive reinforcers. Otherwise, therapists may find themselves in a position where an excessively valuable reward has been promised, or a client has negotiated a therapeutic boundary break (e.g., the reward is to drive the young client over to a local fast food restaurant for tacos).

Wagering on behavioral alternatives. Similar to generating alternative social cognitions, traditional cognitive-behavioral procedures for aggression control and social skill training usually require young clients to generate numerous behavioral alternatives. Ideally, the behavioral alternatives that young clients generate are constructive and adaptive behaviors that, during the heat of the social moment, can be recalled and implemented quickly, instead of relying on aggression or automatic and socially unskilled responses. Challenging or wagering young clients to produce new behavioral alternatives increases motivation for generating prosocial responses. We use positive reinforcement procedures in conjunction with the challenge or wagering procedures: "You will receive one baseball card (or 5 cents or 1 minute of computer time) for every behavior option you can produce in the next 60 seconds."

Additionally, we use time pressure procedures: "Quick, quick, give me some options. What could you do?" Time pressure procedures are designed to assist young clients in quickly identifying behavioral alternatives in a manner similar to how they will need to generate such responses in the real world. It also lowers resistance by using a gamelike format and minimizing time available to respond with oppositional verbalizations.

REDEFINITIONS AND REFRAMING

Cognitive therapists and developmental psychologists often comment on teenagers' capacity to rigidly think in terms of black and white, night and day, yes and no (Curry & Craighead, 1990; Wilkes et al., 1994). Of course, this tendency is increased significantly when teenagers are in conflict with adult authority figures or when they are experiencing a depressive mood. The purpose of using redefinitions in therapy with young clients is to help them let go of maladaptive erroneous beliefs which restrict their ability to resolve personal problems and conflicts. Similarly, redefinitions are useful with parents whose beliefs and definitions of particular situations are restricting their ability to creatively solve family problems. Finally, redefinitions and reframes redirect motivation by changing rigid perceptual sets held by many young clients.

Brown-nosing

When working with irritable teenagers, therapy discussions inevitably focus on why the teenager insists on treating his or her family members, teachers, etcetera, with disdain and disrespect. In such cases, it may be useful to explore with the teenager what might happen if he or she began behaving in a friendly and kind manner toward his or her family. Specifically:

> What if you woke up every morning and said "Good Morning!" to your father? And then, what if you told your little sister you'd be glad to take her to the mall after school? And then, after a day of being nice to everyone in the family, what would happen if you told your parents something you appreciate about them?

We have had many teenagers respond to this line of questioning with a statement like, "I would never act that way because I'm not into *brown-nosing!*" or "I don't suck up to anybody!"

At this point, it is important to know how the client really feels about his or her parents and sister. If he or she sometimes has loving or positive feelings toward other family members, then focusing on redefining "brown-nosing" is warranted. On the other hand, if he or she clearly is unable to generate any positive feelings about other family members, then it is probably best to move on to a different therapeutic tact.

Some young clients may have positive feelings toward family members, but these feelings remain unspoken, partly due to a negative adolescent attitude toward brown-nosing adults and perhaps partly due to positive affective communication skill deficits or anxiety. If a negative adolescent attitude toward brown-nosing is contributing to the adolescent's inhibition about expressing positive feelings, the true definition of brown-nosing should be explored: "Now, what does brown-nosing mean anyway? Really, I'm interested in what you think brown-nosing means." Many teens can accurately define brown-nosing. Basically, the key components are insincerity and an underlying motive to obtain favored status or preferential treatment. In other words, brown-nosers act nice toward someone only because of what they might get from that person.

Once the definition is obtained and discussed, it is natural for therapists to be supportive of the teen's "I will not brown-nose!" value. However, it is also natural to question whether or not treating other family members with kindness and respect is really brown-nosing. In the end, comments similar to the following can be made:

> So, let me get this straight. There are some things you like about your sister, right? (*"Yeah, I guess so."*) And there are some things you like about your parents, right? (*"uh huh."*) Okay, then if you said something nice to them, it wouldn't be insincere *and* it wouldn't be brown-nosing unless you were saying it *only* to get something back from them. Am I right about this? (*"Yeah, you're right."*) Okay then. Let's talk about some nice things you might say to your family that you really believe, then I won't be suggesting that you brown-nose anyone... and believe me, after talking with you about brown-nosing, I'm more clear than ever that I don't want to encourage you to do that.

Another goal of this procedure is to develop insight or understanding regarding motives underlying client behavior or lack of behavior. Specifically, any one of the following interpretations might be true: (a) the youth is withholding positive information from his family because he or she is angry or seeking revenge; (b) the youth is generally depressed, so it is difficult and/or awkward to say anything positive about anything or anyone; (c) the youth has been socialized in the family system to refrain from making positive or affectionate statements; (d) the youth is disengaged and apathetic toward his or her family and so he or she genuinely does not care about them; and/or (e) the youth is afraid to talk openly about his or her affectionate or positive feelings due to fears of rejection or ridicule.

Regardless of which preceding interpretation is accurate, subsequent therapeutic interventions may be designed to address maladaptive qualities of the client's thinking and behavior, or family systems interventions can be utilized to address familial dysfunction or disengagement.

Risks of Honesty and Risks of Deception

A characteristic common among disruptive or delinquent children is the tendency to seek out excitement or stimulation (Quay, 1987; Weiner, 1992). Disruptive, behavior-disordered adolescents consistently engage in risk-taking behavior; this behavior includes both death-defying or health-impairing acts (or both; e.g., jumping off bridges into rivers, tobacco/alcohol/drug use) *and* risks of deception. Generally, risk-taking behaviors fit into two categories: physical or health risks, and/or interpersonal or deception risks (trust violations).

Reframing physical risks. A key component of redefining physical or health risks involves emotional reframing; this also can be referred to as emotional confrontation. The motto among stimulation-seeking youth is often consistent with contemporary fashion and advertisements for soft drinks containing caffeine. For example, t-shirts with the "NO FEAR" label and Mountain Dew or Mello Yello advertisements emphasizing "BEEN THERE, DONE THAT" often capture the adolescent stimulation-seeking mentality. Unfortunately, this mentality inappropriately encourages young people to take dangerous risks, to seek excitement, and to ignore important and useful physical and emotional warnings associated with a fear response. Further, contemporary fashion and advertising takes advantage of young clients' natural developmental inclinations; adolescence is a time when strong needs to prove oneself, to establish a strong identity, and to engage in behaviors designed to question authority prevail. These developmental needs and behavioral impulses require a certain amount of emotional denial in general, and fear denial in particular. Thus, the immense popularity of "NO FEAR" clothing among young clients is not particularly surprising.

NO FEAR clothing and other clothing brands that promote anti-authority or stimulation-seeking behavior (e.g., Bad Boy clothing) provide therapists with an excellent opportunity to use emotional confrontation techniques. A dialogue similar to the following has been used with some success with a number of young clients in our practice.

> *JSF:* I notice you have one of those FEAR t-shirts on... what are you afraid of?
>
> *Client:* It's a NO FEAR t-shirt.
>
> *JSF:* "I know its a NO FEAR t-shirt, but it means the same thing. It means there is something you must be afraid of, otherwise it wouldn't have the word FEAR on it.
>
> *Client:* "It means I do not have FEAR. That's the whole point of the shirt. NO FEAR. Get it. NO FEAR.

At this point, the client is slightly frustrated. He thinks his therapist is a ditz who doesn't get it. What most adolescent clients do not understand is that their t-shirt can be interpreted from two levels or two perspectives. The purpose of this intervention is to help clients see t-shirts from a new perspective. It is a minor exercise in perspective-taking and redefinition or reframing that can have significant implications.

> *JSF:* Okay, okay, I get it. You wear NO FEAR t-shirts because you are not afraid. It is a symbol of being so cool that you can handle situations without fear.
>
> *Client:* That's right.
>
> *JSF:* And I also understand you are very cool.
>
> *Client:* That's right.
>
> *JSF:* Now you know I get it from your point of view, but I still don't think you get it from my point of view... and you have to admit there can be more than one point of view on things. So do I get to explain my point of view until you understand it?
>
> *Client:* Okay, Okay, if you have to.
>
> *JSF:* I don't have to, I just figured you'd be interested because you're a smart guy and you can see lots of things from different points of view and I think you probably can understand my point of view too.
>
> *Client:* Okay. Go ahead. I'm listening.

The purpose of this interaction is to get the young client hooked into listening and trying to understand the meaning of his t-shirt from an alternative perspective. As is often the case, this client agrees to listen *after* his perspective has been articulated by his therapist and *after* his intelligence has been validated.

JSF: Okay. Even though the shirt says NO FEAR, it really IS talking about fear. It's like that saying "Don't think of an elephant." As soon as someone says that, what do you think of?

Client: Yeah, I think of an elephant.

JSF: So you see, you can't have a NO FEAR shirt without thinking of fear. Another example is Michael Jordan. He doesn't need a t-shirt that says "Best basketball player in the world." He knows it, everybody knows it. He doesn't have to wear something to prove it. So I figure that everybody who wears a NO FEAR t-shirt is trying to say or trying to prove that he isn't afraid. So it's like I see that shirt and right away I'm wondering "What is he so afraid of that he has to say he's not afraid of it?"

Client: That's pretty weird.

JSF: I know it's weird. I'm a psychologist. I get paid to think weird.

Client: For sure.

JSF: So tell me what you think my point of view is?

Client: As soon as you see a NO FEAR shirt, you think the person is afraid of something. It's like you ignore the "NO."

JSF: Yeah. That's pretty much it. Also, I think the reason this t-shirt is so popular is because *everybody* feels fear. And *everybody* tries to get around their fear... because if a person is too afraid, he would never do anything but stay home and watch Sesame Street. And so really my point is... because you can relate to the shirt too, after all you're wearing it... *What's your fear?* What's the worst thing that could happen to you?

The overall goal of this interaction is to get the young client to stop engaging in fear denial and talk about something he or she is afraid of. In most cases, clients will not talk openly about their fears until a comfortable therapy alliance has been established. This technique is designed to normalize fearful feelings, to normalize fear denial, and to facilitate perspective taking. Also, the somewhat argumentative or point–counterpoint nature of this interaction can be intriguing or exciting for young clients; to some extent, it stimulates them. Consequently, after the point–counterpoint and perspective-taking discussion, therapists should slow the discussion pace and focus on *the fear*. Asking "What's the worst thing that could happen to you?" is a nice way to get young clients to focus on their fears. But, to allow them to do so, reflective listening is essential at this point in the interaction. Finally, we believe, consistent with cognitive therapeutic perspectives and psychodynamic principles, that if the client can view his or her fear differently *and* talk about it openly, it is less likely that he or she will need to act on the fear in a phobic or counterphobic manner. In other words, we are undermining the young person's motivation to act in such a way as to prove that he or she is adequate and brave.

Reframing interpersonal deception. Interpersonal deception risks common among young clients include lying, withholding information from adults, stealing, and generally living a portion of one's life "undercover" to avoid responsibility for one's behavior. Although it is difficult to determine the precise purpose of behavioral deception in every case, generally deception occurs to avoid responsibility, to maintain a sense of invulnerability, and to enhance stimulation or excitement (Ekman, 1989). In many cases, risks of deception result in legal trouble, violations of trust in relationships, and the evolution of antisocial behavior patterns (Rutter & Giller, 1983; Rutter & Rutter, 1993). Obviously, addressing deception is an important part of counseling young clients who are exhibiting delinquent or conduct-disordered behavior patterns.

When working with risk-taking young clients, it can be useful to redefine the concept of risk to include prosocial behaviors. For example, risk-taking qualities of honesty or honest behavior can be discussed. Further, a common aspect of honesty involves facing threats to one's vulnerability; focusing on how it requires emotional strength to be honest and vulnerable may help young clients begin to view honesty (rather than deception) as an attractive behavior alternative. The emphasis on risk associated with "coming clean" or confessing one's delinquent or dishonest behavior begins the process of redefining prosocial behaviors as exciting, stimulating, or anxiety-provoking.

If there is an adequate therapeutic alliance, a young client probably will begin to make disclosures to his or her therapist about delinquent or dishonest behavior patterns. These disclosures may be boastful and they may constitute tests of trust which the client uses to evaluate the therapist and confidentiality (Fong & Cox, 1983). Initially, the therapist should simply listen to client boastful disclosures to understand motivations underlying the adolescent's deceptive behavior. Later, the therapist should initiate questioning of deceptive practices. For example:

> I guess for you it is actually safer to be dishonest about what you stole from the mall. I don't blame you for being afraid to admit that you went ahead and stole something again after you told your parents you wouldn't steal anything anymore.

Adolescents, particularly delinquent adolescents, do not like admitting fear or anxiety (Rutter & Giller, 1983; Weiner, 1992). Therefore, the above intervention places them in another bind; they must admit to using the safe strategy of deception or they must deny that deception is a safer strategy. If the adolescent admits that deception is safer, then the therapist can urge the adolescent toward taking risks of honesty. The therapist can accomplish this in many ways, including using "dares" or "wagers" (e.g., "I bet you can't admit to your parents that you're stealing again"). Admission of inappropriate behavior to a parental figure may result in a shifting of deeply ingrained family systems interpersonal patterns (Szapocznik et al., 1990).

If the adolescent denies that deception is safer, then the therapist can encourage a "confession" because it is the safest option anyway ("Seems like the best thing to do here is tell your parents what you did before the possibility of you getting in trouble gets even worse"). This latter situation is the most problematic because young clients who claim to be taking the more "dangerous" behavioral path, simply because it is more exciting, probably are "characterological delinquents" and thus have a poorer prognosis (Weiner, 1992, p. 336). Nevertheless, subsequent discussion of considering honesty and renouncing a dangerous and self-destructive lifestyle is still warranted.

Escape from Weakness

Another cognitive technique for enhancing motivation among young clients is what we refer to as the "escape from weakness" ploy. This procedure capitalizes on the fact that most adolescents want to prove their strength and adequacy to themselves and to those around them (Church, 1994). Basically, the procedure entails reframing adaptive social and emotional responses as requiring and demonstrating strength, while framing current maladaptive responses to social situations as demonstrating weakness.

Case example. Sarah, a 15-year-old European American female, was referred for therapy due to repeated legal problems including tickets for running away, being a minor in possession of alcohol, being a minor in possession of marijuana, and shoplifting. At the time of the referral, she had recently changed from living with her mother to living with her father. Sarah indicated that she liked to "get high" and that she might quit smoking pot during the period of time when she was required to provide urinalyses, but that she planned to return to her old habits in 2 months after her required urinalyses were over. Sarah's peer group was uniformly into drugs and she indicated that she could not imagine attending a party "straight." One of the interventions used with Sarah involved framing her need to drink alcohol and use drugs in social situations as a weakness and the ability to deviate from the social norm within her peer group as a strength. After the therapist had established initial rapport and an alliance, and they had together explored Sarah's problems, the following interaction occurred in therapy:

> *T:* It's too bad you feel so weak, so unable to be yourself with your friends. I mean, having to drink or smoke when you're at a party... it doesn't even sound like you have a choice of whether

or not you get stoned at a party. I guess it would take a pretty strong person to go to a party and let everyone know you weren't going to drink or smoke all night.

S: I can be myself with my friends. It's not like I have to drink or smoke to have them as friends.

T: Really? I'm not so sure. Why don't you try that this weekend and then report back to me on what happens.

Using the escape from weakness technique may not result in an immediate behavioral experiment such as the one proposed above. However, we have found that it is sometimes effective at a later date. It is almost as if the challenge to escape a possible weakness interpretation incubates within the teenager's mind until a point when he or she conducts an experiment similar to the one suggested in the preceding dialogue.

Termination as Motivation

For some young clients, the biggest incentive associated with therapy is termination. These clients usually are brought to therapy by their parents, their probation officer, or their group home counselor. These clients are usually disinterested in establishing a close interpersonal relationship with anyone, especially an adult authority figure. They are typically defensive and sometimes simply refuse to speak or interact for substantial portions of therapy. We believe that therapists who work with these clients have limited potentially therapeutic choices. First, they can refer the client back to the parent, probation officer, or group home counselor, indicating to all parties including the client that it appears therapy is not indicated at this time. Second, they can struggle through early resistance phases of therapy, hoping that eventually the young client will establish trust and begin talking and working on his or her issues. Third, they can use the young person's resistance to therapy as a motivating factor. We refer to this last option as "termination as motivation."

Case example. Peter, a 14-year-old Asian American male, was referred to therapy by his probation officer. Although he had previously been in legal trouble for stabbing another student, most recently he had been caught selling Ritalin to other students in his middle school. Peter's probation officer had given him the choice between substance abuse counseling or psychotherapy and Peter had chosen psychotherapy. Peter had previously been in therapy and upon referral he clearly expressed resistance to therapy and would not acknowledge having any therapy goals. Fortunately, his mother was able to identify a number of reasonable goals and therapy commenced despite Peter's disinterest. The therapist determined that "termination as motivation" was the most appropriate general strategy for working with Peter:

> *T:* So, Peter, obviously you don't want to be here.
>
> *P:* Yeah. You got that right.
>
> *T:* Alright. So we can do this slow, or we can do this fast. You decide. Either we work together for 15 to 20 sessions or we work together for 6 to 8 sessions.
>
> *P:* How about 1 session?
>
> *T:* That's fine. So after today's session I call your probation officer and tell him you're not interested in therapy. Then, I'd guess he'll send you to the substance abuse program.
>
> *P:* You wouldn't have to tell him.
>
> *T:* But I would. I'm not going to lie for you. What'll it be, 15 to 20 sessions with me, 6 to 8 sessions with me, or substance abuse counseling?
>
> *P:* Okay.
>
> *T:* Okay what?
>
> *P:* Okay, I'll take 6.
>
> *T:* You mean 6 or 7 or 8.
>
> *P:* Yeah, okay already.
>
> *T:* So, if we do 6 to 8 sessions, that means you have to have goals and you have to work hard. If you have no goals and we just sit here staring at each other, then we go for 15 to 20 sessions, got it? So what are your goals?
>
> *P:* I don't know. I can't think of any.
>
> *T:* Well, we've got your mom's goals. Are they okay?
>
> *P:* Yeah, I guess.

T: Let's see. She said she wanted you to have a good attitude at home and at school. And she said she wanted you to do your best at school. And she wanted you to stay clean and sober. And she wanted you to talk to her more about what's going on. What do you think of those goals.

P: They're alright I guess.

JSF: Well, I guess these goals are okay, but we need to make them measurable. I mean, I don't know what "do your best at school means." What would be your best at school.

P: Probably Cs and Bs.

JSF: Okay. A C average is 2.0 and a B average is 3.0. So we're talking 2.5 grade point average (GPA)?

P: Yeah.

JSF: Alright, how about 2.5 GPA and no Fs. Is that realistic?

P: Okay.

JSF: Are you bored in therapy?

P: Yeah.

JSF: Okay, so we'll make therapy more exciting. If we do 6 to 8 sessions and you have goals, we also meet at the University and we'll videotape the sessions. And I'll pay you for accomplishing your goals. That should be more exciting. Let's see, I'll pay you $5.00 a session. But I'll only pay you if you attend all the sessions, you let me videotape them, and you accomplish all of your goals. If you miss a session, then you pay me $5.00. Okay?

P: You're gonna pay me? Five bucks a session? You gonna pay me or my mom?

JSF: I'll pay you. You're the one who's gonna come to therapy and accomplish some goals.

P: Do we have to videotape?

JSF: I think it will help keep you from getting bored. It's always more exciting when what you're saying is going down in history.

P: I guess.

JSF: Alright, I have your first homework assignment. Because we need clearer goals, you take those goals your mom gave us and make it so we can measure each one of them. Just like we did

with the one about you doing your best in school. Now we'll know, if you get at least a 2.5 GPA with no Fs, you will accomplish that goal. Your homework is to write out each of the other goals so that we will know if you achieve them or not.
P: (Gets out notebook on his own) What were those goals again?

Peter's response to termination as motivation was excellent. Suddenly, after the therapist described the way in which therapy would proceed, Peter became visibly and behaviorally motivated. However, the key to this procedure is that there are clear terms for termination. Peter can get out of therapy and receive financial reimbursement only if he accomplishes the terms of the agreement. Further, because Peter is a stimulation seeker (i.e., skate boarder, snow boarder, etc.), I (JSF) strongly suggested he agree to being videotaped as a part of therapy. Being in front of the video camera was formulated as a method through which Peter might receive some minor stimulation in therapy. Additionally, video playback with individuals like Peter has been used with some effectiveness (Webster-Stratton, 1996).

Aggression Control Short Cuts

As noted previously, young clients frequently have irritability and anger problems that contribute to their being referred for therapy. The following two techniques are modifications to traditional aggression control treatments. They are designed to enhance client motivation to participate in aggression control therapy.

Termination as Motivation and Self-Control Self-Statements: Case example. The following case of Tyler, a 12-year-old boy who had been placed in a classroom for the severely emotionally disturbed due to intermittent and unpredictable aggressive outbursts and learning disabilities, illustrates one way in which therapists can modify traditional aggression control techniques for particularly difficult populations.

Prior to referral, Tyler had, reportedly without provocation, suddenly punched his teacher and a girl on his bus on two separate occasions. Unfortunately, Tyler was an extremely difficult client. He refused to focus on potentially productive therapeutic issues (i.e., precipitant behaviors, cognitions, etc.) and spent most therapy sessions talking about computer games, fantasy books, and electronics. For Tyler, controlling his aggression was of little importance or relevance; he was, not unlike many teenagers, just interested in what he was interested in. Consequently, I (JSF) sought to appeal to Tyler's penchant for short cuts (he was used to finding short cuts through computer games, through the halls at school, and through chores at home). Basically, I found that the only way to approach aggression management with Tyler was to respect the fact that he wanted to "waste" only minimal time on the subject. Tyler and I agreed on a short cut, basically a variation on termination as motivation.

> *JSF:* Today we could start focusing on the techniques for controlling aggression… and I think in 3 or 4 sessions you might get the hang of it and then you could quit therapy. But we would have to really just sit and work on this aggression control stuff during our whole time together. No more talking to me about computer games and stuff like that. What do you think?
>
> *T:* You know what I think. I think that's stupid. I've already told you I don't want to waste my time talking about all this psycho crap.
>
> *JSF:* That's kind of what I figured. So, I came up with a plan. I can give you the short course for anger management. I can give you the fastest version of anger management available. We'll have to spend 20 to 30 minutes talking about it each week for the next 3 weeks. And I'm counting on you being quick at catching on. What do you say?
>
> *T:* Let's do it. But make it quick.

Tyler's primary motivation to engage in aggression management training was to save time. When I previously tried to integrate anger management training into a therapy hour with him, he had become instantly disagreeable and resistant. This particular client's moodiness seemed to stem from him having people get in his way

of being able to do what he wanted, and because I did not want
Tyler to punch me for getting in his way (and I wanted him to work
productively on his problem), I chose to make a deal with him to
work especially quickly.

Traditional anger or aggression control strategies typically employ a series of self-statements designed to aid aggressive clients with
preparation for provocation, coping with provocation, and self-reinforcement after successful aggression control is achieved (Feindler &
Ecton, 1986; Novaco, 1979). Tyler was totally unwilling to commit
time to learning traditional aggression control strategies. Consequently,
I selected several specific skills from the cognitive-behavioral therapy
procedures and hoped that Tyler could generalize from these skills to
more general applications of that skill. I based my hope on the fact
that Tyler was a computer game whiz. He was well trained at picking up specific weapons for use as a part of his computer game arse-
nal. One of the single skills I selected was the generation of
self-statements for use during provocation (Feindler & Ecton, 1986).

> *JSF:* Okay Tyler, I'm counting on you being quick at this. For
> most people, when they get angry and punch someone, they
> usually have triggering thoughts. Let's not waste time on what
> your personal trigger thoughts are. Instead, tell me what you
> could think, what you could say to yourself, instead of an an-
> gry thought, when you're feeling like punching someone.
> *T:* I don't know... I guess I could think about what's gonna hap-
> pen next time I get into trouble. I'll end up in Pine (the juve-
> nile detention center).
> *JSF:* Alright. So next time you're in a tough situation, you should
> just imagine yourself in Pine. What does that look like?
> *T:* It looks like me in a ball and chain. What do you think it
> looks like?
> *JSF:* So, try that out. I'll pretend I'm the girl on your bus. I'm
> bugging you somehow and you want to hit me. Then, imag-
> ine yourself in a ball and chain at Pine.

Obviously, the implementation of aggression control strategies
with Tyler was quick and crude. In our first 15 minutes he was able

to generate his own consequential image and I managed to drag him into a role-play scenario to practice the consequential image. We elaborated on this theme with other specific skills for two more sessions and then we agreed to take a month's break from therapy to see if he could implement the minimal skills he had acquired. Although less than optimal, Tyler's new aggression management skills proved adequate for the next 6 months (I managed to follow his progress through his special education teacher; he subsequently moved to high school and I lost track of his progress).

Another mood-focused, aggression control procedure we have implemented involves the generation of humorous self-statements. We refer to this technique as "using internal jokes." Generally we use this technique after young clients have begun learning traditional aggression control procedures (e.g., identify personal hassles or anger triggers, identify and monitor physiological arousal signals). At this point, we assist young clients in the generation of silly statements, jokes, and riddles that they can use to quickly shift moods and/or distract themselves from aggressive responses. Two of our favorites with young clients include:

1. Never argue with a pig because you get all muddy and dirty and the pig loves it.
2. Q: "Why did the ant crawl up the elephant's leg for the second time?" A: "He got pissed off the first time" (Sommers-Flanagan & Sommers-Flanagan, 1995c).

The purposes of using humorous self-statements instead of traditional coping self-statements are twofold. First, humorous self-statements assist clients with mood shifting. Second, humorous self-statement generation facilitates treatment participation. Whether humorous self-statements are more effective than traditional coping statements awaits empirical evaluation.

Hand Ownership and Hand-to-Hand Conversation. Angry and disruptive young people frequently strike out aggressively in ways that are destructive to themselves and others. A typical example is the adolescent who, out of anger, smashes his or her hand into the wall. This behavior is clearly self-destructive and foolish. However, stating this fact simply and directly to the client usually decreases rapport and increases resistance. Some clients may brag about how they "smashed" a hole in the wall or how they will hit anything when they are angry enough; it does not matter to them how hard the object is. With this type of client, the challenge is how to encourage examination of his or her self-destructive behavior without sounding like a typical adult authority figure.

As usual, we recommend that counselors begin by listening empathically to clients' statements about their anger expression. There is always time, after listening, to focus on self-destructive qualities of the behavior. After listening to the client's story, make this request: "May I look at your hands?" Sit next to the client and examine his or her hands. At times, if it seems that the client is comfortable, counselors may touch the client's hands gently and point to marks, moles, scabs, and scars, and inquire about them. However, always take care before using touch in psychotherapy. As we have stated elsewhere: "... you need to be absolutely sure your touch will not feel invasive or overbearing and that it will not be misinterpreted. If you have any doubts, do not touch your client" (Sommers-Flanagan & Sommers-Flanagan, 1993, p. 117).

The counselor may choose to take a personal history of the client's hands. If the client acts uncomfortable, it may be necessary to stop or to simply state: "I'm just checking out your hands; everybody has unique hands, just like they have unique fingerprints." It is also useful to ask which hand he or she usually uses to hit objects or people.

After completing a brief hand interview, gently grab or point to one of the hands (i.e., as in a handshake or high five) and ask: "Who's hand is this anyway?" The client almost always indicates ownership. Further gentle discussion of taking care of one's hands should follow. For example: "These are great hands. How is it they keep hitting things (or people) and hurting themselves?" This procedure should be pursued to the point where the client may engage in self-talk with his or her hands: "Now tell your hands how much you like them, because of all the things they do for you; you might even want to make a deal with them about you taking care of them." Finally, the counselor can work with the client to identify simple behavioral alternatives to physical aggression and to establish a set of cues that serve as a reminder to take care of his or her hands. For example, clients can be encouraged to "put hands into pockets" or "hold hands" when in situations which might provoke aggressive behavior.

INTERPERSONAL CHANGE STRATEGIES

The following techniques focus more specifically on interpersonal behavior patterns.

Teaching "Strategic Skills" to Adolescents

Weiner (1992) describes many delinquent or "psychopathic" adolescents as inherently understanding the importance of using strategies to obtain their desired goals (p. 338). Despite this general understanding, disruptive, behavior-disordered adolescents frequently utilize ineffective interpersonal strategies and thereby obtain outcomes opposite to what they desire. For example, increased freedom is commonly identified by adolescents as one of their primary therapy goals. However, attention-deficit and disruptive, behavior-disordered adolescents consistently engage in behaviors that eventually restrict their personal freedom (e.g., curfew violation, disrespect toward parents, illegal behavior). The "strategic skills" intervention is designed to help adolescents understand how their own behavior contributes to their inability to attain personal goals (e.g., perhaps by producing increased limits and restrictions).

The therapist must provide two relationship-based explanations to implement the strategic skills procedure. First, the therapist must directly inform them of a willingness and commitment to assist them in personal goal attainment. For example:

> It sounds like you would like more freedom in your life. I imagine it is a drag being 15 and still having all the restrictions you have. I want you to know that I'm willing to work very hard to help you have more freedom. We just have to put our heads together and think of some ways you can get more freedom.

The purpose of this statement is to reduce resistance and distrust. Many, if not most, adolescents expect therapists to side with their parents, teachers, or authority figures. The process of valuing the adolescent's pursuit of freedom can surprise the adolescent and thereby reduce resistance.

Second, therapists must set clear limits on the type or quality of behaviors they are willing to support and promote. This is because adolescents may try to manipulate therapists into supporting illegal or self-destructive behavior patterns (Weiner, 1992; Wells & Forehand, 1985).

> I need to tell you something about what I am willing to help you accomplish. I'll help you figure out behaviors that are legal and constructive *and* help you get more freedom. In other words, I won't support illegal and self-destructive behaviors because in the end, they won't get you what you want. And there may be times when you and I disagree on what is legal and constructive; we'll need to talk about those disagreements when and if they arise.

If adolescents respond positively to their therapists' offer of support and assistance, the door is open to providing feedback about how to engage in freedom-promoting behaviors. Therapists can then tell their clients: "Okay, let's talk about strategies for how you can get more of what you want out of life." Subsequent discussions might include the following problem areas that frequently contribute to adolescents' restrictions: staying out of legal trouble, developing respect and trust in the adolescents' relationships with parents and authority figures, and analyzing and modifying inaccurate social cognitions. Essentially, therapists have facilitated client motivation and cooperation and can move on to analyzing faulty cognitions, modeling and role-playing strategies, and other effective psychotherapeutic interventions.

Case example. A 12-year-old boy entered the consulting room in conflict with his father over how many pages he was supposed to read for a specific homework assignment given to him by a teacher whom he "hated." The boy was disagreeable and nasty in response to his father's comments; direct discussion of issues while both father and son were present was initially ineffective. Therefore, the father was dismissed. After using distraction strategies and a mood-changing technique (See Chapter 3), the boy was able to focus in a more productive manner on the conflict he was having with his father. The boy indicated that his father was partially correct in his claims about the reading assignment, but that the boy's "hate" for this particular teacher made him want to resist the assignment.

The individual discussion between the boy and his therapist focused on (a) how the boy's dislike for the teacher produced a "bad mood," which subsequently produced his resistance to the assignment, (b) how the boy's bad mood and resistance to the assignment had produced disagreeable behavior toward his dad, and (c) how the boy's bad mood, resistance to the assignment, and disagreeable behavior had produced a bad mood and disagreeable behavior within the father (who was now resisting the boy's request that the assignment be modified). Consequently, after the boy's mood was modified, the boy and therapist were able to brainstorm strategies for helping the father change his mood and become more receptive to the son's request.

With assistance, the boy chose to tell the father "You were right about the assignment..." when his father returned to the room. This "improved" interpersonal strategy (which had been role-played prior to father's return) had an extremely positive effect on the father. Additionally, the boy was able to introduce a compromise ("I'll do the assignment if my dad will listen to me without disagreeing when I bitch about how unfair and stupid this teacher is"). In response to his son's admission "Dad, you're right," the father stated (with jaw open): "I don't know what happened in here when I was gone, but I've never seen Donnie change his attitude so quickly ever before." Donnie and his father successfully negotiated the suggested compromise, and before Donnie left, the therapist pointed out (by whispering to the boy) how quickly he had been able to get his father's mood to change in a positive direction. In this case scenario, the therapist helped to modify the son and father's usual reciprocal negative interactions in a manner similar to one-person family therapy advocated by Szapocznik et al., (1990).

Interpreting Interpersonal Relationship Patterns

Disruptive adolescents are notorious for their interpersonally abrasive, hostile behavior patterns (e.g., negative body posture, eye rolls, etc.). Psychoanalytic theorists suggest that such adolescents have core feelings of being unloved and uncared for (Willock, 1986, 1987). Consequently, "...they may strive to bring down on themselves what they consider inevitable rejection, often provoking others to be furious at them" (Kernberg & Chazan, 1991, p. 5). Because adolescent clients can provoke countertransferential anger through their interpersonal behavior designed to resurrect early childhood rejection experiences, it is important for therapists to intervene by pointing out these qualities through interpretation, feedback, or confrontation (Luborsky, 1984; Sommers-Flanagan & Sommers-Flanagan, 1993).

Troubled adolescents are often resistant to accepting responsibility in most life areas, including accepting responsibility for how their interpersonal behavior affects others. Therefore, as suggested by psychoanalytic theorists, preparing the adolescent for interpersonal interpretations is crucial (Luborsky, 1984; Weiner, 1975). Two different paths of interpretation preparation may be useful, one emphasizing empathy and the other initially utilizing a third-person format.

Empathize with how the adolescent is treated by others. After experiencing the client's hostility, therapists may be inclined to confront his or her behavior patterns. Additionally, when exposed to adolescent hostility, therapists have countertransference reactions; put simply, therapists may feel like being mean or aggressive when they confront adolescents (i.e., they may feel like rejecting and abandoning the adolescent in a manner that would fulfill the adolescent's core beliefs of being unlovable and repugnant; Meeks, 1980; Willock, 1987). Although confrontation can be successful, it carries the risk of diminishing rapport and of having an adverse impact on the crucial (and often tenuous) therapeutic alliance.

Instead of using confrontation, we recommend Meier and Davis' (1996) basic rule of confronting only as much as you have supported. While trying to see the world through the client's eyes, the therapist might state something like: "I've been wondering if other people are treating you okay?" This question often will elicit a litany of complaints from heretofore verbally resistant young clients. Then, only after exploring and empathizing with the young person's interpersonal world, can the counselor initiate a gentle focus on the client's contribution to how others treat him or her. The process involves starting with empathic listening, moving to open support and appreciation of the youth's experience, and ending with gentle probing into his or her personal contribution to the problem, such as the following:

> What you are describing is that other people are very critical of you, they get angry with you easily, and they are consistently getting in your face or restricting your freedom. That sounds like a major pain. Of course, I know you are smart enough to know that every relationship is a two-way street. So, I am wondering what you do that might be related to producing these nasty responses from other people?

This approach can be amplified if the client has engaged in hostile interpersonal interactions with the therapist. In such cases personal disclosure of countertransference reactions can be used to facilitate the feedback process:

> Do you know why I asked you earlier if other people were treating you okay? (*Client responds with a shrug*). The reason I asked that is because I had an impulse to be mean to you too. For just a few minutes, earlier in our session, I wanted to put you down—and that's pretty unusual for me. I don't usually like to insult people. Do you have any ideas why I might have been wanting to insult you?

Pointing out previous hostile stares, eye rolls, and insulting comments which the adolescent made toward you can serve as data to further support the triangle of insight necessary for effective inter-personal interpretations (Luborsky, 1984; Strupp & Binder, 1984; Weiner, 1975).

Begin in the third person. Young clients frequently are skilled at criticizing their friends or family for interpersonal defects, while remaining blind or defensive regarding their own deficits. Thera-pists can take advantage of the client's critical skills and later shift the focus to him or her. Use simple statements like, "Tell me more about how your friend Bill gets himself in trouble so often. How is it that he always seems to get into situations where he ends up in legal trouble?"

Of course, adolescents may quickly defend or justify their friend's problems. In such cases a more distant example can be useful: "So you are saying that Bill's parents actually contribute to Bill's prob-lems and therefore to their own difficulties. How does that work? What do they do that is so ineffective?"

When exploring third-person interpersonal problems, take care to prevent simple explanations, such as: "Well, if Bill's parents would just give him more freedom, there would not be so many prob-lems." A good way to avoid simple explanations is to appeal to the adolescent's complexity and intelligence. Most adolescents consider this a compliment and therefore respond positively. For example: "I know you're smart—good at figuring out complicated situations. What else might be happening in Bill's situation to contribute to his troubles?"

Transition to the first person. Making the transition from third-person interpersonal analysis to first-person analysis can be diffi-cult. Humor (and another complimentary reference to the client's intelligence) can aid the transition: "So you have probably already figured out what I am going to ask next (*pause*). (*If client does not respond*) I bet you've figured out that I am going to ask you how all this applies to you?"

Note that the preceding intervention puts the young client in a bind. He or she will not want to admit being caught off guard. Alternatively, in cases where he or she has already figured out where the therapist is headed, the therapist's complimentary comment may reduce resistance. Whether the therapist begins with empathy or in the third person, the most important phase of this intervention is getting the adolescent to accept the interpretation/confrontation. If the adolescent denies the importance or existence of the interpreted material, a limited amount of direct rational argument may be required. When using direct argument, focus on two issues: "Why would I lie to you about this?" and maintaining respect for the adolescent. In other words, avoid the countertransference trap of acting demeaning toward the adolescent. Finally, after the client accepts an interpretation, cognitive-behavioral work on eliminating the problematic interpersonal behavior can begin.

Interpersonal Simulations and Inverse Examples

Goldstein, Glick, Reiner, Zimmerman, and Coultry (1987) have reported success using group discussion of realistic moral dilemmas in treating aggressive young people. Active therapeutic discussion of the adolescent's daily moral dilemmas during individual therapy can also be useful. Daily moral dilemmas include, but are not limited to whether to use alcohol or drugs, to engage in or abstain from sexual intercourse, whether or not to confront friends or family about their alcohol or drug abuse, to cheat or not to cheat on examinations, and deciding whether or not to host a party while one's parents are out of town on vacation. Each of these daily dilemmas can provide therapeutic grist for the mill.

Interpersonal simulations are designed to identify perspective-taking abilities, parent–child trust, and deception tendencies of adolescents (Rutter & Rutter, 1993; Spivack & Shure, 1982). This procedure takes advantage of the fact that adolescents generally enjoy using formal operations skills when solving hypothetical problems (Meeks, 1980). There also may be moral components to the simulations, which make them similar to portions of Goldstein's aggression replacement training program (Goldstein et al., 1987). It is important to make simulations relevant to teenagers' life situations. Theoretically, this procedure is designed to stimulate cognitive development in general, and moral reasoning in particular (Goldstein et al., 1987). The following is a description of one of our favorite interpersonal simulations. We generally use this simulation with teenagers.

The Out-Of-Town Parent Simulation. Many teenagers look forward to having their parents out of town because of the opportunity for increased freedom. This is particularly the case with delinquent young people, as they commonly plan parties at their homes during periods when their parents are away. The out-of-town parent scenario seeks to evaluate what effect parental absence and a concomitant increase of freedom might have on adolescent behavioral impulses. We begin the procedure with a statement such as the following:

> I have a little survey I've been taking and I'm interested in your answer. It's a question about a situation that I've asked other teenagers about and I'd like to get your input too. Is that okay with you? (*the adolescent usually agrees to this, especially when informed that "other teenagers" have been asked the same question*).
> What would you be likely to do if your parents were leaving town for the weekend, and you were going to have the house to yourself? (*adolescents often spontaneously indicate that they would have a party; if the adolescent does not indicate that he or she would have a party, the following question should be asked*).
> Some other teenagers I know have said they would have a party if their parents left town. Would you?

The first step of this procedure involves determining whether or not the adolescent would have a party in their parents' absence. If the adolescent indicates that he or she would have a party, several follow-up questions should be asked.

> I have some questions about the type of party you would choose to have with your parents gone. How many friends (kids) would you invite to the party? Would you allow alcohol, provide alcohol, or allow or provide any other drugs? What pre-

cautions, if any, would you take to ensure that your parents'
home is not damaged or messed up too badly?

As the adolescent proceeds deeper into the party scenario, exploration about potential parental reactions is useful. This is followed
by exploration into the adolescent's rationale for having a party against
his or her parents' wishes:

> How would your parents feel about you having a party at
> their home while they are away? (*In most cases, adolescents indi-
> cate that their parents would not approve of such a party*). I guess
> I'm wondering why you would go ahead and have a party at
> your home, even though you know your parents would disap-
> prove and perhaps even punish you if they found out about it?

The next step in this simulation is to determine if there are any
conditions that would cause the adolescent to go along with his or
her parents' wishes and refrain from having a party.

> What if your parents had a serious talk with you before
> they left town, and they asked you nicely: "Please don't have
> a party." Would you still go ahead and have one? How about
> if they asked you to sign a contract, a contract that basically
> said you would not have a party in their absence; would you
> sign it, and if you did, would you have a party anyway?

The final step in this procedure is to provide an inverse example for
the adolescent to explore with you.

> Okay, now let's say the situation were somewhat reversed.
> What if you were planning to go to the school dance with a
> girl (boy) whom you really liked? And what if your parents
> wanted to come to the dance to watch, or maybe to serve as
> school-appointed chaperons? And, let's say you really didn't
> want your parents to show up at the dance. Would it be okay
> if they ignored your wishes and showed up at the dance any-
> way? And what if they did show up? Would you be angry at

them? Would you punish them in some way? Would you trust them the next time (maybe the next time you wouldn't even tell your parents about the dance)?

The preceding questions should be asked one at a time to determine how the adolescent deals with a situation where he or she is, depending upon his or her parent(s) respecting his or her wishes. A discussion of how to build mutual trust in parent–child relationships may follow this assessment procedure. Also, the therapist may ask follow-up questions. For example:

When you look at this situation from the other perspective, does it have any affect on what you would do if your parents left town? Would you still have a party? If so, how do you justify having your wishes respected, but not being willing to respect the wishes of your parents?

In our practice, adolescent clients have provided a range of responses to the out-of-town parents scenario. Specifically, one 17-year-old girl indicated: "Teenagers aren't supposed to be honest to their parents." Others have backed off their "party plans" after being provided with the inverse example. Obviously, those adolescents who are able to quickly see the situation from their parents' perspective tend to be those who have better relationships with their parents, who are more capable of empathy and perspective taking, and who also tend to do better in therapy (Rutter & Rutter, 1993). In contrast, adolescents who adamantly hang on to their choice to party behind their parents' backs often have little trust or respect for their parents and/or are exhibiting behavior patterns consistent with conduct disorder.

As noted previously, it is helpful to use analogies and parallel examples when discussing specific moral dilemmas with adolescents. Recently, a boy discussed his plans for hosting a party at his parents' home (without their permission). He had complained previously about his parents' lack of trust for him and had even identified "improving trust" as one of his therapy goals. When confronted with the inconsistency of his party plans with his goal of improving trust, the client stated: "What my parents don't know won't hurt them." He held to this line of thinking until provided with the following parallel example:

> You have a girlfriend, is that right? I guess that's a relation-ship where trust is important too. What if your girlfriend decided to make out, or even have sex with another guy? I guess what you are saying about you and your parents might apply. That is, as long as you never find out about what she did, it won't hurt, will it?

Providing a very personal variation of the moral dilemma with which the adolescent is struggling can assist in shifting the level or style of moral reasoning.

CONCLUDING COMMENTS

This chapter focused on behavioral and cognitive approaches de-signed to increase the difficult young client's motivation for en-gaging in therapy. To increase motivation may require some manipulation of behavioral contingencies associated with atten-dance and involvement in therapy. Additionally, therapeutic ma-nipulation of how young clients view or perceive contingencies associated with attendance and involvement in therapy may be nec-essary. However, we should emphasize that we are referring to the word "manipulation" in a positive manner. To some extent thera-pists must manipulate or control behavioral reinforcement and cognitive appraisal of reinforcement associated with therapy to enhance motivation for therapy. If young clients do not experience the process of going to therapy as minimally reinforcing and/or do not view it as potentially adding positive dimensions to their lives, they will be more likely to resist attending therapy sessions and will be more likely to resist becoming involved in and influenced by therapeutic processes.

5

Communication Strategies and Altered Consciousness:
Therapeutic Storytelling and Hypnotherapy

When I saw him coming and heard him mention the dog pound, I canceled the invasion and sounded the retreat. "To the house, pups, run as fast as you can, retreat!"

They peeled off and headed north down the alley as fast as their little legs would take them. I waited until the last pup had made his escape and then I looked up at the cat.

"We'll meet again, cat, and when we do that fence won't be worth the paper it's printed on." Don't know why I said it that way. If you think about it, it don't make a lot of sense, I mean, fences aren't exactly... in the heat of battle a guy sometimes... never mind.

The old hag had a big grin on her face, looked so smug and self-satisfied I was tempted to risk capture and teach her some manners. (from The Adventures of Hank the Cowdog, *Erickson, 1984, p. 88)*

In the preceding excerpt, Hank the Cowdog illustrates thinking and behavioral problems often associated with the intense
emotions of anger and fear. First, he makes a statement that is basically incoherent. Hank shows us how fear and anger can cause
people to sound and act foolish. Second, Hank observes within himself
the impulse to "teach" the old hag of a cat a lesson. This is a strong
impulse commonly associated with aggression control problems
(Novaco, 1979). Although like most children's books, the *Hank the
Cowdog* series is written for entertainment purposes, it also can be
used educationally; the fact that children learn from stories and
storytelling is beyond debate.

This chapter describes two major approaches to facilitating change
in difficult young clients. These approaches include storytelling
and hypnotherapy; they are grouped together because they emphasize procedures that primarily involve the therapist talking while
the young client listens in what some theorists would refer to as
an altered state of consciousness (Erickson & Rossi, 1980; Wallas,
1985). Essentially, the methods are similar in that they emphasize
divergent communication strategies for delivering therapeutic messages to young clients. These techniques differ in terms of the
level of directness in communication. For example, some therapists who advocate storytelling and metaphor strategies with children generally avoid direct discussion of the story's or metaphor's
meaning. Instead, they believe that young clients will integrate
the story's meaning into their development by unconscious processes. In contrast, other storytelling procedures can be more directive, and the hypnosis procedure discussed in this chapter is a
fairly directive procedure. Overall, variations on storytelling and
hypnotherapy techniques included in this chapter have as their
goal the successful delivery of a message to young clients, the content of which we design to shift client thinking processes to more
adaptive levels and/or to facilitate cognitive or moral development.
Various forms of storytelling work particularly well in school settings both because of their efficiency in use of time and because of
their potential for interactive use with academic work (Thompson
& Rudolph, 1992).

THERAPEUTIC STORYTELLING

There are numerous well-known approaches to using therapeutic storytelling in treating young clients (Bettleheim, 1977; Gardner, 1971; Lankton & Lankton, 1989). These approaches generally base their effectiveness on children's natural interest in and responsiveness to stories. Storytelling appears most appropriate when more directive cognitive and behavioral approaches have not proven successful. This is because most storytelling procedures are less directive than more traditional treatment approaches. Put simply, storytelling allows counselors time to make their point in a manner that is nonthreatening and is therefore less likely to provoke resistance in young clients. In addition, it provides a way for counselors to focus on values without directly referring to values in a manner that might seem accusatory or overbearing. Although there is little systematic research on the effectiveness of storytelling in child/adolescent counseling and psychotherapy, anecdotes and positive case reports attesting to storytelling procedures abound (Brandell, 1984; Davis, 1986; Kestenbaum, 1985; Lawson, 1987).

For the purposes of this discussion of storytelling procedures, we distinguish between indirect and directive storytelling approaches.

Indirect storytelling

Indirect storytelling approaches were developed in an effort to bypass client resistance. This type of storytelling approach may be especially appropriate with clients who are typically resistant to counseling interventions. Lankton and Lankton (1989) stated:

> Metaphors in therapy constitute an indirect form of treatment. Like other forms of indirection, therapeutic metaphors do not engender the kind of resistance to considering new ideas that direct suggestions often can. They are experienced as gentle and permissive, not a confrontive or demanding way to consider change. At one level, a metaphor is "just a story" that doesn't require any response, but at another level, it stimulates thinking, experiencing, and ideas for problem resolution. (pp. 1–2)

Further, Lankton and Lankton (1989) suggested that indirect storytelling is an alternative to more directive methods:

...what are the options for therapists trained only in direct approaches when they experience the familiar frustration of working with clients who seem "stuck," "resistant," "noncompliant," "incongruent," or otherwise unable to respond to direct suggestions, assignments, or authoritative challenges to irrational thoughts? (p. xv)

Unfortunately, in our opinion, indirect therapeutic storytelling is too often used by counselors as a sort of vague last resort. Because nothing else has worked, a counselor tells his or her young client a therapeutic story and hopes that, through some mysterious process, positive attitudinal and/or behavior change might occur. Further, counselors and writers advocating storytelling and metaphor as a primary therapeutic modality are frequently rather antiscientific in their approach; they even complain that "direct approaches lend themselves more easily to current research methodologies, general accountability, and training programs" (Lankton & Lankton, 1989; p. xv). Our view is that indirect storytelling is best viewed as an alternative communication strategy. As such, it should be used as a technique within the context of an overall treatment plan, rather than as a treatment approach in and of itself.

Storytelling goals. When using storytelling techniques, we suggest focusing on both treatment process and treatment outcome goals. Specifically, treatment process goals may include increasing client openness (as measured by verbalization and emotional expression), improving client mood (as measured by positive affective expression within sessions), enhancing the counseling relationship (as measured by client desire to see the counselor and/or references to the counselor as being "cool"), increasing client hope for positive change (as measured by observation of affect and by acceptance of, and/or generation of, hopeful statements), and cooperation with treatment as measured by compliance with in-session activities and homework assignments.

Treatment outcome goals are generally derived from problem and goal lists generated by young clients and their parents or teachers during initial sessions. In the subsequent example client goals include decreasing argumentativeness and learning to use constructive communication skills when talking with others. We recommend that stories used by counselors be specific and aimed at a problem behavior, attitude, and/or emotion (Lankton & Lankton, 1989).

Story construction. Some mental health professionals are natural storytellers and need few structured techniques for developing interesting therapeutic stories. Others become better storytellers when there is a guide or structure for story construction and development. One possible guide is the acronym S-T-O-R-I, developed by William Cook (personal communication, April 12, 1993).

S: *Set the stage for the story.* This part of story development involves creating a scenario involving a child who is living in a particular situation. We recommend that you describe the central child figure in the text in a positive manner. For example:

> Once upon a time there was a really smart boy. His name was Lancaster. Lancaster was not only smart, he was also a very cool dresser. He wore excellent clothes and most everyone who met Lancaster immediately was impressed with him. Lancaster lived with his mother and sister in the city.

In this example, the client's name was Larry. It is often helpful to give the story's central character a name that sounds slightly similar to the client's name and to begin developing a story that has other similarities to your client's life (e.g., a similar family constellation).

T: *Tell about the problem.* This stage includes a problem with which the central character is struggling. It should be a problem similar to the client's. This stage ends with a statement about how no one knows what to do about this very difficult problem.

> Every day, Lancaster went to school, just like he was supposed to. But he didn't like going to school all that well. You see, Lancaster didn't like having people tell him what to do. He liked to be in charge... to be the boss. Unfortunately, his teachers at school liked to be in charge too. And then, when

he was at home, his mother liked to be the boss. So Lancaster ended up getting into lots of arguments with his teachers and mother. His teachers were just about to kick him out of school. And to make things even worse, his mother was so mad at him for arguing all the time that she was just about to kick him out of the house. Nobody knew what to do. Lancaster was arguing with everyone and everyone was mad at Lancaster. This was definitely a very big problem.

O: *Organize a search for helpful resources.* During this portion of the story, the central character and his or her family try to find help for solving their problem. This search usually results in identifying a wise old man, wise old woman, or wise old animal or alien as a special helpful entity. The wise entity lives away from everyone else and has a kind, gentle, and mysterious quality.

Because the situation kept getting worse everyday, almost everyone was looking for help for Lancaster. Finally, Lancaster's principal called Lancaster's mom and told her of a very wise old man who lived in the forest. The man's name was Cedric and, apparently, in the past, he had been helpful to many young children and their families. When Lancaster's mother told him of Cedric, Lancaster refused to come with her to see Cedric. Lancaster laughed and sneered and said: "The principal is a Cheese-Dog. He doesn't know the difference between his nose and a meteorite. I'm not doing anything *he* suggests."

Eventually, Lancaster's mom got Lancaster to agree to come with her to visit Cedric. Of course, she had to offer to buy him his favorite ice cream sundae every day for a week, but he finally agreed to come.

After hiking for 2 hours through the forest just outside the city, they arrived at Cedric's tree house late one Saturday morning. They climbed up the steps and knocked at the door. A distant voice yelled: "Come in... come in, it's about time you got here!" As Lancaster and his mom stepped into the tree house room, they were greeted by a delicious smell and Cedric waved to them to take a seat at the kitchen table. They sat.

And Cedric served them toasty-hot strawberry waffles, complete with whipped cream and fresh maple syrup. They ate and talked about mysteries of the forest for what seemed like an hour. Finally, at the end of their brunch together, Cedric pushed his chair back from the table, leaned back, and asked: "Now what was it the two of you came to see me for? I think it would be safe to say that when you got here, you were looking for something more than just strawberry waffles."

Lancaster suddenly felt shy and looked at his mom. His mom, being a sensitive and cooperative type of mom, looked up at the big, hulking face of Cedric and described how Lancaster could argue with just about anyone, anytime, anywhere. She described his tendency to call people mean names and how Lancaster was in danger of being kicked out of school. Of course, Lancaster occasionally burst out with: "No way!" and "I never said that," and even an occasional "You're stupider than my pet toad."

At the end of Lancaster's mom's story, Cedric looked at Lancaster and grinned. He let out a little chuckle. Lancaster usually didn't like it when people laughed at him, but he found he was more curious about Cedric's reaction to his mom's story than he was mad about the fact that Cedric was chuckling at him. So he asked: "What are you laughing about?" Cedric replied:

"I like that line. You're even stupider than my pet toad. You are really a pretty funny guy. I'm gonna try that one out. How about if we make a deal. Both you and I will say nothing but "You're even stupider than my pet toad" in response to everything anyone says to us. It'll be great. We will have the *most* fun this week *ever*. Okay. Okay. Make me a deal."

Lancaster, somewhat dazed and confused over Cedric's enthusiasm, simply reached out and took Cedric's outstretched hand and said: "Uh, okay." Cedric then quickly ushered Lancaster and his mom out his front door, smiling and saying... "Hey you two toad-brains, see you next Saturday!!"

The search for helpful resources is a process similar to what many children and parents have experienced during their search for a counselor. It also can be similar to how school personnel search for resources to help a troubled child. However, the therapeutic helper in the story has tremendous advantages over ordinary counselors. Specifically, he or she can propose paradoxical strategies without risk, because realism is unnecessary. Further, young clients can learn vicariously and perhaps more quickly from observing exaggerated maladaptive behavior patterns based on their own behavior problems. Although the present storyline initially utilizes a paradoxical strategy, depending upon counselor preference and the clinical situation, a variety of initial vicarious treatment strategies may be employed.

R: *Refine the therapeutic intervention.* In this storytelling model, the initial therapeutic strategy is ordinarily not expected to be effective. Instead, the strategy provides a vicarious learning opportunity. It is during the fourth stage of this storytelling process that the central character learns an important lesson and subsequently begins to modify his or her problem behaviors.

It turned out to be a long week for both Lancaster and Cedric. Both of them called just about everyone they saw a "stupid toad-brain" and when appropriate, they used their agreed-upon phrase: "You're even stupider than my pet toad." Unfortunately, Lancaster ended up getting kicked out of school, and the morning when they were on their way to Cedric's, Lancaster got slugged in the mouth for insulting their taxi driver and he was sporting a fat lip.

Upon entering Cedric's tree house, Lancaster noticed that Cedric had a black eye.

"Hey, Mr. Cedric, what happened to your eye?" asked Lancaster.

"Probably the same thing that happened to your face, fish lips!" replied Cedric. "I think it's pretty obvious that not everybody thinks toad comments are particularly funny. In fact, just about everybody I ran into this week ended up getting mad at me. Is that what things are usually like for you?"

"Uh, well, this week was a little worse than usual. Even my best friend said he doesn't want to see me again and my principal got so mad at me that he put my head in the toilet of the boys' bathroom and flushed it."

And so it was back to the drawing board for Lancaster and Cedric.

"Well, Lancaster, mind if I call you Lanny?"

"Uh, yeah whatever, just nothing that has to do with toads."

"Well Lanny, the way I see it, we have three choices. First, we can keep on arguing with everybody and insulting them, every chance we get. Maybe if we argue even harder, people will eventually back down and let us have things our way. Second, we can work on being really nice to everyone most of the time, so they'll forgive us more quickly when we argue with them in our usual mean and nasty way. And third, we can learn to argue more politely, so we don't get everyone upset by calling them things like 'toad brains' and stuff like that."

After talking their options over with each other and with Lancaster's mom, Cedric and Lancaster decided to try the third option: arguing more politely. In fact, they practiced with each other for an hour or so and then agreed to meet again the next week to check on how their new strategy worked.

As seen in the narrative, Lancaster and Cedric learn some harsh lessons together. The fact that they learn them together is something that could, of course, never happen in real life. However, the storytelling modality allows counselor and client the opportunity to truly form a partnership and enact Beck's concept of collaborative empiricism (Beck et al., 1979).

I: *Integrating the lesson.* In the final stage of this storytelling model, the central character articulates the lesson learned.

Many months later, Lancaster got an invitation from Cedric for an ice cream party. When Lancaster arrived, he realized the party was just for him and Cedric. Cedric held up his glass of chocolate milk and offered a toast. He said: "To my friend

Lanny. I could tell when I first met you that you were very smart. Now, I know that you are not only smart, but you are wise. Now, you argue politely and you only argue when you really feel strongly about something. And you are back in school and, as far as I understand, your life is going great. Thanks for teaching me a great lesson."

As Lanny raised his glass for the toast, he noticed how strong and good he felt. He had learned when to argue and when not to argue. But most importantly, he had learned how to argue without making everyone mad at him. And the funny thing was, Lanny didn't feel all those mad feelings inside him anymore.

The extent to which counselors directly articulate the story's lesson or moral generally depends on the counselor's theoretical orientation. Some counselors prefer to leave the story's basic message unstated; this constitutes the indirect storytelling approach described earlier. Other, more directive counselors like to describe part or all of the story's message. Whatever the case, although the story may inspire behavior change, it may more importantly inspire renewed cooperation with learning prosocial interpersonal skills.

Evaluating the effects of storytelling. We have conceptualized storytelling as an alternative communication strategy within the context of a larger therapeutic context. Therefore, it is more appropriate to evaluate storytelling effectiveness in terms of counseling process variables, rather than counseling outcome variables. These variables, or goals, are listed below. When observed subsequent to a story, these behaviors are likely indicators that a storytelling technique has had a positive effect:

1. Verbalization and emotional expression increases (sometimes there may be a short period of quiet, followed by talkativeness or increased emotional expression).
2. Expression of positive affect is increased.
3. The client indicates a desire to see his or her counselor and/ or refers to the counselor as being "cool".

4. Client reports increased hope for positive change.
5. Client becomes more cooperative with treatment; there is greater compliance with in-session activities and homework assignments.
6. The specific behavior targeted by the story shows clear improvement.

Directive storytelling

Many counselors tell stories to young clients in an attempt to influence their thinking in a direct and obvious manner. In other words, stories may be told to make a point or to deliver a message, and children are expected to verbalize the message content or "moral of the story" shortly after the story's conclusion. Directive storytelling includes a real or imaginary person or character who experiences a problem situation similar to that being experienced by the client. The story may involve one of three themes: (a) positive problem resolution, (b) a negative outcome or warning story wherein the main character suffers from shortsightedness or poor decision making, or (c) an interactive storyline during which client and counselor take turns developing the story. We describe each approach briefly below.

Positive problem resolution stories. "The Security Guard" is a positive problem resolution story based on an actual experience reported to me (JSF) while I was working as a psychologist at a nuclear reservation. We use the story with young clients who have aggression control problems. Generally, we use it within the context of a standard aggression control protocol (see Feindler & Ecton, 1986, for an excellent description of such a protocol).

> Let me tell you about a guy I worked with several years ago. He was a security guard at a nuclear reservation. When I was working there as a psychologist, it was my job to interview all the security guards and give them tests to make sure they were mentally "okay" and fit to work on the nuclear site. The security guard had a simple job. His job was to check to see if

people who came to work were wearing proper identification. You see, everyone who worked at this place had to wear a badge. The badge was either clipped on, or worn on a plastic chain around the neck. This particular guard had to stop cars at the entrance and look at everyone's I.D. One time, he stopped a car and a guy who had been through the gate hundreds of times had forgotten his I.D. card. The guy said: "Hey, I forgot my I.D. card today. Can you let me pass through anyway?"

The security guard said: "Sorry, it's the rule. I can't let you go in. You'll have to go back and get your badge."

At this point, the guy without his badge started getting angry. He swore at the security guard. He complained that he would have to drive back 40 miles to pick up his card. He stated:

"Don't be so stupid. You know me. I come by here and show you my card every day. Why don't you just let me through? I'll bring my card tomorrow."

Despite complaints and insults, the security guard refused to let the man through the gate. So, the man jumped out of his car, got face-to-face with the guard... and spat on him!

This story illustrates an intense provocation. Toward the story's end, we usually ask young clients: "What do you think the guard did?" or "What would you do if you were the guard in this situation?" Often, aggressive young clients tell us the security guard should "punch the guy's lights out." Or, sometimes they insist that if they were the guard, they would just let the guy through. Of course, we explore what might happen if the security guard punched the other man or if he let him through without his I.D. badge. Either of those responses are likely to get the security guard in trouble and perhaps even cost him his high-paying job (we usually mention that the guard is getting paid 40 to 50 thousand dollars a year). Finally, in conclusion, we describe what the security guard actually did.

When the guard told me the story, I asked him what he did. I wouldn't have blamed him too much if he had punched the guy. But, he didn't. I said, "So what did you do?" He replied, "Nothing. I did nothing. Just stood there. I mean, it was his problem, not mine. He really had a problem... I didn't want to make it mine."

This story is an excellent example of how a person can resist strong provocations; the security guard did not get hooked into a conflict. The story can provide a foundation for discussing mental or physical techniques that young clients can use to stop themselves from reacting aggressively to difficult provocations.

Counselors can also use provocation stories such as the security guard story to articulate the "fool in the ring" concept (see Feindler & Ecton, 1986). Essentially, the "fool in the ring" idea identifies the provocateur as "a fool" standing in the middle of a circle or ring. The fool's intent is to draw someone else into the ring with him, to get someone else to act like a fool also. Eventually, if the fool is successful, whomever he or she draws into the ring with him or her becomes controlled, like a puppet, by the fool. Ordinarily, most aggressive young people can understand this scenario and are motivated to avoid being controlled by another person (especially someone who is described as a fool).

In a different vein, I (RSF) have used "realistic" storytelling to communicate my strongly held value that gay and lesbian people are to be treated equally and with respect as important members of our society. Often, if there is even the slightest hint that sexual identity or orientation is an issue for my client, I will manage to tell a short story about one of my gay or lesbian friends, or about attending a gay or lesbian support meeting, or about seeing and hearing Chastity Bono or some other famous figure talk about the coming-out process. When young gay or lesbian clients hear a story implying acceptance of alternative sexual orientations, it can help them open up and discuss their sexuality. Alternatively, if the young client is heterosexual, we may initiate a discussion of sexual values or the story may simply pass by without comment.

Warning stories. Warning stories are directive in the sense that they are thinly veiled cautions related to known client behaviors.

Again, we have found "real life" stories to be most effective, and unfortunately, they are all too easy to accumulate. An example I (RSF) recently added to my collection goes as follows:

> I knew a girl who started dating a really cool guy this past July. I'll call them Jill and Jack. They hit it off right away and had some great talks about their lives and their hopes and fears. Both of them were seniors. Jack had broken up with his last girlfriend, Penny, in April and she was still pretty hung up on him. Well, it turns out that Jack and Penny had sex right before they broke up—he even told Jill all about it— and Penny told Jack she had an implant for birth control... so he hadn't used anything. And—guess what?
>
> Well, sure enough, about the third week in August, Jack gets a call from Penny, and she's three and a half months pregnant. Jack called Jill. He was crying. I guess his folks think he should marry Penny. They are pretty old-fashioned. They won't pay for Jack's college unless he goes along with them. Penny wants to give the child up if Jack doesn't marry her. Jill is sick about it. She's fine, really, but she can't believe how one day, she's just dating this interesting guy, and the next day, he's going to be a dad, maybe get married, and somehow, be a family guy. He wanted to be an attorney. Penny wanted to be a nurse. Now, I guess the first thing they'll be is parents.

With warning stories, it is best to commiserate with the unfortunate protagonists and exclaim about how unfair life can be, how little risks can sometimes blow up in your face, and so on. Blaming the "victims" is best left to the client, if any blaming occurs. The heart of the warning story is that sometimes, bad things happen to basically good people if they don't take precautions and don't heed warnings... and of course, sometimes, bad or difficult things happen anyway.

Interactive stories. Sometimes referred to as incomplete stories (Semrud-Clikeman, 1995), in this technique the counselor begins a story and then takes turns with the adolescent or child in making up subsequent segments. We introduce the idea and sometimes even give the client the option of starting first. A case example follows.

Cindy was a 13-year-old gifted young woman who struggled with her family dynamics and her image as an oddball at school. I (RSF) often provided her with doodle materials (paper, markers, and clay) to supplement our verbal interactions. One day, she drew a stick figure leaping through the air.

> *RSF:* Boy, that person looks energetic. Hey, let's tell a story together about her. Okay if I start?
>
> *C:* Sure. Are you sure it's a girl?
>
> *RSF:* No. Would it be okay if it's a girl?
>
> *C:* Yeah. It was anyway.

I (RSF) proceeded to begin a story about a girl who had walked around with weights on her ankles all her life, until one day, for some unknown reason, she tried taking the weights off, just to experiment. Cindy picked up the story from there and said the girl was so light, it scared her. And she walked funny. And people made fun of her. We enjoyed the process of creating a story together, stopping and commenting on various choices our main character made and other aspects of the story. I also noted themes we could discuss later.

Interactive storytelling can span more than one session, with both child and counselor assigned the task of making up one or two possible endings. Giving the client control over the story's development provides interesting assessment information and the child often perceives this as empowering. Simply discussing the fact that endings can come out different ways and exploring the real-life elements that come into play as the story of each of our lives goes along can open many fruitful areas in the counseling process.

In some instances it may be possible to work with storytelling and reactions to stories within the context of the client's classroom assignments. It would be important to have the child's permission to involve the teacher in any aspect of the counseling process, but within the context of certain counseling goals such involvement might be welcomed and quite beneficial.

HYPNOTHERAPY

Hypnotherapy can be a very desirable approach for young clients who are resistant to becoming engaged in therapy. Despite information in the literature to the contrary, we have found that hypnotherapy is a reasonably effective tool for working with children diagnosed as having ADHD (Gordon, 1991). Just as is the case with standard cognitive-behavioral treatment approaches, hypnotherapeutic approaches are more likely to be effective if they are individualized and tailored not only to a child's specific problem, but also to his or her family background, personal strengths and weaknesses, personal preferences, and other qualities. However, in addition to individualizing therapeutic techniques, the following hypnotic technique emphasizes that young clients sometimes view hypnotherapeutic procedures as more exciting and appealing than other procedures which are virtually identical, but labeled differently (i.e., imagery or relaxation).

The premise that hypnotherapy is more exciting or stimulating to resistant clients is similar to how we described motivational techniques in Chapter 4. That is, with treatment-resistant young clients, the question is not so much whether a particular technique may or may not be effective; rather, the question is whether or not the client can be motivated to try to engage in the technique. It is our observation that many young clients, perhaps because of their stimulation-seeking temperaments, respond with greater enthusiasm and motivation to the prospect of experiencing hypnosis than to the prospect of participating in mental imagery or progressive muscle relaxation (Quay, 1966, 1986). Consequently, we use the "hypnosis" label when working with young clients who are resistant to directive cognitive-behavioral therapy, even though it might be accurate to identify the technique as relaxation and mental imagery combined with suggestive statements (Kohen & Olness, 1984). With this treatment population we emphasize the label "hypnosis" partly to capture young clients' interest, cooperation, and motivation.

The following section describes a general approach titled "Wizard of Oz" hypnotherapy for use with 8- to 13-year-old children who are generally difficult to treat because of their intermittent inattentive, impulsive, and oppositional characteristics. We have utilized this approach as an adjunct to cognitive-behavioral therapy individually and within a small group format. We integrated the Wizard of Oz metaphor into a hypnotherapy approach designed to facilitate personal problem solving, improve self-regulation skills, and enhance self-esteem and self-efficacy (Sommers-Flanagan & Sommers-Flanagan, 1996c). As an adjunct to cognitive-behavioral therapy, goals include improving the therapeutic alliance, heightening young clients' interest in therapy procedures, and improving overall cooperation with treatment.

Wizard of Oz Hypnotherapy

The Wizard of Oz hypnotherapeutic approach is an individualized treatment procedure which specifically highlights personal strengths or attributes that may partially or completely exist within a young client's behavioral repertoire. Similar to the Wizard of Oz storyline, clients formulate and clarify their personal goals and desires, review evidence that they may already partially possess some positive attributes they desire, complete homework and/or posthypnotic suggestion assignments that assist in "proving" they have particular positive attributes, and receive concrete symbols attesting to their personal attributes and accomplishments.

Preparation. Preparation is always an important step when conducting clinical hypnosis. Our preparation procedures include the following components.

Building rapport and alliance. When using this (or any) hypnotic approach, it is especially important for therapists to gather sufficient information about client strengths and preferences and to establish an initial young client–therapist bond. For example, information about the child's hobbies, particular likes/dislikes, and hopes/wishes should be obtained. Additionally, with younger children (10 and under) we use playful interactions followed by brief feedback (e.g., a drawing activity accompanied by comments like:

"I see you are really good at including everybody in your drawings" or "I notice that you erase a lot, so you must like to get things just right").

Introduction to hypnotherapy as a personal change strategy. As described by Gardner (1974), counselors should educate parents of children receiving hypnotherapy regarding the nature of hypnosis and how it will be used with their child. In our practice, when we use hypnotherapy with disruptive, behavior-disordered clients, we use it primarily as adjunctive treatment. In other words, we use it in combination with other treatment methods and modalities.

Although most parents are accepting of hypnosis as a therapeutic procedure, others may express surprise and a minority of parents express negative reactions to potentially using hypnosis with their children. Overall, we emphasize that hypnosis is an interesting and appealing procedure through which children can learn to control themselves more effectively. Of course, hypnotherapy should not proceed unless parents and children consent to the use of the technique (Gustafson et al., 1994). In cases in which children are treated individually, we give children the option of having their parents present for reassurance during initial inductions (Gardner, 1974).

Coaching (within group therapy format). Therapists may need to coach and remind children who routinely display disruptive behavior patterns to take hypnotic procedures seriously. This is especially true when hypnotherapy is used as an adjunctive technique in a group setting with children who exhibit inattentive, impulsive, and uncooperative behavior patterns. In such cases, we recommend two therapists for a group of four to five children. This therapist–client ratio ensures that the therapists can deal with practical behavior management issues effectively. When introducing the Wizard of Oz approach, one therapists states (referring to the other therapist): "Do you want Dr. John to hypnotize you?"

Within the context of a group for disruptive youths, we have found that young clients invariably respond enthusiastically to this offer; this may be partly because young clients who are often disruptive are sometimes strongly attracted to experiences they expect will be exciting and stimulating (Quay, 1966, 1986).

We also recognize that asking children if they "want Dr. John to hypnotize" them is an authoritarian hypnotherapy model, generally avoided when using hypnosis with young clients. We inquire about being hypnotized in this manner with this type of child for any of the following reasons: (a) these children generally have self-control problems and sometimes do not see themselves as having control over private imagery and/or physical calmness; (b) these children are sometimes attracted to people or experiences that will impose external control on them (e.g., gangs or military service); (c) these children sometimes have more confidence in the "other" person controlling them than they have in themselves exercising self-control; (d) the eventual purpose (consistent with the "Wizard of Oz" metaphor) is for the attractive and powerful authoritarian figure to help the children discover that they had self-control and power within themselves all along; and/or (e) these children usually find it very empowering to eventually discover that they produced the changes within themselves and are able to take personal ownership of those changes despite the initial authoritarian statement.

Pre-hypnosis problem solving. Following an initial enthusiastic response to the offer of a hypnotic experience, therapists may need to remind young clients in a group setting that hypnosis is not a recreational endeavor; instead, hypnosis is a clinical procedure designed to help people overcome personal problems or undesirable habits (Olness & Gardner, 1988). Within individual or group settings, we use the "offer of a hypnotic experience" as a springboard for personal goal setting and discussion of problem-solving procedures associated with desirable and adaptive behavior change.

Okay. If you want to be hypnotized, you have to take it seriously. Also, you have to have goals. As you probably know, people aren't hypnotized just for fun. You have to have a reason to be hypnotized. So, take a few minutes to think of something about yourself or something about the way you feel or act that you would like to change through hypnosis.

Further explanation of hypnosis and a description of its therapeutic uses (e.g., overcoming undesirable habits, establishing desirable habits, improving athletic performance, and improving academic performance or concentration; Watkins, 1987; Wester & O'Grady, 1991) is a crucial component of preparing children for hypnotherapy (Olness & Gardner, 1988). As suggested above, we have observed that children who are generally off task and resistant suddenly become focused and cooperative when we present them with a hypnotherapy opportunity. We take advantage of this focused cooperation and use it as an effective means to enable otherwise difficult clients to engage in goal setting and problem-solving activities. As we have emphasized throughout this book, having difficult young clients take ownership of therapeutic goals is a significant accomplishment in and of itself; it also may facilitate positive treatment outcome (Locke, Shaw, Saari, & Latham, 1981).

Examples of goals children have chosen when engaging in hypnosis include: improving math performance, obtaining a girlfriend or learning how to talk with girls, concentrating better in class, handling teasing better, gaining greater control over arm and leg movement (i.e., decreasing motor restlessness), and stopping saying insulting things to other kids at school.

After the goal-setting procedure, therapists and clients discuss each problem and generate ideas (before hypnotic induction) regarding how the children might achieve their goals. This procedure also assists in later individualization of hypnotic suggestions. The therapist explains that "because hypnosis isn't magic, we'd better come up with some of our own ideas about how to solve these problems."

In the case of a 12-year-old boy who wanted to learn how to "get a girlfriend" through hypnosis, the prehypnosis problem-solving phase produced several potential solutions to his problem. These included breathing deeply and relaxing when talking with girls, reminding himself (with internal statements) that "I am friendly and have a good personality," asking questions about what the girl might be interested in, and practicing effective listening skills (e.g., paraphrasing). Of course, an underlying purpose of agreeing with a 12-year-old boy to assist him to "get a girlfriend" (which we reframe as "developing social skills") is to have him develop cognitive and self-regulation skills that will aid him in other areas of his life (e.g., speaking up assertively to teachers, calming himself before examinations, etc.).

Induction. Our purpose in describing this technique is not to train therapists regarding how to use hypnosis. Instead, we recommend that therapists who desire such training attend classes or workshops, obtain supervision, and read texts on clinical hypnosis. Consequently, our recommendations regarding induction procedures will be general.

Therapists have used a wide variety of induction approaches successfully with children (Olness & Gardner, 1988). We have generally used ideomotor or eye fixation approaches with small groups of 10- to 13-year-old children. For example, both the hand levitation and fixation at point on hand techniques, as described by Olness and Gardner (1988), have been very effective in our practice. We have found imagery-based approaches, such as the favorite place or favorite activity, to be useful as well (Olness & Gardner, 1988). We also use repeated arousal and rapid reinduction (i.e., fractionation) within both individual and group therapy formats (see Watkins, 1987).

Suggestions. The core metaphor for suggestions in this approach is the "Wizard of Oz" storyline. Most children are familiar with the *Wizard of Oz* story, but familiarity with the story is not a prerequisite. The Wizard of Oz storyline is provided in the following suggestive metaphor.

> In the *Wizard of Oz,* the Straw Man wanted brains, the Tin Man wanted a heart, the Lion wanted courage, and Dorothy wanted to take Toto and go home to Kansas. They wanted these things very badly. So, they went to the Wizard for help. At first the Wizard seemed bothered. He called himself the "great and powerful Oz" and sent them away. Later, he sent them out to bring back the witch's broom. When the Straw Man, the Tin Man, the Lion, Dorothy, and Toto returned with the broom, they were surprised at their own success. They

discovered that the Wizard was just a regular man and wasn't really a wizard after all. They also discovered that they already had brains, a heart, and courage. Then, the Wizard gave them each something to show they were smart, loving, and brave. And Dorothy discovered that she had within herself the power to get herself and Toto back to Kansas.

Throughout this hypnotic procedure, children are intermittently aroused by the therapist and then inquiry regarding their feelings, thoughts, and sensations is conducted. The therapist also asks about which specific procedures helped them become most comfortable and relaxed. Subsequently, the therapist rehypnotizes them (e.g., "go back to the comfortable place with the comfortable feelings"). Therapists then give individualized and group suggestions when the children are in trance states.

When using hypnotherapy in small groups, the counselor addresses each client individually for a portion of the suggestion procedure. The counselor explains this process to children before providing suggestions:

> For the next few minutes I will be talking to Amber. As you all know, Amber indicated that she would like to stop having her feelings hurt so easily when others tease her. She also wants to stop herself from hitting or hurting other kids after her feelings have been hurt. While I talk to Amber, each of you can listen whatever amount you want. Maybe some of what I say to Amber may apply to you. After I finish talking with Amber, I will, one by one, take time to talk with each of you individually.

We include sample suggestion content below.

Self-control, calmness, and relaxation suggestions. A significant portion of this procedure focuses on affirming children's self-regulation or relaxation skills. One particularly overactive boy accurately complained after an initial induction that his "arms and legs were all twitchy and not at all relaxed." Although being "twitchy" might not ordinarily interfere with hypnotherapy in children, this particular boy's goal (noted above) was to decrease motor restlessness. He previously had been picked on by other students (and teachers) because of general fidgetiness and difficulties sitting still in class. Consequently, the therapist provided to him individually during the next hypnosis phase a mild numbing or analgesic suggestion, during which the therapist rubbed the boy's arms and hands with a finger. Afterward he exclaimed, "It worked! That was great. My arms were limp and relaxed. Can you do my legs too?"

During the next phase of hypnosis, the therapist noted the boy's role in controlling his own arms and he was gently directed to replicate the process in his legs. Subsequently, he was able to obtain mastery over his "twitchy" legs, using his own finger, and he was very enthusiastic in reporting his success to other group members.

The therapist also gives other, more general relaxation and self-control suggestions:

> Congratulations on becoming deeply relaxed! Hypnosis is very interesting. For you to become as deeply relaxed as you are now, you have to allow it to happen. Even though at first, you may think the hypnotist is doing the work, you eventually realize that you are the one who has to listen closely and cooperate with the hypnotic procedure. This is a great accomplishment. You have listened well, cooperated, and so now, like you mentioned when we were all alert a few minutes ago, you are feeling very relaxed, maybe even more relaxed than you have ever let yourself feel before. And you have allowed yourself to let go and feel this great feeling of comfort. Also, because you have achieved this comfortable and relaxed state once, you can do it again.

Positive attribute reframes. The therapist provides each child with individualized reframes of their personal attributes. This is because children who have been disruptive and have experienced repeated negative feedback from teachers and fellow students often view their personal characteristics negatively. For example, a therapist provided a girl in one group who was very sensitive and reactive to the comments of others with this positive reframe of her personal characteristics, followed by a posthypnotic suggestion.

You say you want to stop yourself from insulting other kids at your school. Like you said before we started, one reason why you feel the impulse to insult classmates is because they've hurt your feelings. What you don't realize is that the reason other people can hurt your feelings is because of a very special quality you have. You are very sensitive. Sensitivity is a very nice quality; more people should be sensitive. I am glad you are sensitive. Being sensitive means that you can sense, you can figure out what people mean more quickly than most people can. Many people don't even notice the things you notice. You get hurt easily and then you want to hurt others back and sometimes other people don't even know what has happened.

Problem-oriented post-hypnotic suggestions. After a positive attribute is identified, a post-hypnotic suggestion is attached to the attribute. The posthypnotic suggestion is often a competing emotional and/or behavioral response. When a child is feeling positive about him or herself, it is more difficult to feel hurt, angry, and vengeful. Consequently, as in the case example, it is more difficult to behave aggressively.

Being sensitive is a gift. Next time you notice your feelings are hurt, you may also notice some good feelings about yourself; you could remember you're a sensitive person and that's a positive quality. You could have new ideas about what to do when someone else hurts your feelings. You might look around and figure out who else in the room is sensitive and who else has had their feelings hurt. Then, you might just go and be friendly to the other person who is feeling hurt... even if it is the same person who insulted you. The reason you can do this is because you have a special gift for sensitivity and compassion.

Suggestion goals. The goals of these hypnotic suggestions are three-fold. First, we design the procedure to provide children with knowledge of, and confidence in, their self-regulation skills. Disruptive children often feel as though they cannot relax, slow down, or calm themselves. Using this procedure, they often have an experience of laying quietly, listening to induction and suggestion instructions, and intermittently feeling deeply relaxed for up to 45 minutes. The fractionation procedures also seem to intensify their perception of being able to apply hypnosis (and self-regulating relaxation) quickly and efficiently. These skills can be generalized to previously problematic classroom and social settings.

Second, the procedure provides young clients with specific self-esteem and self-efficacy enhancing reframes. The self-esteem enhancing suggestions generally focus on special qualities that the therapist knows the child/adolescent already has within him or her. There also may be some behavioral implications associated with the positive quality. Another example:

> One thing you don't realize about yourself is that you have within you an incredible creative ability. Now that you notice your creativity, you have more of a chance to use it. Creative people can transform what someone says about them into other possible meanings. Creative people think the words "Could be..." a lot when they are solving a problem. So, it's kind of like when another boy says to you: "You're stupid" and you know you're not, it pushes your creativity button and you start thinking "Why did he say that? Could be..." Well, it could be that he's actually worried about how smart *he* is instead. Or it could be that he's been called stupid by someone else and so he's trying to take it out on you. Or it could be that he's jealous of you and really thinks you're smart. When your creative button is pushed you might realize that the mean things other people say don't really have as much to do with you as it does with them. The more you practice this in your mind and in real life, the more likely you'll start acting the way you really want to. That way, pretty soon, you will probably notice that when you hear an insult it is even easier to be calm.

Third, suggestions focus on behavioral self-control and self-management procedures. Specifically, four behavior change content areas can be identified: (a) the child/adolescents' previously identified goals (e.g., "I remember you said you want to work on how to handle it when other children tease you"); (b) problem-solving approaches discussed before the induction (e.g., "You already identified some methods for dealing with children who tease you. These methods included counting to 10, walking away, thinking of humorous ways to interpret what the other kid said, and using a fogging technique"); (c) behavior rehearsal imagery (i.e., "Now you see yourself responding calmly to an insulting comment another boy in your class has made about you"); and (d) triggers or cues for eliciting a relaxation response (e.g., "Whenever you hear an insult, no matter who it is directed toward, more and more often your response will be to get calm and thoughtful. That way you can use your creativity to figure out what the insult really means").

Arousal. Use standard arousal techniques to conclude the hypnotherapy procedure. Counting up from 1 to 5 is our most common approach. In group settings, when one child may be competing with others and not opening his or her eyes, we use a casual statement as suggested by Gardner and Olness (1981): "I wonder who will be the first one to be able to get fully alert again" (p. 75–76).

Generally, we have observed a very positive client response to this procedure. For example, one boy enthusiastically stated at the end of a session: "Can we have group again tomorrow and do this again?" This boy, at the beginning of group, had complained about how attending group therapy was interfering with his after-school plans.

Post-hypnotic and Post-homework Rewards. Similar to the *Wizard of Oz,* we often give our clients gifts which symbolize or represent their positive achievements. For example, we usually keep a stack of award certificates available and write in statements pertaining to relevant accomplishments (e.g., "Amber has earned High Honors in relaxing in the face of insults"). We also allow children to choose their own rewards (e.g., basketball cards, X-men cards, Pogs, Slammers, Dairy Queen treats, etc.).

CONCLUDING COMMENTS

Storytelling and the Wizard of Oz hypnotherapy approach described above are especially suited for children and early adolescents who have tendencies toward disruptive behaviors and who act resistant to what they perceive as more "boring" and traditional treatment. However, as noted, we generally use these procedures as an adjunct to standard cognitive-behavioral social skill and self-control programs. It has been our experience, as described by others (Kohen & Olness, 1984), that clinical responsiveness to hypnotherapy and storytelling is fairly rapid and can be observed after only a few (1–3) sessions.

Narrative techniques, such as storytelling and hypnotherapy, provide a metaphoric vehicle for helping young people discover, practice, and apply some of their most positive attributes to their personal difficulties. The overall goals of these procedures include increasing involvement and interest in counseling or psychotherapeutic techniques, teaching effective skills for modifying negative and undesirable mood states, facilitating maintenance of the therapeutic alliance, increasing perceptions of self-control and relaxation skills, enhancing self-esteem/self-efficacy, and learning vicariously of maladaptive and adaptive responses.

6

Ecological Theory and Parent Education Strategies

"Mummy," Matilda said, "would you mind if I ate my supper in the dining-room so I could read my book?"

The father glanced up sharply. "I would mind!" he snapped. "Supper is a family gathering and no one leaves the table till it's over!"

"But we're not at the table," Matilda said. "We never are. We're always eating off our knees and watching the telly."

"What's wrong with watching the telly, may I ask?" the father said. His voice had suddenly become soft and dangerous.

Matilda didn't trust herself to answer him, so she kept quiet. She could feel the anger boiling up inside her. She knew it was wrong to hate her parents like this, but she was finding it very hard not to do so. All the reading she had done had given her a view of life that they had never seen. If only they would read a little Dickens or Kipling they would soon discover there was more to life than cheating people and watching television. (From Matilda, Dahl, *1988, pp. 28–29)*

Matilda is suffering from a problem that is not unusual among young client referrals; she is stuck in a family system that is all too frequently capricious, vindictive, and irrational. Matilda's response to being stuck in her particular family system is multifaceted. First, she avoids contact with her family by reading books. As the storyline proceeds, she begins to brood. Eventually, she seeks and exacts revenge on her parents by punishing them for their misdeeds.

As we have suggested in previous chapters, counseling *can* empower young clients. Through individual counseling, young clients can learn to influence their family, school, and social systems by responding to various situations in increasingly adaptive and constructive ways. However, sometimes, no matter how much a young client strives toward adaptive emotional, cognitive, and behavioral responses, significant change does not occur because powerful family or external forces maintain and perpetuate dysfunction.

This chapter focuses on methods for dealing with parents and families in counseling. First, this chapter briefly describes the importance of viewing children/adolescents within the context of their social ecology. In the *Matilda* example, her development and behavior are simultaneously influenced by numerous external factors, including her school, family, and social relationships. However, as illustrated in the opening excerpt, her family is concurrently and continuously influenced by other powerful external factors, such as television. Consequently, whether referred to as multisystemic or ecologically informed therapy, it is important to view child/adolescent development from a wholistic or more inclusive perspective. Brofenbrenner (1986) describes this perspective in terms of his research: "... the focus of the present analysis can be described as 'once removed.' The research question becomes: How are intrafamilial processes affected by extrafamilial conditions?" (p. 723). Essentially, much of what has been discussed previously in this book, and certainly what follows within this chapter, should be considered under the broad umbrella of human developmental ecology.

Second, after a general discussion of developmental ecology, we describe specific parent education and training strategies which directly address dysfunctional family dynamics and maladaptive parenting behaviors. Recent research supports parent education and training techniques as effective components of counseling with children in general and with those with ADHD, ODD, and CD (especially adolescents; Anastopoulos, Barkley, & Sheldon, 1996; Kazdin, 1996; Long, Forehand, Wierson, & Morgan, 1994; Schaefer & Briesmeister, 1989). As suggested from ecological theory, it is important to implement child and adolescent behavior change strategies from multiple focal points.

ECOLOGICAL CONSIDERATIONS

In Chapter 1, we reminded readers that children are culturally different in many ways from adults. Adults, to greater or lesser degrees, recognize their interdependence with other adults and are free, within limits, to negotiate relative degrees of autonomy and dependence in their lives. However, the social world of the developing child or adolescent allows very little of this same freedom. The child's social ecology (e.g., parents, school, peers, neighborhood, authority figures; Brofenbrenner, 1986; Diamond & Liddle, 1996) dictates a far greater portion of the child's functioning than we remember or experience as adults.

The power of family ecology provides a golden opportunity for change, growth, and healthy development advocated by family systems theorists and therapists. As pointed out recently by an esteemed colleague, "Because children and adolescents are deeply effected by their families and extended social environments, it is almost inconceivable that a counselor should treat a child or adolescent without attending to ecological considerations" (D. Scherer, personal communication, October 24, 1996).

Urie Bronfenbrenner (1977, 1979, 1986) has detailed what he describes as human ecological principles. His and others' research has identified central ecosystemic factors affecting human development. Citing research on family interactions with peers, schools, hospitals, daycares, and adult work environments,

Bronfenbrenner (1986) demonstrated convincingly that a given child's development—social, intellectual, and emotional—is a complex, interactive process influenced by multiple layers of contingencies and relationships to which the child and the child's family are subject.

There are many situations in which it is neither appropriate nor practical to work exclusively or primarily with young clients in individual or group therapy. In fact, many family therapists strongly advocate working, if at all possible, primarily or exclusively with families when addressing child/adolescent problems (Diamond & Liddle, 1996; Satir, 1972). Family therapy has several advantages over individual therapy in the treatment of young clients. These include the following: Specific children are not identified as primary patients and therefore are spared potential negative self-esteem effects sometimes caused by such identification; family dynamics that may be contributing to or maintaining child problem behaviors can be directly observed; family interventions can be designed to directly address family dynamics problems; and, finally, in a case in which a particular child has difficulties, the therapist can assist the family in learning better ways to cope with and enhance the child's functioning.

When a counselor is working within a family systems or ecological framework, it is possible to work with many configurations of the family system as part of the counseling process. However, the counselor should carefully explain this orientation and potential interactions with various family members at the beginning of the counseling relationship.

While we did not design this book to teach mental health professionals the fine (and complex) art of working systemically or ecologically, we want to stress that it behooves most, if not all such professionals to seek such training. Even though we do not always have direct access to children's families or to broader ecosystems, acknowledgment of the centrality of these systems is essential in relating to and assisting individual children. In addition, it is sometimes possible to select a particular aspect of the child's world and make significant changes within the system. As an example, the following section outlines strategies for addressing problems present in one of the child's most powerful shapers of behavior, attitudes, and feelings: his or her parent(s).

APPROACHES TO PARENT EDUCATION AND TRAINING

Parent education and training is a common, nonpathological approach to resolving childhood and adolescent problems (Braun, Coplon, & Sonnenschein, 1984; Kazdin, 1996). Parent education and training approaches assume that parents are motivated to provide their children with environments designed to facilitate optimal physical, emotional, and social development. Although such is not always the case, counselors sometimes can be too quick to conclude that a family or set of parents is resistant without first attempting educational interventions (Schaefer & Briesmeister, 1989).

When to Use Parent Education and Training

Parent education and training may be a crucial component of counseling when:

1. The child displays characteristics of difficult temperament such as argumentativeness, irritability, or aggression.
2. Parents are insecure or underconfident.
3. Parents are experiencing difficulty implementing basic and consistent disciplinary systems.
4. Parents express a willingness or openness to parenting education opportunities.
5. Parents appear able and willing to receive support and encouragement from other parents and/or parent educators.
6. Parents overrely on punitive responses to their children, ignoring prosocial behavior, and/or are emotionally and physically un- or underuninvolved in their children's lives.

Parent education and training may be used to enhance family functioning in a number of ways.

Parent Education as Separate from Counseling

Parent education can occur separate from therapy. In such cases, the counselor or therapist may simply refer parents to a relevant local parenting class. For example, one might state:

> Because we have talked about how important it is for you to use firm and loving discipline with Jeffrey, I wanted to recommend an upcoming class offered through the Adult Education Center. It's called "Love and Limits: Positive Approaches to Discipline." It lasts four sessions and is fairly inexpensive. I think you would find the class helpful. Also, there will be other parents enrolled in the class who are working on issues similar to yours.

The main advantage of sending parents to classes outside of therapy for parent training is that it allows therapists to maintain a clear and exclusive therapy relationship with the child or adolescent. This is useful because sometimes young clients will feel betrayed if their *own personal therapist* or (God forbid) *their school counselor* meets separately with their parents to make plans about managing the child/adolescent more effectively. Another advantage to sending parents to parent education classes is that classes help parents build a support network of people interested in improving parenting skills and coping with problematic child behaviors. Such a support network is often very helpful to parents who may have been previously isolated and/or uninformed regarding the stresses and challenges of childrearing (Braun et al., 1984).

Of course, there are also disadvantages to sending parents to parent education classes. One distinct disadvantage is that some parenting classes advocate childrearing principles much different than those advocated by the therapist. Obviously, discontinuity regarding suggested childrearing options can be detrimental to therapy progress and confusing to parents and children. Consequently, we recommend careful screening of parent educators and class content prior to referring parents to classes outside of therapy. Another disadvantage is that outside parenting classes generally cannot provide parents with individualized feedback and planning regarding the specific child behavior problems they are experiencing. Finally, in some communities, adequate parenting classes may simply not exist.

Parent Education as a Part of Counseling

The therapist him- or herself also can implement adjunctively parent education and training. For example, after one or more individual sessions, the therapist may schedule a separate session or a series of sessions with parents to conduct parent training. This arrangement is advantageous because it allows greater individualization of parent training than could be provided through enrollment in a generic parenting class. However, as noted above, some young clients may experience distrust over having their parents meet privately with their therapist—or embarrassment at having their parents come to the school to see their counselor.

Generally, we recommend caution when a single therapist is considering a shift from individual therapy to parent training or therapy involving family members. In some cases, practical considerations may require that treatment with young clients shift between individual, family, and parent training approaches. If so, therapists should consistently remind all parties of the rationale and specific goals associated with each meeting. Ideally, this information should be stated (and repeated) when parents and child are present. For example:

> For the next two sessions, I will be meeting privately with your parents (*looking at youth*). During this meeting we will discuss ways that your parents can respond better when you have arguments about things. Like we've all talked about, sometimes your parents yell and sometimes they threaten to ground you and sometimes they spank you. One of the reasons you all came here is because yelling, grounding, and spanking haven't been working very well. So, I will meet with your parents and we will figure out better ways of handling the arguments... Okay?

When discussing goals and objectives of parent education, it is important to use language that minimizes blame (Braun et al., 1984).

Obviously, if parents or children perceive themselves as being blamed for family problems, they are likely to become more defensive and resistant. In the preceding example, we chose the words "yelling, grounding, and spanking" because the parents and child had previously identified them in the joint portion of the initial interview. Further, the therapist gently pointed out that these procedures "haven't been working very well," a conclusion upon which all participants can readily agree.

Additionally, as suggested above, if a therapist initiates a primary therapeutic relationship with a young client, he or she should avoid subsequent or concurrent individual counseling or psychotherapy with other family members. Engaging in multiple individual therapy relationships within a family can compromise objectivity and may cause competition among family members for the therapist's time and favor. We believe that becoming the individual therapist for more than one family member within the same family system risks the efficacy of the original therapeutic relationship, and in some cases, it may be unethical (American Counseling Association, 1995; American Psychological Association, 1992).

However, involving other family or members of the child's social system is certainly possible and potentially helpful. The counselor simply needs to be very clear about who the client is and why others would be involved. The following statements may be used by therapists and counselors to clarify relationships and to maintain professional boundaries:

1. "I want everyone to understand that I am *Sally's* therapist. Although sometimes I may meet with others in the family, I am not meeting with you as your therapist, I am still Sally's therapist and I am meeting with you to further *her* therapy goals."

2. (*At the end of an initial assessment meeting with a family*). "In my practice, I have a policy of being either an individual therapist, a family therapist, a group therapist, or a marital therapist. I do not mix those roles. In other words, I will not be Max's (dad's) personal therapist *and* the family's therapist. I will be one or the other. If I become Max's therapist and you

decide you want family therapy, I will be glad to give you some names and telephone numbers of other therapists who might become your family therapist. Or if we decide it's best for me to work with you all as a family, then the family is my client. If one of you feels you would like individual counseling, I will help you find someone to work with individually. Is everyone clear on how that works?"

Parent Education in the Context of Family Meetings

Parent education and training can occur within the context of what we refer to as "family meetings." Family meetings are therapy sessions during which all family members or all relevant family members are in attendance. We refer to these sessions as family meetings instead of family therapy because they are implemented within the context of the young client's individual therapy. In other words, as described above, the therapist is maintaining a primary therapy relationship with the child and is conducting a family meeting to further the individual child's therapy goals. Additionally, the emphases in family meetings are on parent–child communication and parent training, using the child or children as assistants. Family meetings use a child empowerment model wherein children have input regarding appropriate limits, consequences, behavioral choices, etc.

When conducting family meetings we utilize the following procedural guidelines:

1. The therapist and child meet before the family meeting to establish a plan regarding *what* will be discussed during the family meeting and *how* it will be discussed.
2. Therapist and child have established goals for the family meeting. Additionally, they may have made predictions regarding how the parents will respond to topics that are to be discussed and they may have made contingency plans based on those predictions.
3. Therapist and child meet briefly together immediately before the family meeting to review plans and goals for the family meeting.

4. The meeting proceeds using a problem-solving format wherein the family identifies, defines, discusses, and brainstorms potential solutions for a single problem. Family members agree on which potential solution to implement and how to evaluate its effectiveness.
5. The counselor may give incentives or rewards to the child and/or parents for using effective communication skills.
6. Therapist and child meet briefly together at the conclusion of the family meeting to debrief the session.

PARENT EDUCATION CONTENT

There are a number of content areas for which counselors might choose to conduct parent training or refer parents for parent education classes. These areas primarily include ineffective or maladaptive parenting strategies that have been identified as risk factors significantly associated with aggressive or delinquent child behavior (Kazdin, 1995; Patterson, Reid, & Dishion, 1992). Specifically, these content areas include: inadequate or ineffective discipline; inadequate parental involvement, monitoring, or supervision of children; negative modeling; and divorce adjustment. Although there are other significant risk factors, such as parental substance abuse, dysfunctional family communication and/or relationships, and early childhood neglect/abuse that require parent education and remediation, we limit our focus here to the specific and teachable parenting behaviors listed above. Generally, more pathological parent behaviors such as substance abuse or dependence require specific therapeutic intervention aimed at the parent *in addition to* parent education and training.

Inadequate or Ineffective Discipline

When discussing parenting strategies and techniques with parents, it is crucial to consider and address parental defensiveness. This is particularly important when discussing effective disciplinary strategies with parents. Most parents are naturally defensive about their parenting style and strategies. This is normal and consequently, whether working with parents individually or within the context of a parent education group, counselors should compliment parents for consulting a counselor or parent educator to learn more effective parenting behaviors. Also, counselors should be empathic and acknowledge that effective parenting is an extremely challenging task.

I want to welcome you to our first session. The reason you are here is because you care a lot about your child and want to be the best parent possible. To be honest, it is hard to really know if we are good parents; parenting is hard and lots of times when we parent well, our children are not appreciative. I guess that's why some parents say "You'll thank me for this later" when they discipline their children.

Many parents do not know the definition of discipline; it is common for parents to mistakenly confuse discipline and punishment. Therefore, when discussing discipline, we always introduce a common working definition:

In order for us to work together effectively, we need a common definition of discipline. Discipline involves teaching and education. We use discipline to educate our children on what behaviors are okay and what behaviors are not okay. Ideally, if we are good disciplinarians our children will eventually internalize our discipline and become self-disciplined. In other words, they will learn to make good decisions regarding their own acceptable and unacceptable behaviors. Eventually, effective discipline will be reflected in what behavior decisions your child ends up making as a young adult.

It is also important to remember that discipline is not the same as punishment. Discipline includes a wide range of both positive and negative responses to children's behavior. In contrast, punishment is simply the application of something negative or aversive or painful to a child after he or she has engaged in an unacceptable or undesirable behavior. Discipline is more than just punishment and punishment is simply one type of response that can be categorized as discipline.

Physical punishment. Parents referred for parent education commonly over-rely on physical punishment as a method for managing or modifying child behavior. Parents may be especially defensive about their "right" to spank, hit, and scold their children. As stated in Chapter 1, parenting practices in general constitute an area requiring special sensitivities to personal and cultural beliefs and values. In particular, the use of physical punishment in childrearing is a very delicate area, touching on core value systems for parents and professionals alike.

For example, while conducting workshops in another country, we encountered many professionals and parents who strongly believed in the benefits of physical punishment and said so publicly. Although personally and professionally we believe in using nonphysical forms of discipline to manage and influence child behavior, other individuals and especially individuals from different cultural backgrounds *may* believe otherwise (Deyoung & Zigler, 1994). (The research in this area is inconclusive, but our experience suggested a need for sensitivity and caution.) While working with these citizens, it became clear to us that their negative view of North American childrearing techniques made it difficult for them to accept suggestions of eliminating physical punishment from their parenting repertoires. Specifically, they indicated that North Americans are too soft on children and that our children grow up spoiled and without adequate morality. Many individuals indicated that their own parents and teachers used harsh physical punishment and a few expressed a desire to understand alternatives. Most, however, adamantly claimed their rights to use similar punishment techniques and indicated resentment against "U. S. citizens telling them how to raise their kids."

When discussing physical punishment with parents from any culture, it is important to place physical punishment within the context of an overall discipline strategy. This means acknowledging that children can learn a great deal from physical punishment. It also means clarifying that physical punishment involves using bodily pain as a means of teaching children about acceptable and unacceptable behavior patterns. When educating parents about discipline, we try to help them accurately categorize and label the operant conditioning approaches they are using with their children (See Figure 6.1). Consequently, when discussing physical punishment, we clarify differences between physical pain and physical punishment.

Technically speaking, spanking (the administration of physical pain as a behavior modifier) may or may not qualify as a pure punishment. In fact, in many cases, spanking functions as a reinforcer, especially in families in which positive reinforcement within the home is limited or rare. In addition, we generally find that many parents are confused about time out, response cost, and other aspects of behavior modification. Discussing definitions and categorizations of punishment, pain, reinforcement, time out, etcetera, can help parents understand more clearly the potentially negative implications of using physical pain as a behavior modifier. We offer the following guidelines to help parents understand discipline alternatives.

Figure 6.1. A grid explaining behavioral contingencies.

When parents apply a positive stimulus or reward to children's behavior, they are using positive reinforcement. When a positive stimulus, or an opportunity for reward, is taken away (i.e., withdrawn) the parent is using response cost (e.g., time out from reinforcement). When a negative or aversive stimulus is applied to children, the parent is using punishment. Finally, when negative or aversive stimuli are taken away, the parent is using negative reinforcement.

	Positive	Negative
Apply	Positive Reinforcement	Punishment
Withdraw	Response Cost	Negative Reinforcement

1. Use a grid (see Figure 6.1) to illustrate and explain differences between positive reinforcement, negative reinforcement, response cost, and punishment.
2. Inform parents that physical punishment is a misnomer. In cases in which they use spanking, slapping, Tabasco sauce on the tongue, etcetera, to modify behavior, this is the administration of physical pain (which may or may not be functioning as a punishment).
3. Inform parents that techniques such as time out and grounding are theoretically designed as response cost procedures because they involve withdrawal of a specific type or reinforcement opportunities. However, parents sometimes inappropriately combine them with punishment when they use scolding, shaking, insulting, or hitting in conjunction with time outs or grounding.
4. Review with parents positive and negative aspects of positive reinforcement. Specifically, inform parents that positive reinforcement is the strongest behavior modifier. However, also warn parents that excessive positive reinforcement designed to control child behaviors can undermine intrinsic motivation (Ryan, 1983).
5. Review with parents positive and negative aspects of punishment in general and the use of pain as a punisher in particular. Make particular note of the way pain can become reinforcing, particularly in the absence of alternative positive reinforcers such as attention, verbal comments, and concrete rewards.
6. Remind parents that to be satisfying, research suggests that the ratio of positives to negatives in a relationship should run at least 5:1. Parents can learn to focus on catching their children "doing something good" (D. Scherer, personal communication, October 24, 1996) to keep the ratio balanced.

Collaboration and support. If parents have come for counseling or parent education, they are often doing so because current discipline techniques are not working effectively. In other words, their children may be defiant or noncompliant, despite the parents' best efforts at producing cooperation and compliance. After being supportive, empathic, and establishing a common working definition, counselors should focus on children's problem behaviors and parents' discipline goals. Questions like, "How would you like your child to behave?" or "When you ground your child, what are you are trying to teach her?" can help parents focus on what they are trying to accomplish, instead of what they may be doing wrong.

Counselors should explore and identify the effectiveness of current discipline strategies used in the home. Include a systematic review of what parents have tried in their efforts to reduce or eliminate their child's undesirable behaviors. This is true whether problem behaviors are occurring with an infant or toddler (e.g., hitting and biting) or with an adolescent (e.g., refusal to follow family curfew guidelines). Generally, if counselors do not adequately inquire about all of the disciplinary strategies previously employed by parents, parents will be unlikely to listen to and try potentially useful alternative parenting behaviors.

Beck's concept of collaborative empiricism is useful when working with parents regarding effective disciplinary strategies (Beck et al., 1979). The purpose of this strategy is to engage parents in a constructive relationship wherein specific discipline techniques can be formulated, implemented, and evaluated. We make statements similar to the following:

> There is no way for us to know, in advance, what discipline strategies might work best with your child. As you know, every child is different and the way each parent implements discipline techniques can be very different as well. So, to determine what works best for you and your child, would you be willing to try out some techniques that we identify as potentially being useful? Then, we can evaluate the effectiveness of each technique on a weekly basis.

Most parents agree to experiment with different disciplinary alternatives if there is an adequate therapeutic alliance.

Meier and Davis's (1996) rule for counseling—confront only as much as you have supported—is especially important in parent education. In fact, when working with parents who are feeling insecure about their parenting skills, this principle is crucial. Specifically, counselors should effectively and efficiently point out positive parenting attitudes and behaviors *before* gently confronting parents regarding ineffective strategies they may be using. It is important to recall that parents may be as sensitive as their children to criticism from a higher authority. Also, many parents feel guilty, threatened, and angry about having to consult with a professional regarding their child's behavior. Also, it is not uncommon for parents to be required—ordered by the court—to complete parent education classes or parent training with a counselor. Recall that just as positive reinforcement is more effective than punishment in raising children, it is also an effective tool for working with parents (Braun et al., 1984).

Sometimes, parents have inappropriate goals regarding their children's behavior. In such cases it is important for counselors to support underlying parental intent, but not parental strategies. For example, one set of parents we worked with wanted their 10-year-old son to cooperatively and agreeably complete 12 chores within their home on a daily basis. Although these expectations might be reasonable within specific settings and among specific cultural groups, within the context of this boy's family and neighborhood, complete compliance with this rather rigorous chore list was unrealistic. The boy was overwhelmed, defiant, and depressed over his chore requirements. Consequently, our approach involved supporting the parents' goals of raising a child with a positive work ethic while modifying their beliefs regarding how many chores were required to increase the likelihood of their son becoming a productive worker as an adult. In cases such as this, unrealistic parental expectations may be based on the parents' difficult or traumatic personal experiences during their own childhoods; referral for individual therapy may be necessary.

Inconsistent discipline: Coercive family process. Consistency is another key to effective discipline. Patterson and colleagues (1992) have identified a type of inconsistent discipline pattern referred to as "coercive family process" which strongly contributes to aggression and delinquency (p. ix). Coercive family process consists of

repeated interchanges between parent and child which reinforce increasingly aggressive child behavior . The following sample interaction between "Sally" and her mother "Barbara" captures the essence
of coercive family process:

> *S:* Mom, I want to go out with Brenda and some other friends
> tonight. We'll be home by midnight. Can I go?
>
> *B:* No, you can't go out tonight. You've been out late three nights
> in a row. It's time for you to stay home for a change.
>
> *S:* I told Brenda that you'd probably be a bitch about this. You
> are such a f---ing bitch, I can't believe it. I said I'd be home by
> midnight. You never let me go out and have any fun. F---
> you!!
>
> *B:* Don't you dare talk to me that way, young lady. I'm the par-
> ent and I make the decisions about how things run around
> here.
>
> *S:* Yeah, right. Stick it up your tight ass. I can do whatever I
> want to do. (*Child leans up into her mother's face*) I hate you,
> you ugly f---ing bitch, I'd like to smack your ugly face. If
> you make me stay home, I will make your life miserable all
> night.
>
> *B:* (*beginning to cry*) Oh, just get out of here and leave me alone.
>
> *S:* I'm gone.

In this example, the mother begins to try setting a limit. However, she is neither kind nor positive in her initial approach. In
response, her daughter Sally becomes verbally aggressive. Eventually, although it often takes longer than in the preceding illustration, Barbara gives in to her daughter's aggression and threats. The
message that Sally receives is simple: Aggression works, people back
down, and she can get what she wants by threatening her mother.
Not surprisingly, once verbal renditions of this coercive process begin,
it is not long until physical aggression follows.

Measuring the effectiveness of discipline strategies. We should
emphasize two final points when working on discipline techniques
with parents. First, parents benefit from using a specific evaluation

strategy. This is because parents need reminders and reinforcement for their discipline efforts. If parents do not know specifically what to look for, they may inadvertently conclude that their children's behavior has not changed. Second, parents should be educated and prepared about the tendency for child behavior to persist and be resistant to new disciplinary strategies. For example, parents should be informed: "Sometimes, especially if you begin using a potentially very effective strategy, children may become exceptionally resistant; they will yell, scream, refer to you as mean, and want to go back to the old disciplinary strategy. For example, a child may ask to be spanked or behave in ways designed to provoke parents into using physical punishment." These possible scenarios should be explained in advance to parents who are receiving parent education and training. Guidelines for discussing discipline strategies with parents are outlined in Table 6.1.

Inadequate Parental Involvement/Supervision

Research indicates that parental involvement and supervision are essential to the development of prosocial behaviors in children and adolescents (Patterson et al., 1992; Rutter & Giller, 1983). Conversely, children and adolescents who do not have adequate adult supervision and involvement are more likely to develop socially deviant and delinquent values and behavior patterns than are their better-supervised counterparts (Kazdin, 1996; Rutter & Giller, 1983). Inadequate involvement and supervision are also associated with higher levels of substance abuse among youth (Kazdin, 1995; Robins, 1991). In some cases, simply informing parents of these facts can inspire them to monitor their children's behavior more thoroughly. However, in other cases, parents require stronger incentives. Individual counseling for parents may be necessary to change their values, priorities, and parenting behaviors.

One of the most powerful socializing factors in children's lives is media representations of specific products, values, and lifestyles. Of course, the primary source of media socialization is television, but magazines, music, toys, movies, and various forms of advertis-

Table 6.1. Guidelines for Discussing
Discipline Strategies with Parents

1. No matter how ineffectively or inappropriately parents have behaved, make some supportive and empathic statements concerning the parents' disciplinary efforts.

2. Develop a common working definition of discipline. This includes defining and clarifying punishment and its negative attributes.

3. Focus on the children's problem behaviors and parental goals.

4. Explore and identify the effectiveness of parents' current disciplinary strategies.

5. Use collaborative empiricism when having parents utilize new discipline strategies (Beck, Rush, Shaw, & Emery, 1979).

6. Confront parent discipline behaviors only as much as you have supported them (Meier & Davis, 1996). Recall that parents probably feel guilty, threatened, and possibly angry about having to seek professional assistance for their parenting.

7. Identify a simple evaluation strategy that parents can use to monitor their success.

8. Emphasize persistence and patience with regard to child behavior change. Remind parents that children may strongly resist changes in the status quo and may misbehave in an effort to return to the old familiar (but ineffective) system.

---

ing all strongly contribute to our childrens' developing value systems (Huston et al., 1992). Generally speaking, to effectively supervise children's access to and input from various media sources parents must exert a certain amount of control over their children; they also must remain present when their children watch television, listen to their children's music selections, and screen movie, magazine, and toy selections.

Parents may complain that they do not have access to their children's television viewing habits. For example, they may indicate that a television or video cassette player is available to their children at times and in locations not monitored by an adult. Sometimes the television is even located in their children's room. Further, many people contend that television viewing does not cause violence or delinquent behavior. Nonetheless, parents should be informed that allowing children to have televisions and/or video equipment available for private viewing basically abdicates a significant portion of their child's social education to the media.

Television viewing does not necessarily cause aggressive behavior in specific instances (Huston et al., 1992). However, virtually every research study ever conducted on the relationship between viewing television violence and subsequent violent behavior patterns and tolerance of violence has confirmed that viewing violent television shows or movies significantly contributes to later violent behavior and the acceptance of violence (Huston et al., 1992). Ann Caron, in her book titled *Strong Mothers, Strong Sons* (1993), reports:

> After he had killed six women, Nathaniel White told reporters that he had committed his first murder after seeing the movie Robocop. "I did exactly what I saw in the movie," he said.
>   ...in surveys of young male prisoners, 22 to 34 percent had consciously imitated crime techniques learned on television. (1993, pp. 149, 151)

Box 6.1 presents a parents' guideline for supervising and monitoring television viewing and other media influences. Provide it to parents who are interested in managing the input their children receive through the media.

Parental Modeling and Indirect Messages

Parents frequently communicate the classic "Do as I say, not as I do" message to their children. Unfortunately, modeling is generally a more powerful teaching tool than is verbal instruction or lecturing (Bandura et al., 1963). Children are quite adept at noticing double standards and often are not shy about pointing out to their parents discrepancies such as:

Box 6.1. Supervise and Monitor Your Child's Television Viewing

Regardless of your child's age, television can be a powerful source of learning personal and social values. Unless parents take steps to manage their children's television viewing behavior, your child may end up spending more time in front of a television set than in the classroom by the time they graduate from high school. In general, excess television viewing is associated with increased violence tendencies, a propensity toward obesity, and unrealistic and destructive viewpoints on alcohol, drugs, sexuality, and relationships. If you are interested in having control over the messages your child receives through television viewing and other media sources, follow these guidelines.

1. Supervise your children's television viewing by watching *with* him or her. Parents should discuss values, behaviors, and feelings promoted by specific movie scenes or television shows.

2. Be a positive role model for your child. Often, children learn more from what parents do than from what parents say. Therefore, *show* your children that there are activities other than television which are interesting, healthy, and worthwhile.

3. Recognize that television viewing can become habitual and almost addictive. Many people begin missing out on important life activities because they want to watch television instead. Break the television habit by observing television-free periods. Consider saving money by disconnecting the cable and renting selected videos instead of simply viewing what various networks or stations offer your family.

4. Set clear limits on the amount of television your child is allowed to watch. Offer incentives for your children when they make choices to do something instead of watch television. Some children may prefer earning computer time, time with you, or a family trip over viewing television.

5. Never allow children to have a television in their own room. Doing so promotes social isolation from the family and the adoption of media-based social values.

6. Teach your children about the persuasive techniques utilized by advertisers. Children can become smart consumers. They can also learn to buy generic products; advertised products are more expen-

continued on next page

sive because of advertising costs. Children should be taught to be suspicious of great deals offered via advertising.

7. Institute family reading time (or any other constructive activity) instead of family television viewing time.

8. Be stronger and more interesting than the television. If it comes down to it, do not be afraid to turn it off, unplug it, disconnect the cable, or sell it at your next garage sale. News is available through the radio, newspaper, and weekly magazines. Remember that television is a notoriously poor form of recreation.

"Why do you get more ice cream than me?"

"You drink beer, but I'm not supposed to, is that fair?"

"Right mom, you say I'm supposed to always let you know where I'm gonna be… but you don't do the same for me!"

Whenever parents complain about particular aspects of their children's behavior, we make it our policy to gently explore parental behavior within those same areas. For example, when parents complain that their children are drinking alcohol, we find ways to ask parents about their own alcohol use. Somewhat to our surprise, we have found this policy especially useful in the area of emotional modeling.

Emotional modeling. There are both genetic and environmental theories available for explaining the presence of depressive, anxiety, and aggressive disorders (Olweus, 1979; Patterson, 1982). Although we tend to believe more strongly in environmental explanations for emotional disorders, even theorists who advocate genetic explanations acknowledge the influence of emotional modeling (Olweus, 1979).

We routinely teach parents how to be positive emotional models for their children. For example, we give parents emotional expression homework assignments similar to the following:

You've said that your daughter has lots of trouble with anger. As you probably know, when you are angry, it is often easier to just blow your top and throw a fit than it is to calm yourself down and express yourself constructively. It takes both effort and skill for people to stop themselves from expressing anger destructively. To help your daughter become more motivated and more skilled at dealing with and expressing her anger, you will need to teach her. And the best way to teach her and motivate her is for you to show her how to deal with anger. So we want you to try what we call an emotional modeling assignment. Here's what you should do. On a few nights, perhaps at the dinner table, one of you should identify something you're angry about. Describe the situation, state you're angry about it, and tell the family how you dealt with it constructively. Then, some day or evening when someone within the house does something that you find irritating, rather than let it pass, demonstrate to your daughter how to express irritation by using "I" statements and owning your feelings. We have found that if parents can show their children how to express their feelings appropriately, children are more likely to follow suit.

Of course, the preceding assignment requires more explanation, practicing, and a few statements of caution, but the main point is clear. That is, parents must become aware of their own emotional management and expression behaviors and they must begin to model appropriate handling of emotions. To facilitate this process in the area of anger management, we recommend that parents read Carol Tavris' (1989) book *Anger: The Misunderstood Emotion.* Additionally, we recommend Haim Ginott's (1969) classic book *Between Parent and Teenager* for parents who are working toward developing positive emotional relationships with their children.

To support parents in their efforts at managing children's difficult emotions, we sometimes provide them with handouts on different topics such as television viewing (see above). Because challenging children and adolescents we frequently see in therapy are usually angry and sometimes aggressive, we provide a handout titled "Parental Responses to Children's Anger: Strategies for Anger Management and Violence Prevention" (see Box 6.2).

Box 6.2. Parental Responses to Children's Anger: Strategies for Anger Management and Violence Prevention

1. Communicate and maintain family rules, limits, and consequences. One important family rule is that anger is acceptable, but aggression is not acceptable. Remember that the most effective parenting style is the "authoritative" style. This means that parents are the final authority, but that children's ideas and wishes are respected, acknowledged, and sometimes followed.

2. Model effective ways of coping with and dealing with your own anger. This may involve role-playing and "dinner discussions" of anger, fear, or sadness.

3. Seek first to understand the meaning and purpose of the anger (without, if possible, asking direct questions). Be nondirective and listen as well as you can to your child's anger.

4. To the extent possible, communicate understanding of the anger's meaning. This should be communicated through summary, paraphrase, or emotional reflection. It is also appropriate to share a time when you felt in a similar manner. Parents should avoid saying "I understand how you feel" because children and teenagers may react negatively to that statement.

5. If appropriate and safe, let your child continue to be angry. In other words, do not push or pull your child out of his or her emotional state before the child is ready to move on.

6. If the situation allows and if you can think of an appropriate story, commiserate and empathize with your child's anger by thinking of a story when you were similarly angry over a similar situation. Share the story with your child *if* your child stands a reasonable chance of hearing it.

7. If your child's anger is directed toward you, do *not* further escalate the problem by becoming angry in response. It may help to recall that the angry or insulting statements your child may direct toward you probably have little or nothing to do with you.

8. Maintain a house rule about decision making. Specifically, decisions at home are not made during a time of anger. Similarly, discussions or debates are not held when one or both parties are too angry to reason rationally. If one or both parties cannot be

continued on next page

civil and reasonably kind, problem solving or decision making should not occur.

9. Offer your child alternative times and places for a calm and rational discussion of the issue.

10. In cases of extreme anger, manipulation, or verbal abuse, techniques such as deflection (e.g., "nevertheless, you will not be going out tonight") or sponging ("Yes, I know, you already told me you hate me") may be used to handle your child's anger.

11. Never give in to a child's request or demand when your child is behaving in an angry or abusive manner. To do so perpetuates the coercive family process discussed by Patterson and colleagues (Patterson, 1982; Patterson et al., 1992).

12. Be prepared to protect yourself and other family members. This may mean calling the police, self-defense training, psychiatric hospitalization, residential or wilderness treatment, etc.

Divorce Education

There are a number of problems associated with divorce which can and do have adverse effects on children of divorce. These include but are not limited to unresolved parental grief; under- or overinvolvement with one parent or the other after divorce; ex-partners' fighting and hostility that involves children or is viewed by children; parents placing children in the middle of their conflicts by using them as messengers, counselors, or spies; and short- or long-term disruption of living arrangements. As the adverse effects of divorce on children become more and more recognized, court systems within some states have begun to require that parents enroll in and complete a course on divorce adjustment. Although we are supportive of this divorce education movement, we also believe that counselors should scrutinize divorce education course content and procedures.

A reputable parent educator or licensed counselor should facilitate divorce education classes. Given the emotional nature of divorce, the facilitator should interview or screen potential participants prior to acceptance into the course. Additionally, there should be a course curriculum, recommended readings (we recommend *Mom's House, Dad's House* by Isolina Ricci, 1980), and participant hand-outs or workbooks. If ex-partners are allowed into a course together, there should be a procedure for determining whether or not these ex-partners are able to minimally communicate with each other and whether or not either may be verbally or physically dangerous or abusive. Finally, some parents who are divorcing need more support and counseling than a psychoeducational course can provide. In such cases, a postdivorce support group or individual counseling may be necessary.

CONCLUDING COMMENTS

Numerous factors powerfully influence childrens' behavior. This chapter focused on family and developmental ecology as a perspective for viewing and understanding child/adolescent development. Specifically, this chapter emphasized methods for directly influencing parents of children who have been referred for counseling.

Children are surprisingly resilient and frequently they develop healthy and adaptive behavior patterns despite unfortunate or abusive family circumstances (Rutter, 1979). Some parents may use this fact to resist parent education or belittle the parent education process. Despite child resilience, our position is that parent education is a useful procedure, particularly in cases in which children have exhibited difficult temperament characteristics. Further, there is ample clinical research attesting to the potential benefits of parent education and training, especially with children diagnosed as having disruptive behavior disorders (Schaefer & Briesmeister, 1989).

PART III

Special Topics in Treating Young Clients

7

Assessment and Management of Young Clients Who Are Suicidal

See what you lost when you left this world?
This sweet old world...
The breath from your lips,
the touch of fingertips
and sweet and tender kiss,
the sound of a midnight train,
someone calling your name,
wearing someone's ring,
somebody so warm
cradled in your arms.
Didn't you think you were worth anything?
Millions of us in love
promises made good
your own flesh and blood
looking for some truth
dancing with no shoes
the beat, the rhythm, the blues
the pounding of your heart, strong
together with another one.
Didn't you think anyone loved you?
(from "This sweet old world," *Lucinda Williams, 1995)*

Many mental health professionals would prefer to skip this chapter. It might be easier and it certainly would be more pleasant if we could refer all potentially suicidal young clients to some other counselor, agency, or treatment alternative. Children and adolescents who for whatever reasons express a desire to end their lives, or who engage in suicidal gestures, self-mutilation, high-risk behaviors, or conversations centered on death themes can be unsettling to all those close to the youths, including parents, friends, teachers, and counselors. Often, mental health professionals are expected to assess the seriousness and lethality of young clients' suicidality and quickly "fix" whatever is causing suicidal urges. Of course, these are difficult, even unrealistic expectations. Nonetheless, it is essential that all mental health professionals be informed of and trained in basic suicide assessment procedures. Further, basic training in management, treatment, and referral of suicidal young clients is also essential because therapists can never know in advance when their next new client will be suicidal (Sommers-Flanagan & Sommers-Flanagan, 1995c).

This chapter reviews major issues associated with assessing and managing young clients who are suicidal. We chose to include a chapter on suicide assessment and management in this book for two reasons. First, suicide attempts are among the most common of all psychiatric emergencies, occurring in 2% to 10% of adolescents (Brent, 1995). Second, suicidal ideation, attempt, and completion are even more likely within the population of difficult or challenging youth who are the focus of this text. Obviously, we believe that it is imperative for counselors who work with this difficult population to have adequate knowledge and skills for working with suicidal youth.

SUICIDE ASSESSMENT

Determining whether or not a difficult adolescent is at risk for suicidal behavior ranks as one of the most stressful tasks a mental health professional can undertake (Kleepsies, 1993). In fact, whereas there are guidelines for professional behavior along these lines, statistics indicate that even utilizing the best information available, we will have a large number of false positives (we will hospitalize or take other precautions with young people we believe are suicidal but who would not eventually make a suicide attempt), and approximately one out of five of us will, at some point in our career, face the tragedy of a false negative. In other words, eventually we may overlook signs of suicidality, if there were any to notice, and one of our young clients may kill him- or herself (Lewinsohn, Rohde, & Seeley, 1994).

In the general population, completed suicides are a low base rate phenomenon. The exact rates are difficult to state with certainty, given that it is an underreported event. For example, Berman and Jobes (1991) reported a rate of 12.9 suicides per 100,000 youth between the ages of 15 and 24. Suicide is often regarded as reflecting poorly on the victim, or on surviving members of the victim's family; therefore, obvious suicides may be reported as accidents (Capuzzi, 1994; Garland & Zigler, 1993). Some officials estimate that true rates may be twice or more as high as the reported rates (Berman & Jobes, 1991). Epidemiological and demographic data are both important sources of information regarding risk factors associated with a given individual. In addition, these data reflect trends in the culture which should help inform social policy and preventive efforts.

Most sources report dramatic increases in suicide rates among youths (ages 15 and 24) between the years 1960 and 1987, with a subsequent leveling off and slight decline since then (Berman & Jobes, 1991). Researchers who study these trends have identified a correlation between U.S. youth suicide rates and corresponding increases and decreases in the proportion of adolescents in the U.S. population (Berman & Jones, 1991). An upturn in suicide rates is predicted for the last few years of this century. Currently, at the national level, suicide is the third leading cause of death for people between the ages of 15 and 22, after accidents and homicides.

Demographic data also provide information regarding risk factors. Statistics presently suggest that young males are still more likely to complete suicide, whereas young females are more likely to attempt suicide. This gap may be narrowing as females begin to use more violent and lethal methods to kill themselves. European Americans are still more likely to kill themselves than are African

Americans, but again, the gap appears to be narrowing. American Indian youth are a subgroup with high rates of violent death, including suicide, although rates vary significantly from tribe to tribe (Berman & Jobes, 1991).

Some researchers have reported that gay and lesbian young people commit suicide more often than does the general young population and these researchers claim suicide to be the leading cause of death for this population (Gibson, 1994). Others contend that the research in this area is not methodologically sound and that there is little evidence supporting the gay and lesbian lethality hypothesis (Muehrer, 1995; Shaffer, Fisher, Hicks, Parides, & Gould, 1995). Regardless of the statistics, sexual orientation issues in young people are very important for counselors to treat with compassion and acceptance, and asking about the level of turmoil and possible suicidal thoughts when working with gay and lesbian young clients is a wise choice.

In addition to epidemiological and demographic risk factors, there are a number of important risk factors to consider in assessing suicide potential with clients. Some research has been conducted specifically with young people, but much has been conducted with the population at large, and as such, it must be extrapolated for relevance for child/adolescent clients.

Assessing Suicide Risk Factors

Because difficult young people may be masterful secret keepers, it is especially important for mental health professionals to become and stay informed of suicide risk factors. In the absence of direct disclosure from young clients, therapists must assess young clients' suicidality indirectly. This indirect assessment process partly involves gathering information pertaining to the following potential suicide risk factors.

Psychiatric diagnosis. Brent (1995) reported a general consensus among researchers to date that over 90% of all youthful suicide victims suffered from at least one major psychiatric disorder. Not surprisingly, mood and substance abuse/dependence disorders are the most common psychiatric disorders associated with suicidal behavior. However, some studies also indicate that CDs in youth and personality disorders in general also increase the likelihood of suicide attempts or completions (Brent, 1995). Consequently, while interviewing young clients, therapists must pay close attention to symptoms associated with various mood disorders (i.e., major depression, dysthymic disorder, and bipolar disorder). As suggested by Shaffer and colleagues (1995), the presence of psychiatric disorder is most probably the single strongest predictor of suicide.

Hopelessness. In addition to the presence or absence of psychiatric disorder, careful assessment regarding the presence or absence of hope in a young client's life is essential. Hopelessness, although probably most often manifest as a subset of depression, is an important risk factor in and of itself. A youth may *not* technically meet the criteria for major depression or dysthymic disorder, but may feel completely hopeless about life, the future, and him- or herself. Some studies have shown measurements of hopelessness as more significant predictors of suicidal behavior than measurements of depression (Beck, 1986; Beck, Brown, & Steer, 1989). Hopelessness can be evaluated directly by interviewing and observations, or by using a self-report scale (e.g., the Beck Hopelessness Scale; Beck & Steer, 1993).

Substance use/abuse. It is more difficult, especially early in the assessment or treatment process with adolescents, to obtain accurate information pertaining to substance use and abuse. Young clients are notorious for either exaggerating or minimizing their alcohol and drug use, depending upon underlying motivations. Nonetheless, listening to parental complaints, asking about social activities, and asking about the client's general attitude toward drug and alcohol use can be helpful. Additionally, we employ various directive or confrontive strategies when interviewing young clients about alcohol and drug use such as the ones outlined below.

1. Assume your client has at least experimented with drugs and ask very specific questions: When was your last drink? Exactly how much did you drink then? What were you drink-

ing? Beer? Wine coolers? Whiskey? Vodka? And when was the time you drank before that time? And when was the last time you were drunk? Passed out? And when you were last drunk, were you a sloppy drunk? Did you throw up? Black out? Etc.

2. Try to manipulate your client into admitting to drug/alcohol use: My impression is that just about everyone your age drinks quite a bit, how about you? When did you first try smoking marijuana? You know, its pretty normal for young people to experiment with drugs. Have you?

3. Using confrontation and statements about normal behavior, try to help your client admit to whether he or she is minimizing or exaggerating his or her substance use: Whenever I ask boys how much they drink, I usually take what they tell me and divide by two. In other words, I believe they drink about half as much as they tell me. But, when I'm asking a girl, like yourself, I usually take what you tell me and multiply by two. You said you drink once a week and that you usually have about 4 beers at a party, so I'm going to double that. I figure you either drink 4 beers twice a week or 8 beers at a typical party. Is it okay for me to write that down?

Cognitive variables. A history of impulsivity and observed impulse control problems are important risk factors in assessing suicidality (Berman & Jobes, 1991). It is important to listen and watch for signs indicating difficulties with behavioral control. Asking a young person about what usually gets her or him in trouble often sheds light on this area, or asking about friendships and what goes wrong within them can be informative as well. Research also has identified negative attitudes toward one's body, dissociation, impaired problem-solving ability, and mental constriction as cognitive variables that may be associated with suicidal behavior (Orbach, Lotem-Peleg, & Kedem, 1995; Wilson et al., 1995).

Social functioning. Family background and family factors have often been noted in the suicide literature, but there are no definitive "suicidal families." Two multivariate analyses (Joffe, Offord, & Boyle, 1988; Lewinsohn et al., 1994) indicate that disorganized, unsupportive family typologies are associated with increased suicide risk. Lewinsohn and colleagues (1994) reported that lower income and younger age of parenthood (child born before parent was age 20) were associated with suicide or suicidal behavior in youth. Joffe and colleagues (1988) report a relationship between parental substance abuse and parental criminality and youthful suicide risk. Also, children from single parent families and families with less education are more likely to attempt suicide (Andrews & Lewinsohn, 1992; Garrison, Jackson, Addy, McKeown, & Waller, 1991; Kashani, Goddard, & Reid, 1989; Shafii, Carrigan, Whittinghill, & Derrick, 1985).

Stressful life events. Many studies support the notion that suicide risk increases when difficult life events occur. Parental or personal legal or disciplinary difficulties, physical or sexual abuse, job loss, interpersonal conflicts or losses, and exposure to suicide are all more common in suicide victims than in controls (Brent et al., 1993). Young people are often susceptible to suggestion, especially when the suggestion comes from the media or from idols or good friends. The suicide of a close friend or of a famous role model provides powerful suicide modeling that, if nothing else, increases young clients' awareness of their own suicidal impulses and suicide options.

Prior suicide attempts. There are a number of difficult young people for whom nonlethal suicide attempts seem to be a means of attracting attention and alleviating stress in their lives. However, even these "nonlethal" attempts tend to become more lethal over time, and can, by mistake, result in a completed suicide. In general, more attempts and more lethal attempts are associated with later suicide attempts and sometimes eventual suicide completion (Brent, 1995). Prior suicide attempts remains the most reliable predictor for eventually committing suicide for both adults and adolescents. Therefore, even though the attempts may be stressful and irritating to counselors and family members, these parties must take them seriously (Lewinsohn et al., 1994).

Assessing Suicide Thoughts and Plans

In assessing suicide risk, counselors must "pop the question" regarding suicidality. We consider the direct approach: "Have you had thoughts of hurting yourself or killing yourself?" to be most appropriate when interviewing teenagers. For younger clients, a question like: "Did you ever feel so upset that you wished you were not alive or wanted to die?" (Jacobson et al., 1994, p. 450) is more appropriate.

In addition to queries regarding suicidal ideation, if it has been determined that a young client is at risk for suicide, therapists must inquire about potential suicide plans. Again, for teenagers the direct approach is appropriate: "Almost everybody has thought about how they might kill themselves, if they ever felt like doing it. If you were going to kill yourself, have you thought about how you might do it?" A slightly different approach is recommended for assessing suicide plans among prepubertal children: "When you were really upset and wanted to die, how did you think you might make yourself die?" Further, we recommend a handy mnemonic devise for assessing critical components of suicide plans. The word S-L-A-P, the letters of which stand for *Specificity, Lethality, Availability,* and *Proximity,* is very helpful (Miller, 1985).

Specificity. Specificity refers to the details of the plan—the more specific and clear, the higher the risk. Some youth will resist sharing their plans. Again, Wollersheim (1974) recommends a procedure wherein the therapist states questions in a manner that helps make deviant responses seem more normal and acceptable: "Just about everyone your age who has thought about suicide has also thought about how she might do it. What's your plan for it if you decide to kill yourself?" Of course, therapists should use this type of questioning only with postpubertal young clients who have already admitted to suicidal ideation.

Lethality. Lethality refers to the likelihood that the plan, if implemented, would bring about death, and how quickly it might do so. The higher the lethality, the higher the risk. If it seems the youth is high risk in other ways, counselors should query beyond the client's identified method. Ask about the specifics (e.g., how many and what type of pills?). In other words, specific information about suicide plans is necessary to determine lethality.

Availability. This term refers to availability or accessibility of the identified suicide method. RSF once had a very distraught young woman admit that she wanted to drive a car off a cliff and die in the long crash down. However, the young woman did not drive, did not have access to a car, and there were no cliffs in the region. On the dimension of availability, this plan did not get a very high score, but it still provided important clinical information. Similarly, it is important for counselors to ask about availability of pills, firearms (and ammunition), knives, and other lethal suicide methods.

Proximity. This term refers to proximity of helping resources. Are there family members, friends, teachers, or neighbors watching over the distressed person? Of course, depending on relationships involved, such individuals may be either a great asset or a great liability in the healing process, but their presence and watchfulness can be a mitigating variable in overall suicide risk.

Assessing Suicidal Intent

Another important aspect of suicide assessment involves evaluating a client's intent to commit suicide. This assessment issue is somewhat related to lethality. For example, adolescents who have used highly lethal means in a previous suicide attempt often have high intent to kill themselves. However, evaluating suicidal intent is more than just evaluating lethality of previous attempts or potential suicide plans; it also involves evaluating desires or consequences associated with suicidal behavior.

It is important to understand desired and/or anticipated consequences of potential suicidal behavior from the young person's perspective. Specifically, therapists inquiring about suicidal intent seek to answer some of the following questions:

1. What does he or she want or expect to have happen as a result of killing him- or herself?
2. Does she or he mainly intend to die?
3. Is there anyone with whom she or he would like to "get even"? For example, does she want to make her parents sorry for something they have or have not done?

In situations in which there have been previous suicide attempts, exploring intent is important both for assessment of risk and for treatment, management, and suicide prevention.

There is a vast difference between the young person who defiantly cuts her arm and lets blood drip on the carpet in front of her angry mother and the young person who quietly removes a gun from a locked cabinet late at night and drives into the woods to shoot himself. One appears intent on getting a reaction from her mother; the other appears intent on killing himself. However, simply because a particular suicide attempt is not associated with the intent of death, it would be wrong to assume that further attempts will not occur, often with increasing lethality.

Consultation

As discussed at the outset of this chapter, suicide assessment and management is complex and stressful for counselors. Consequently, we recommend that counselors routinely obtain consultation regarding assessment and management of suicidal youth. Additionally, to aid counselors working with suicidal youth, a checklist of general suicide assessment procedures is provided in Table 7.1.

MANAGEMENT AND TREATMENT OF SUICIDAL YOUNG CLIENTS

There is no such thing as a "typical" suicidal youth. Suicidal children and adolescents come in all sizes and shapes, from all backgrounds, and with all sorts of reasons for their suicidality. Most therapists will find that they can work comfortably and effectively with some young clients who are suicidal and cannot do so with a

Table 7.1. Checklist of General Suicide Assessment Procedures

_____	1. Assess risk factors
_____	2. Ask about suicidal thoughts
_____	3. Assess suicide plans
_____	4. Assess client intent or goals associated with suicidal be-haviors
_____	5. Obtain psychiatric or collegial consultation
_____	6. Determine appropriate action (degree of intervention)

small subset of one type or another. Accurate assessment is an important component of determining the appropriate treatment approach and setting for young suicidal clients. Honest self-scrutiny is another. We believe that it is better to refer early if referral is likely in working with a suicidal youth. As mentioned earlier, the literature suggests that young clients who attend therapy because of suicidality do not usually stay long, and they handle mid-therapy referrals even worse than do most clients (Pfeffer et al., 1991). The following information is designed to facilitate therapeutic management of young suicidal clients.

No Suicide Agreements

A technique commonly used by therapists working with suicidal clients is the "no suicide agreement" or contract. This agreement or contract may be implemented verbally or in written form. Drye, Goulding, and Goulding (1973) first advocated the no suicide agreement. They initially recommended having clients make a short verbal statement: "No matter what happens, I will not kill myself, accidently or on purpose, at any time" (p. 172). Further development of no suicide agreements has produced additional clauses. For example, clients may be asked to indicate that they will talk or meet with their therapist or some other designated loved one or professional if they feel the urge to harm themselves (Mahoney, 1990;

Sommers-Flanagan & Sommers-Flanagan, 1995a). They may also agree to contact local crisis intervention service providers if their therapist is unavailable when suicidal impulses occur.

Research on using no suicide agreements is sparse. Initially, Drye and colleagues (1973) reported strong positive results using their no suicide agreement method. Of course, their studies were not well controlled, so it is difficult to know how effective no suicide contracts might be if more sophisticated research methodology were utilized. However, at this point, using no suicide contracts with suicidal clients is both routine and a virtual ethical mandate. For example, in a recent report on clinicians' attitudes toward no suicide agreements, Davidson, Wagner, and Range (1995) stated that "...no researcher in good conscience would compare the suicide rates of a group of patients with a no suicide agreement with a group without such an agreement" (p. 411). Using no suicide agreements with adolescent and adult clients has simply become state-of-the-art with regard to managing suicidal clients.

Not surprisingly, we strongly urge using no suicide agreements. With younger children (ages 8–11) it is more appropriate to establish an agreement with parents and child, rather than solely with the child him- or herself. This would include the parent agreeing to provide vigilant direct or arranged supervision of the child and locking away knives, guns, or medications that might be used destructively by the child. In addition, parents would agree to set up an appointment if the child articulated feelings of being out of control or made any kind of attempt to hurt him- or herself. Of course, we would also ask the child to call us directly if she or he felt at imminent risk of trying to hurt her- or himself; but at younger ages, direct parent involvement is crucial.

With adolescents, establish a no suicide agreement directly with the youth. However, in most instances, parent(s) should be informed of and involved in no suicide agreements as well. Although it is hard to prove that no suicide agreements actually help, it is extremely unlikely that they are harmful. In fact, in addition to providing a link between therapist and client, we consider the manner in which young clients react to no suicide contract requests as crucial assessment information.

Word no suicide agreements carefully. Unless you are able and willing to be available 24 hours a day (which is impossible), identify alternative support persons and/or facilities in the agreement. For example, you might state that "in the event I am not available to speak or meet with you when you are feeling suicidal, you agree to contact the suicide hotline and/or be transported to the hospital emergency room for evaluation and support." It is important to include that the client agrees *not* to harm her- or himself until she or he has met with you or a designated person face to face (Sommers-Flanagan & Sommers-Flanagan, 1993). We also recommend that you renew or mention no suicide agreements whenever you see a client until the client actually indicates that an agreement is no longer necessary because self-destructive urges are no longer active.

Decision Making

In assessing the suicidality of a difficult youth, the counselor must gather information for both immediate and longer-term decision making. On occasion, the reason a young person is brought to therapy is that he or she has indicated, in some way, an intention to kill him- or herself. Our experience is similar to reported studies (Maris, Berman, Maltsberger, & Yufit, 1992): In many cases it is unlikely that suicidal young clients will stay in long-term therapy. The first responsibility is to determine the extent of the risk and to take measures to protect the youth from killing her- or himself. The second responsibility to is to determine effective interventions within the constraints of the situation, the family structure, and the individual youth (Brent et al., 1996).

A problem created by having both short- and long-term responsibility is that on occasion, acting to protect the youth in the short run (by hospitalizing or breaking confidentiality) can jeopardize the therapy relationship for longer-term change. Nonetheless, when short- and long-term responsibilities regarding potential suicide conflict, the counselor must err on the side of caution, acting to protect the youth's life.

Case Example. Fifteen-year-old Hillary was referred to RSF for therapy because she had taken a nonlethal overdose of painkillers.

She had seen a male therapist for a short time with little progress; he believed that Hillary might benefit from meeting with a female therapist. It took a few sessions of relationship-building activities before Hillary revealed that she had taken the overdose after being raped, while very intoxicated, at a fraternity party that she and her friends had attended. Until she chose to disclose this information, she had not informed anyone else of the incident and she was very clear that she was not interested in informing anyone else of her rape experience.

Therapy focused on rebuilding self-esteem, recovering from trauma, and gently exploring a potential substance abuse problem. Hillary needed parental support in her efforts to stay in school, to calibrate her social activities, and to rebuild a sense of hope in the future. I asked if the family would come in occasionally for supportive family meetings. Hillary's mother willingly agreed to attend sessions. In contrast, Hillary's father attended only on one occasion, making it clear he had no time for "counseling." Hillary was adamant that I not reveal her rape, and I complied with her wishes until she had a second sexually abusive experience.

The circumstances were similar. Once again, Hillary had gotten drunk and one or more male partiers forced her to have sex with them. Her suicidal ideation was reactivated, and her ability to protect herself from further sexual exploitation seemed limited at best. We had a no suicide contract and I believed that she was safe on a short-term basis. I set up our next meeting, telling Hillary that I wanted to have her mom come along for part of the session, but that we would talk first.

We met the following week. Nothing much had changed. I knew from phone calls that Hillary's mother was mystified regarding her daughter's demolished self-esteem and suicidal urges, and I knew that it was time to help Hillary inform her mother of the rape experiences. I also knew that I would need to take a firm stand, basically telling Hillary that if she did not tell her mother what had happened, I would do so myself.

Hillary was furious. She cried, swore at me, and threatened to walk out of my office and kill herself. I told her I cared a great deal about her, and would therefore have to call the police if she left with that intention. Finally, her mother came back to the office, and while everyone in the room cried, Hillary was able to tell her mother about the rapes.

I only saw Hillary for two more sessions. Her mother rallied to her side and began attending a parents-of-teens support group. The school counselor became involved and was able to negotiate special accommodations for Hillary at school. I was able to tell Hillary how sorry I was that it became necessary to force the issue of her secret, and she was able to say she understood why I did it. But she wasn't interested in any more therapy—especially with me.

After therapy, Hillary finished high school, was able to date, and has held down a steady job successfully. However, I do not know whether she has sought additional counseling or whether she ever will do so in the future.

This case had many complicated dynamics other than the client's suicidal threats and attempts. However, we believe that most suicidal adolescents will be experiencing difficult life situations in addition to specific psychiatric disorders. The preceding case illustrates that there is often a cost associated with choosing to break confidentiality with young clients. Although in different situations, young clients may experience relief when secrets associated with their suicidal behavior are disclosed, it is ordinarily difficult to predict in advance whether disclosure of an adolescent's secret will result in a negative emotional reaction and eventual termination. Obviously, the pros and cons of breaking confidentiality must be seriously considered.

Alternatives to Suicide

Suicidal young people are often acutely experiencing a lifelong battle between dependence and independence. Further, they are likely to be ambivalent about many areas of their lives. They are disappointed in their life and family circumstances, but they are not confident in their ability to make it on their own. They may want to trust authority figures and loved ones to come through for them, but are unable to openly trust adults. They want to be assured of their worth—internally and externally—but brief reassuring statements are inadequate. Their emotions range from anger to loneliness to fear to longing. They, like the rest of us, want to believe in a hopeful future. But they are not hopeful about the future. And worse, they may share very little of this with you. In fact, they may not even admit it to themselves.

In our experience, young suicidal clients appreciate straight talk. Similar to most adolescents, suicidal clients will often engage in and enjoy a good argument. Sometimes, during lively discussions of suicide and other alternatives, their views of suicide as a viable or desirable option to life will evolve.

Most adolescents do not like having their choices restricted. Consequently, counselors should openly acknowledge that committing suicide is an option in life. Additionally, sometimes we talk about suicide using old axioms, such as "You can always die"; or, "Suicide is a permanent solution to a temporary problem." Comments such as these provide a launching point for the dialogue aimed at finding alternatives that will achieve the same goal (or even better goals) than death. In certain cases, it helps to appeal to young clients' pride: What if there was a better solution than killing yourself and you didn't take time to try it?

One young male client of RSF's, an aspiring writer, responded avidly to the following question and metaphor:

> What if your life were a book and in the next chapter, the one after this one, the plot takes an amazing turn and you (choose one): fall in love with the perfect person; win the lottery; discover an amazing hidden talent; or make the friend of a lifetime? But if you kill yourself, it's like a book with half the chapters torn out.

We spent the rest of the hour imagining the next chapters. We wrote a list of possible plot developments, and I then asked him to think of at least five more during the week and rank order the entire list.

After going through his rankings, we re-ranked them based on ease of bringing them about, and began strategic planning to see if there were ways to make the next chapter of his life read something like the plot he'd imagined. This case example illustrates the importance of helping clients develop a perception of personal control and personal contribution to their lives. Further, young suicidal clients are easier to engage in discussions about life if the counselor uses their personal interests as a foundation for such a discussion.

In some cases, the child uses suicidal behavior to get parental attention. If the parental attention is available, even to a modest degree, then working with the family on how to get each other's attention—how to express needs and respond to expressed needs—can be a direct and rewarding process. At first, much of the expression will be stored up and shared in the therapist's office, and the needs expressed will be indirect approximations of deeper needs. But with persistent modeling and redirection, young clients can learn to say what they need, and families can learn to listen and respond with enough emotional connection that the suicidal gestures are no longer needed. Family therapy for suicidal youth is often an important and effective treatment option (see Rotheram-Borus et al., 1994).

Suicide Attempters

In contrast to completed suicide, suicide attempts, gestures, and ideation are a much higher base-rate occurrence. Estimates suggest that up to 60% of high school-aged teens report having seriously considered suicide and that 10% to 14% report having made some form of suicide attempt (Mehan, Lamb, Saltzman, & O'Carroll, 1992). While of course, every attempt must be taken seriously, one common reaction to multiple attempts is to feel manipulated by the attempter. Families and treatment professionals can become frustrated and even jaded in dealing with multiple attempts. As noted above, it is important to consult with other professionals when working with suicidal youth. This is especially so when therapists are working with repeat attempters. We have found working with repeat attempters to be a situation ripe for therapist burnout, misjudgments, and perhaps unnecessary referrals.

Working with young clients who repeatedly attempt suicide requires commitment and detachment. Defining the limits of the counselor's role is essential, as is communicating these limits. We recommend communicating something similar to the following:

> I want you to know I value you and I don't believe suicide is the best answer to your problems. I know that sometimes, you want to die. But sometimes, you don't. Sometimes, a large part of you wants to die. But so far, there's been a little part of you that wants to stay alive and work things out for a better life. I'm on that side. The side of that little part of you that wants to hang in there. I can't keep you alive. But I can help the part of you that wants to live work on making things better. I can work with you on staying alive.

With clients who use suicide talk or attempts for attention, or who use suicide talk to express rage, disappointment, or despair, the obvious solution is to find alternative means for that expression. This is easier said than done. Often, situations children are reacting to are difficult or impossible to change.

Case example. Georgia came to therapy after the school counselor panicked and broke confidentiality: Georgia had expressed her suicidal thoughts in a group of high achievers like herself. Without consulting or warning Georgia, the school counselor called Georgia's mother and told her the story. Georgia's mother called and made an appointment with me (RSF). The first Georgia knew of the whole betrayal and subsequent arrangement was when her mother told her, in the car, on the way to see me.

Georgia was understandably furious. After hearing the story, I had her mother in, and explained, with Georgia present, that the school counselor should have talked with Georgia directly. I then wondered aloud why Mom had kept the secret until the trip to my office.

Mom burst into tears and cried the remainder of the session. Georgia and I looked on, talking quietly with each other.

G: Mom and Dad don't believe in therapy. Well. Dad doesn't.
RSF: Really?
G: Yeah. Guess that's why she didn't bring it up.

The next few weeks, it became very clear that Georgia felt trapped in her family. Her parents were consistently in conflict, her siblings were gone, and her giftedness was downplayed and minimized rather than noted or supported by her family. Alternatives began to occur to her as we talked about the lives of gifted kids. Boarding school featured prominently. It was not something she was sure she wanted but at least it was an alternative to suicide.

We began to talk about her mother's deep sadness and how sometimes, kids take over for their parents in doing emotional work. We tried to convince her mother to see someone for therapy. Although her mother refused individual therapy, Georgia was able to see that some of her sadness was actually her mother's sadness. She was able to see that she was carrying some of her mother's emotional burden and that another alternative was to let her mom carry her own burden. We drew what that might look like—a short stick figure, transferring half of her load into the pack of a taller stick figure. We talked about how hard it was to love someone who was always sad. It was affirming for Georgia. Her family situation was not much fun, and she had known that inside, but had never articulated it. It helped immensely for her to have someone else see this pattern with her, and to have someone else help her discover that she had alternatives and ways to individuate without killing herself.

PROFESSIONAL ISSUES

The initial concern of therapists working with suicidal young clients is client protection. A secondary concern is self-protection. We provide the following review to ensure the likelihood that therapists will behave in a professional manner and therefore reduce their potential for liability.

Documentation

For therapists who conduct suicide assessments and/or therapy with suicidal clients, we recommend using the suicide assessment checklist included in Table 7.2.

Table 7.2. Suicide Assessment Documentation Checklist

Check off the following items to ensure that your suicide assessment documentation is up to professional standards.

_____ 1. I discussed limits of confidentiality and informed consent with the client and parents.

_____ 2. I conducted a thorough suicide assessment, including:

      _____ Risk factor assessment

      _____ Suicide assessment Instruments or questionnaires utilized (write in)

      _____ Assessment of suicidal thoughts, plan, client self-control, and suicidal intent completed

_____ 3. I obtained relevant historical information from the client regarding suicidal behavior (e.g., suicidal behaviors by family members, previous attempts, lethality of previous attempts, etc.).

_____ 4. Previous treatment records were requested/obtained.

_____ 5. I consulted with one or more licensed mental health professionals.

_____ 6. An appropriate "no suicide" contract was established.

_____ 7. The patient was provided with information regarding emergency/crisis resources.

_____ 8. In cases of high suicide risk, appropriate and relevant authority figures (police officers) and/or family members were contacted.

Decision Making And Client Recommendations

When it comes to managing suicidal young clients, our policy is almost always to err on the conservative side. For example, if we are in doubt, usually first we consult with a knowledgeable professional, and second, we recommend intensive observation or hospitalization. In many cases we avoid hospitalization because of its potential regressive effects on suicidal youth. Additionally, it has been our experience that many young clients have fairly negative experiences within the confines of hospitals. Consequently, whenever possible, we try to protect suicidal clients from having additional negative life experiences and we assign them a personal observer. The personal observer may be a committed family member or staff members at a local group home or residential treatment center. The role of the personal observer is to prevent impulsive suicidal behavior. However, as you can well imagine, personal observers assume a task fraught with responsibility and potential danger.

In some cases, we have had teenagers express suicidal impulses in provocative or manipulative ways. For example, a 16-year-old girl whom we treated indicated to her parents that if she could not visit her boyfriend, then she would "kill herself." Subsequently, the parents contacted us and inquired as to what action they should take. We informed them of our basic rule: Always take suicidal threats seriously. With regard to this case, taking the 16-year-old's suicidal threat seriously involved restricting her freedom. Therefore, we told the parents to inform her that if she was suicidal, they most certainly would *not* let her visit her boyfriend alone or be alone in general. However, if she wanted to visit her boyfriend and be accompanied by one or both of her parents, then a visit was acceptable. Overall, we have found that taking a stand of protection and maintaining close family contact is a most effective means of dealing with suicide in general and provocative or manipulative suicide talk in particular.

CONCLUDING COMMENTS

Evaluating and providing therapy for suicidal young clients can be extremely stressful. This chapter reviewed procedures designed to help suicide assessment and management proceed more smoothly. Hopefully, if therapists pay close attention to suicide risk factors, assess client suicide thoughts, plans, self-control, and suicide intent, and apply the basic management strategies reviewed in this chapter, then working with suicidal young clients can become more comfortable and unnecessary suicidal behavior can be reduced.

Checklists are included within this chapter to assist counselors who are trying to maintain professional, ethical, and legal standards when working with suicidal young people.

8

Medication Evaluations and Evaluating Medications

"Well," said Mrs. Piggle-Wiggle, "if it were only his older sister who complained about Phillip I would be inclined to let time work things out, but as long as Phillip is annoying his daddy and Miss Perriwinkle who is one of the best fifth-grade teachers in this county, then we had better take steps."

"Take steps?" quavered Phillip's mother. "What do you mean by steps?"

"Oh, it's very simple," said Mrs. Piggle-Wiggle. "Have Phillip come down after school and I'll give him a bottle of Show-off Powder. For the next few days sprinkle a little on him before meals, especially when you are having company, and just before he leaves for school in the morning. I'm sure you won't have any more trouble."

"But what is this show-off powder? Will it hurt Phillip?" asked Mrs. Carmody fearfully. (from Hello, Mrs. Piggle-Wiggle, MacDonald, 1957, pp. 15–16)

N ow, what if Mrs. Carmody dropped by her therapist's office after talking with Mrs. Piggle-Wiggle? It would be highly likely that Mrs. Carmody would ask her therapist about "show-off powder" (i.e., Prozac). And, before reading any further, as a mental health professional specializing in treating children, what would you tell Mrs. Carmody?

On a more serious note, the purpose of this chapter is to provide information on medication treatment alternatives within the context of nonpharmacologic (counseling or psychotherapy) treatments. When it comes to treating young clients, medication treatment may be primary, adjunctive, or irrelevant. Whatever the case, treatment of child and adolescent emotional and behavioral problems with medications is becoming more and more common. As a consequence, basic knowledge regarding pharmacologic treatment options and whether and how to discuss medications with young clients and their parents now constitutes an important body of knowledge for mental health therapists (Fisher & Greenberg, 1989; Littrell & Ashford, 1995; Sommers-Flanagan & Sommers-Flanagan, 1996b). This chapter reviews strategies for discussing medication issues with young clients and their parents, determining when and whether a medical referral is necessary or appropriate, and understanding the relative safety, efficacy, and appropriateness of various psychopharmacologic agents.

SHOULD THERAPISTS DISCUSS MEDICATIONS WITH THEIR CLIENTS?

Littrell and Ashford (1995) recently reviewed whether or not it is ethically acceptable for nonphysician mental health professionals to discuss medication use with their clients, from the perspective of psychologists. Although the specific issue of "show-off powder" was never addressed, they discussed two perspectives regarding whether psychologists should talk with their clients about medications. First, with regard to whether it is legal or ethical for psychologists to discuss medications with their clients, Littrell and Ashford (1995) concluded:

Extrapolating from legal decisions in nursing and pharmacy, there is nothing illegal about psychologists discussing medications with clients. Prudent practice and [the American Counseling Association (1995) and] American Psychological Association (1993) Code[s] of Ethics dictate the need for coordination of care when a client is under the care of two professionals. However, discussion about the care provided by another professional may be necessary when the client's best interests are served by such a discussion. (p. 243; bracketed information added)

Second, with regard to the issue of informed consent and therapists' responsibility to discuss proposed and alternative treatments with their clients, Littrell and Ashford (1995) stated:

Forty-nine states have statutes mandating informed consent. Many state statutes define informed consent as including discussion of proposed as well as alternative treatments. Legal experts believe that state statutes apply to all members of the health care delivery system. If informed consent legislation applies to psychologists, then the statutes mandate that psychologists ensure that clients are informed about the relative merits of pharmacotherapy treatment options. These statutes require that psychologists either discuss medications themselves or refer to a professional who will. To meet the needs of their clients, it is becoming increasingly imperative for psychologists to be knowledgeable about medications. (p. 243)

It is clear from their analysis that nonphysician therapists either should be prepared to discuss medication treatment alternatives with their clients, or should refer their clients to therapists, possibly physicians, who can provide such a discussion. We list other reasons why nonphysician therapists should be informed regarding medical treatments in Box 8.1.

DISCUSSING MEDICATION TREATMENT WITH YOUNG CLIENTS AND THEIR PARENTS

By definition, nonmedical therapists are *not* trained to prescribe medications for their clients. Nonetheless, parents of young clients often bring up the topic of medications for discussion with their

Box 8.1. Why Nonphysician Mental Health Professionals Should Be Informed About Medication Treatments

When outlining this book, we considered: "If this is a book about non-pharmacologic treatments (i.e., counseling and psychotherapy), why include a chapter discussing medication treatment?" In responding to this question, we developed the following rationale for including this chapter:

1. Although nonpharmacologic treatments for children and adolescents are often effective in alleviating specific problems, they are sometimes ineffective. In such cases nonmedical professionals may need to discuss (and/or refer for) pharmacologic treatment alternatives.

2. In some cases, pharmacologic treatment may be effective in alleviating symptoms associated with specific mental disorders (e.g., obsessive–compulsive disorder).

3. Unfortunately, due in part to the remedicalization of psychiatry and the general biological philosophical orientation currently *en vogue* within our popular culture, many clients (and professionals) have unrealistic expectations regarding the usual effectiveness of pharmacologic treatment (Kramer, 1993). This information may confuse or mislead clients and professionals when it comes to making therapeutic decisions.

4. Because there often are no clear answers regarding what form of treatment may be most effective for specific child/adolescent symptoms, it is incumbent upon all professionals to provide relevant and objective information to parents as they try to make decisions regarding whether or not to try psychoactive medications in the treatment of their child. It is also important to provide similar information to young clients themselves. Providing objective information regarding treatment alternatives is essential to obtaining informed consent to treatment from parents and children.

5. Despite the power of the placebo and the self-serving financial interests sometimes inherent in providing counseling, psychotherapy, and/or medical treatment, our ethical standards dictate that we be honest with young clients and their parents regarding the potential effectiveness of various treatment alternatives.

6. Reviewing factual information about medication effectiveness can assist all professionals in becoming aware of their personal biases.

7. Young clients and their parents (and some physicians) will often ask counselors, social workers, and psychologists for opinions and advice regarding medications.

child's counselor, school psychologist, social worker, psychologist, or other health or mental health professional. Sometimes, parents begin asking questions about medications simply because they do not know that counselors or psychologists or social workers are unable to prescribe medications. On other occasions, medication issues come up for discussion because nonphysician therapists are more accessible and perhaps less intimidating than are physicians. In fact, physicians typically spend very little time discussing various treatment alternatives with their patients (Campbell, Manksch, Neikirk, & Hosakawa, 1990). Additionally, either parents or therapists sometimes initiate discussion of medication treatment alternatives when there is frustration or dissatisfaction with the pace and/or progress of nonpharmacologic therapy.

Case Example: Run, Don't Walk, To Dr. Smith's Office

Child and adolescent referrals sometimes have a seasonal rhythm. This seasonal aspect of child/adolescent referrals is closely tied to the school calendar and academic and behavioral progress. Summer and early fall referrals frequently have proactive or preventive characteristics because parents and teachers want children to be prepared for the coming academic year. In contrast, late fall, winter, and spring referrals are frequently reactive or crisis oriented because parents and teachers are trying to help children and adults survive through the remaining school year.

One April, I (JSF) received a consultation referral from a distraught Mr. and Ms. Doe, who wanted to discuss treatment options for their 12-year-old sixth grader. Reportedly, their son, who had historically obtained straight As in school, began a dramatic academic and behavioral tailspin beginning in October of sixth grade. Although the boy (Billy) had always exhibited characteristics of stubbornness and impulsivity, he was quite intelligent and had been, until sixth grade, cooperative and achievement oriented within the school setting. Billy's mother, who was relatively knowledgeable regarding child behavior, suggested that Billy may have always had qualities of "mild attention-deficit disorder." Despite the implementation of classroom and school-based interventions during the fall and winter, Billy's behavior and academic progress continued to deteriorate. Finally, after a late March playground fight, school suspension, and academic warnings, the parents chose to heed the advice of the boy's school psychologist, who reportedly stated: "Run, don't walk, to the closest telephone and call Dr. Jones (a local physician) and make an appointment to get your son some medicine."

When the couple met with me in mid-April, their son's behavior had significantly improved. Billy was diligently taking 75mg imipramine (Tofranil) daily. Nonetheless, Billy's parents were pressing him to submit to counseling and Billy, consistent with his single-minded style, was fending off his parents' suggestions of counseling with substantial verbal prowess (e.g., "You are so lame. Can't you see that you're the ones who need counseling?").

It was clear from the outset that Billy's parents believed, despite possible medical or biological aspects of Billy's problems, that they and Billy might obtain benefits from counseling. Specifically, they stated: "Even if Billy has a biological or medical problem, we want to know how to best handle him; we want to be the best possible parents for Billy." Mr. and Ms. Doe had been informed by Billy's physician that Billy had "a chemical imbalance," that such problems were usually "genetic," and that it was unlikely that counseling would be useful.

Mr. and Ms. Doe were very pleased that Billy's troublesome symptoms had been reduced by the imipramine. However, they also had numerous concerns about Billy and about the medication. Some of their questions included:

1. "How long do children usually need to take this kind of medication?"
2. "Exactly how does the medication work? You know how doctors can be; he really didn't spend all that much time with us. He just said it's a chemical problem and it's genetic."
3. "What if Billy gets worse while he's still taking the medicine? Does that mean he should switch medicines or will the doctor just increase the dosage?"

4. "The doctor said he was giving Billy a small dose of medicine to begin with, but Billy is a pretty small boy for his age and so we wondered how much imipramine would be too much for a boy Billy's size?"

5. "If we can get Billy to come in for counseling do you think he will need to keep taking the medicine?"

This case is an excellent illustration of common client questions about medications, but more importantly, it illustrates how parents and/or children may have grave concerns about taking medications, *even when the medications appear to be working effectively*. Finally, this case also illustrates several issues therapists face when other professionals have been expedient or unprofessional in their approach to clients. For example, why didn't the physician take the time to answer the questions of these apparently reasonable and intelligent parents? Moreover, if the boy was diagnosed as having ADHD, then why did the physician prescribe an antidepressant, when psychostimulants such as methylphenidate (Ritalin) ordinarily constitute first-line treatment (Rosenberg, Holttum, & Gershon, 1994)? Also, if Billy is depressed, then why did the physician prescribe an antidepressant (when there is no evidence that antidepressants are effective for child/adolescent depression) while claiming that counseling would not be useful (Fisher & Fisher, 1996; Sommers-Flanagan & Sommers-Flanagan, 1996b)? Before reading on, take a few minutes and consider how you might respond to the questions posed by Billy's parents. The following sections provide general guidelines regarding how to talk with parents and children about medications.

Focus On Clients' Concerns

In his classic text titled *The Helping Interview*, Alfred Benjamin (1981) outlined approaches for helping professionals who are facing questions posed to them by their clients. He advised:

> I feel certain that we ought not to reply to every question. At times ethics may even prevent us because by so doing we might betray the confidence of someone else. On the other hand, we should, I

feel, respond to every question the interviewee says—by listening to it with as much understanding as possible and being as helpful as we can in our response. Not every question calls for an answer, but every question demands respectful listening and usually a personal reaction on our part. (1981, p. 80)

Benjamin's (1981) advice is especially important when clients ask questions which put us on the spot. As counselors, it is natural to feel responsible and to have strong impulses to help our clients. Nonetheless, Benjamin reminds us that before answering questions, we should first listen very attentively and try to discern our clients' underlying concerns. Specifically, we should address the meaning of our clients, medication questions first, and later, if necessary, we may (or may not) answer their medication questions directly.

In the case example described above, the parents' questions reflect underlying anxiety or fear about making the right decisions concerning their son's mental health care. When parents have underlying concerns about medication use with their children, it is crucial for counselors to clearly identify the nature and quality of parental concerns before giving advice or sharing their own professional views regarding medication use. Obviously, parents sometimes have fears that are unrealistic and unfounded (e.g., that a trial of Ritalin might cause irreversible brain damage). On the other hand, they may have fears that are based firmly in reality (e.g., fears regarding the sexual side effects of Prozac and other serotonin specific reuptake inhibitors (SSRIs) and worries about the effects of long-term antidepressant use). Overall, when questions pertaining to medication use arise in the context of counseling or psychotherapy, the counselor's task is twofold: to explore the parents' underlying feelings (i.e., usually anxiety) and to implement a strategy for coping with feelings associated with medication use. We will first discuss methods for exploring parental feelings and then we will focus on coping with feelings associated with medication use later in this chapter.

Explore underlying concerns. Several techniques can help therapists effectively explore client anxieties about medication use. Illustrations of paraphrasing, reflection of feelings, and gentle inquiry are provided below.

Paraphrase: "You have lots of questions about your son being on this medication. You want more information about how the medicine works, dosage, and how long Billy will need to be on the medicine."

Feeling reflection: "You sound a little worried about having your son take this medication."

Inquiry: "Whenever parents ask me lots of questions about medications, I start wondering about how they're feeling about their child taking medicine. So before I answer your questions, I'd like you to tell me more about your concerns. What do you think might happen if your son keeps taking this medicine?"

The general purpose of these techniques is to gather more information about how parent(s) feel about their child taking medication before answering parental questions and before providing general information about medications. The goal of exploring underlying parent concerns is to identify parents' and/or children's specific fears about medication use. If counselors answer client medication questions immediately, further exploration of client feelings may be cut off.

Inform Clients of Your Professional Limits and Biases

It is crucial for counselors to acknowledge their professional limitations and biases when speaking with parents about medications. If limitations and biases are not acknowledged, counselors run the risk of misleading clients regarding their credentials and expertise. To do so is clearly unethical and must be avoided (American Counseling Association, 1995; American Psychological Association, 1992; American School Counselor Association, 1992). When clients ask nonphysician counselors about medications, a statement similar to the following is mandatory (*after* exploring client underlying feelings and fears):

Before I can address any of the questions you have asked me about medications, I need to be clear about a few things. First, I am not a physician. That means I cannot prescribe medications. Second, I am not a pharmacist, and that means I do not have detailed information about how medicines work. Third, because I am a counselor (or psychologist or social worker), I am trained in using nondrug approaches to help children and families make positive changes in their lives. Therefore, take anything I might say in that context; I am not a medications expert and I have a professional bias toward using nondrug approaches for personal change.

The preceding disclaimer statement brings up an important issue. Specifically, what business do nonphysician mental health providers have making comments about medications to clients when they are admittedly professionally biased and ill-trained in the area of medication treatment? This is an excellent question and one that counselors (as well as physicians) should ask themselves. We frequently have found physicians who are biased toward medication use (as in the case of Billy, described above) and, unfortunately, many physicians do not take the time to provide clients with an adequate explanation about medications or psychosocial issues (Campbell et al., 1990). Finally, after repeatedly having clients ask us questions about medications, we have concluded, similar to Littrel and Ashford (1995), that *sometimes* nonphysicians can provide clients with helpful information about medications. However, we recommend that nonphysicians ask themselves the following questions *before* deciding how to respond to client questions about medications:

1. Am I too biased about this issue to comment constructively?
2. Do I have any helpful information to provide my client on this topic?
3. How can I best address the concerns underlying my client's questions about medications?

Refer Clients Back To Their Physicians

The easiest, and often best, response to client questions about medications is simply to state something like:

> It sounds like you have some excellent questions about the medication(s) your son has been prescribed. I recommend that we write them down and that you schedule an appointment with your son's physician so you can ask him or her directly.

This is clearly the best response if you have confidence that the child's physician will respond to the questions sensitively and responsibly.

Fortunately, there are many physicians who are approachable, professional, balanced, and competent; in such cases, parent(s) can have nearly all of their questions answered directly by the physician, and whether and how nonphysician therapists should discuss medications with clients becomes irrelevant. However, in our experience, physicians dismiss their patients' questions about medications too frequently and the result is that clients come to us for answers or direction. Despite the fact that we sometimes have been disappointed with the manner in which physicians address parents' questions about medicines, we remain optimistic and therefore ordinarily work with clients on how to formulate and ask their questions of physicians directly.

In our relatively small professional community, the reputation and skill of various physicians (with respect to responding to client medication questions) is easily accessible. Consequently, we can often predict in advance how physicians will respond to client requests for additional information about medications. Nonetheless, we generally use the following criteria in determining whether or not we, as nonphysicians, should act as an additional resource for information about medications. Specifically, we ask ourselves:

1. Are the parent(s) assertive enough to schedule an appointment and directly ask their child's physician questions about medication use?
2. Can the parent(s) afford to schedule a special appointment time with the physician to discuss medications?
3. Is the physician willing or able to schedule an appointment with the parent(s) within a reasonable time period (i.e., 1–3 weeks)?

4. Is there a likely chance that the physician will sit down and discuss these questions with the parent(s) in an honest, nondefensive, and unbiased manner?

If there is a reasonable chance that answers to these preceding questions are "yes," then we ordinarily refer clients back to their prescribing physician for further medication discussions. In contrast, if we suspect that the answers to these questions are "no," then we usually address medication questions directly with clients.

Provide General Medication Information (or Information on How to Obtain Information)

Providing information to clients, explaining how a treatment procedure works, or directing clients to obtain a particular type of information can be therapeutic (Sommers-Flanagan & Sommers-Flanagan, 1993). Such procedures are therapeutic partly because clients can experience a greater sense of personal control over their lives when they are provided with or obtain useful information with which they can make informed decisions. Additionally, the information obtained may be reassuring and/or validating, and consequently clients feel more relaxed or more justified in having had negative or anxiety-provoking thoughts (Beck, 1976).

It is often useful to begin a discussion about medications with a generally supportive and reassuring statement. For example:

> The fact that you are unclear and a little nervous about imipramine and how it will or can affect your son is normal. After all, most people know very little about these types of medications and how they affect young people.

Although statements such as this do not answer client questions or solve problems, they constitute a sort of empathic reassurance and contribute to rapport and the development of a working alliance.

Beyond general support and directing parents back to physicians, addressing medication questions can become more problematic. This is because medication use in general, and particularly medication use with young clients, is fraught with controversy. Some professionals are strongly in favor of medicating young clients, while others are strongly opposed (Breggin & Breggin, 1994; Eagen, 1994; Martin, 1995; Sanua, 1995). That being the case, any statement nonphysicians make about medication use with children may be open to debate. Further, it is unlikely that most professionals, especially nonphysicians (or nonpharmacists), are willing to take risks with their professional reputation by making unsubstantiated statements about medication use. Therefore, later in this chapter we include a section on providing basic information.

Refer Clients for a Medical Second Opinion

If, after focusing on and exploring client medication concerns, informing clients of your professional limits and biases, referring them back to their original physician, and providing them with general medication information your clients still have significant concerns about the medications they or their children are taking, they should be referred for a second medical opinion. In such cases, to facilitate referral, it is important for nonphysician practitioners to have a positive working relationship with a few local physicians. Similar to psychology and counseling, it is not unusual for physicians to back away from confronting one another on their professional work. However, it is much more appropriate for physicians to criticize and question each other's medication choices than it is for nonphysicians to step into a professional arena wherein they have little or no training. In other words, it is useful to have some physician colleagues who are aware of and sympathetic to the tendency of other physicians to over-rely on medications for treatment of child and adolescent emotional and behavioral problems.

A checklist for handling client questions about medications is included in Table 8.1.

BASIC MEDICATION INFORMATION

Psychiatric medications are generally prescribed to children and adolescents to control or alleviate troublesome somatic, emotional,

Table 8.1. Checklist (Plan) For Handling
Client Medication Questions

_____   1. Explore and focus on client concerns regarding medication(s).

_____   2. Assist client in how to formulate and ask appropriate questions directly with their physician.

_____   3. State your professional limitations and biases clearly and directly.

_____   4. If #2 is unsuccessful, provide client with general information and/or reading materials.

_____   5. If you and/or the client remain concerned about the medication(s), dosage, side effects, combinations, etcetera, direct him or her to a physician who can provide a second opinion.

cognitive, or behavioral symptoms. Not surprisingly, there is debate regarding whether medication treatment addresses underlying biological abnormalities or whether they simply control surface symptoms, while underlying causes (e.g., emotional trauma, life changes such as divorce, etc.) remain unchanged. Those who adhere strictly to the medical model advocate the following position:

> Proponents of the medical model, whether psychologists or psychiatrists, are committed to their belief that conceptualizing mental illness as a physical illness offers the best hope for diagnosis and treatment... It is argued that the medical model removes, at least in part, the stigma and blame to which emotionally disturbed people may be subjected in society. (Wyatt & Livson, 1994, pp. 120–121)

This section briefly describes psychiatric medications commonly prescribed to children and adolescents. It is organized based on diagnostic or behavioral problems frequently associated with difficult young clients referred for counseling or psychotherapy. We also briefly review information pertaining to expected medication efficacy and associated side effects.

Diagnostic Problems

In psychiatry, medications usually are prescribed to treat symptoms associated with specific psychiatric diagnoses. Additionally, medications are sometimes prescribed on the basis of problematic symptoms that may or may not be associated with a specific diagnostic category (e.g., aggression). Although these are reasonable strategies, there are problems in the diagnosis of mental disorders, and we should acknowledge symptom overlap among youth briefly before describing general pharmacologic practices.

First, and most important, providing specific diagnoses for young clients is a very difficult task. This is because when it comes to child/adolescent psychopathology, comorbidity is the rule rather than the exception (Harrington, 1993). What this means is that many, if not most, young clients referred for treatment qualify for more than one psychiatric diagnosis. For example, McGee and colleagues (1990) reported that about one third of depressed adolescents also suffered from CD, while another one third suffered from an anxiety disorder. Similarly, Ryan and colleagues (Ryan et al., 1987) reported that 58% of depressed children also met diagnostic criteria for moderate to severe separation anxiety disorder. There is also strong evidence for diagnostic overlap among learning disorders, ADHD, ODD, eating disorders, phobias, and substance abuse disorders (Sommers-Flanagan & Sommers-Flanagan, in press). Suffice it to say, it is challenging to identify a single target syndrome when applying medication treatment to young clients.

Second, some child advocates complain that although psychiatric diagnosis is designed adequately for describing and identifying adult disorders, diagnostic categorization for children and adolescents is inadequate or inappropriate. For example, some researchers and clinicians have proposed alternative diagnostic systems specifically oriented toward identifying child and adolescent depression (Carlson & Garber, 1986; Weinberg, Rutman, Sullivan, Penick, & Dietz, 1973). At the very least, it is a fact that significantly less research has been devoted to child and adolescent psychopathology than to adult psychopathology.

Third, research on neurotransmitters associated with various psychiatric disorders or emotional–behavioral symptoms is in its very early stages (George, 1994; Jacobs, 1994). Although this is true with regard to adult neurobiology, the research is even more underdeveloped with regard to child neurobiology. This means that there are a number of scientifically unsupported explanations for the many specific emotional and behavioral problems exhibited by young clients. For example, many physicians explain to parents that child/adolescent symptoms are caused by some sort of amorphous "chemical imbalance" when there is no scientific evidence to support that any specific chemical imbalance exists (Sommers-Flanagan, 1995). Consequently, we recommend that nonphysician mental health professionals exercise caution prior to endorsing any neurobiological explanations of child/adolescent behavior.

Fourth, psychotropic medications are generally designed for treating adult psychiatric disorders. After medications have been approved by the Food and Drug Administration (FDA) for use with adults, they become available for prescription in the United States and subsequently physicians prescribe their use with children even though clinical efficacy research was originally conducted on adults. Consequently, medications prescribed for children often have little scientific research regarding their effects on children. This is the case for antidepressants (including Prozac), which are acceptable treatment alternatives for depression in adults, but have never been approved by the FDA for use in the treatment of childhood or adolescent depression (Fisher & Fisher, 1996).

Conditions Sometimes Warranting Medication Treatment

The following review of child/adolescent diagnostic categories and corresponding medication treatments is limited to diagnostic entities and behavioral problems commonly treated with medications. Space does not allow a systematic review of all child/adolescent symptoms and mental disorders sometimes treated with psychotropic medications. Consequently, we limit our discussion below to the following diagnostic or symptom-focused entities: ADHD, enuresis, unipolar depression, anxiety disorders, and CD and/or ODD.

Attention-deficit/hyperactivity disorder (ADHD). Characterized by inattentiveness, impulsivity, and overactivity, ADHD constitutes one of the most frequent syndromes for which children are referred for therapy (Silva, Munoz, & Alpert, 1996). Further, due to increasing popularity of Ritalin (methylphenidate), various antidepressants, and biogenetic etiologic formulations of ADHD, parents and physicians often view medications as a primary intervention strategy when treating children diagnosed as having ADHD (Barkley, 1990).

Given the large numbers of youths receiving medication treatment for ADHD, it may come as a surprise to nonphysicians that nondrug treatment approaches are the best first approach to treatment (Hancock, 1996). Specifically, Rosenberg and collegues (1994) stated that: "Stimulants should not be used in place of or as an alternative to behavioral interventions, since the few available studies of their long-term effectiveness have failed to demonstrate such effectiveness when used alone" (p. 27). Consequently, initiating behavior modification programs, social skills training, problem-solving skills training, parent training, and in-school interventions before resorting to medication trials constitutes a wise and prudent treatment approach in treating ADHD (Barkley, 1990). Medication treatments should be considered after behavior modification approaches have been implemented, or, in cases of severe ADHD, behavior modification and medication treatments should be implemented simultaneously.

Psychostimulant medications, specifically Ritalin, Dexedrine (dextroamphetamine sulfate), and Cylert (pemoline), are generally (but not exclusively) considered first as medication alternatives for ADHD treatment. We list medication alternatives for the treatment of ADHD in Table 8.2. However, specific physicians often have their preferred medication alternative (e.g., we know some physicians who routinely begin children diagnosed with ADHD on Tofranil [imipramine] and others who often select Catapres [clonidine], Prozac [fluoxetine], or even Zoloft [sertraline] before resorting to a psychostimulant trial).

Most research on treating ADHD with psychostimulants in general and with Ritalin in particular suggests that Ritalin signifi-

Table 8.2. Medication Alternatives in ADHD Treatment

Brand name	Generic name	Classification
Ritalin	Methylphenidate	Psychostimulant
Dexedrine	Dextroamphetamine	Psychostimulant
Cylert	Pemoline	Psychostimulant
Norpramine	Desipramine	Tricyclic AD
Tofranil	Imipramine	Tricyclic AD
Catapres	Clonidine	Beta-Blocker
Wellbutrin	Bupropion	Atypical AD
Prozac	Fluoxetine	SSRI AD
Tegretol	Carbamazepine	Anticonvulsant
Zoloft	Sertraline	SSRI AD

Note. AD = antidepressant; SSRI = serotonin specific reuptake inhibitor.

cantly improves the following behavioral and cognitive character-istics: hyperactivity, distractibility, behavioral compliance, impul-sivity and aggression, motivation, academic achievement, and mood (Greenhill, 1992; Spencer et al., 1996). Overall improvement esti-mates range from about 60% to 80% of children and adolescents treated with Ritalin. However, as noted above, counselors and par-ents should view psychostimulants as secondary or adjunctive treat-ment for ADHD. Professionals should advise parents to always employ nonpharmacologic interventions exclusively or in combination with medications when treating children diagnosed with ADHD (Rosenberg et al., 1994).

Some tricyclic antidepressants (TCAs) have shown promise in treating ADHD symptoms. Specifically, imipramine, desipramine, and amitriptyline may be more effective than placebo in alleviating ADHD symptoms (Gittleman-Klein, 1987). However, as we dis-cuss below in the section on depression, TCAs in general and de-sipramine in particular have problematic side effect profiles with child populations.

Enuresis. Enuresis is defined as "repeated voiding of urine during the day or at night into bed or clothes" (American Psychiatric Association, 1994, p. 108). At the present time, enuresis is the only FDA-established indication for using tricyclic antidepressants in the treatment of children and adolescents. The efficacy of desipramine and imipramine in the treatment of nocturnal and diurnal enuresis is fairly well established. However, TCAs generally constitute a short-term treatment for enuretic youth because some youth become tolerant to the anti-enuretic effect of desipramine and imipramine. In addition, many young clients experience a recurrence of enuresis after discontinuation of TCA treatment. Other medications that have shown promise in alleviating enuresis include Anafranil (clomipramine) and Tegretol (carbamazepine).

Despite the established short-term effectiveness of desipramine and imipramine in treating enuresis, Rosenberg and colleagues (1994) state:

> ...behavioral therapy (such as the bell and pad apparatus) is the treatment of choice for nonorganic functional enuresis. The TCAs are used as a supplement, or when the child is away overnight.... These agents are recommended only after all other behavioral approaches have failed and are likely to be effective only for short-term use. (p. 68)

In addition to the bell and pad apparatus mentioned by Rosenberg and coworkers (1994), clinical hypnosis was as effective as imipramine in the treatment of enuresis in at least one clinical trial. Clinical hypnosis deserves more attention as a potential primary treatment of enuresis (Banerjee, Srivastav, & Palan, 1993).

Unipolar depression. Primarily two types of medications are prescribed to young clients diagnosed with unipolar depression (Kaplan, Simms, & Busner, 1994). These include TCAs (e.g., imipramine, desipramine, amitriptyline, and nortriptyline) and SSRIs (fluoxetine, sertraline, paroxetine, and fluvoxamine). Although lithium and monoamine oxidase inhibitors (MAOs) are sometimes used with depressed youth, these medications are more risky (Ryan, Meyer,

Dachille, Mazzie, & Puig-Antich, 1988; Strober, Freeman, Rigali, Schmidt, & Diamond, 1992). Despite what appears to be widespread general use of TCAs and SSRIs with children and adolescents, neither medication type has been approved by the FDA for the treatment of depression in youth. Additionally, there is limited research data available pertaining to the efficacy of antidepressants in general with youth; in particular, to date, there are no published group treatment studies available that evaluate the efficacy of sertraline, paroxetine, or fluvoxamine for treating depressive symptoms in youths.

Recent reviews of TCA efficacy with depressed youth have reached the same conclusion: There has never been a well-controlled scientific investigation demonstrating that TCAs are more effective than are placebos in alleviating unipolar depression (Fisher & Fisher, 1996; Sommers-Flanagan & Sommers-Flanagan, 1996b). For example, in a recent review we conducted, the reported efficacy of TCA medications ranged from 8.3% to 56% of the treatment population, whereas placebo efficacy within the same studies ranged from 17.0% to 68.7%. Quite simply, TCAs have *not* established themselves as an effective treatment for unipolar depression in youth.

In the late 1980s and early 1990s, Prozac (fluoxetine) emerged as a popular alternative to TCA treatment for depression in adults. Similarly, Prozac has been promoted by some as having numerous advantages over TCA treatment for child and adolescent depression (Eagen, 1994; Ryan, 1990). Unfortunately, similar to TCAs, SSRIs (Prozac, Zoloft, Paxil, and Luvox) have yet to receive any legitimate scientific support for their use in treating children and adolescents with depressive symptoms. Further, both TCAs and SSRIs have side effect profiles that can be problematic among young clients.

Unwanted reactions to medications are generally classified as either side effects or adverse events. Side effects are generally considered "nuisance" symptoms. Nuisance symptoms include, but are not limited to "excitement, irritability, nightmares, insomnia, headache, muscle pains, increased appetite, abdominal cramps, constipation, vomiting, hiccups, dry mouth, bad taste, sweating, flushed face, drowsiness, dizziness, tiredness, and listlessness" (Puig-Antich et al., 1987, p. 83). In contrast, adverse events include more serious symptoms. Examples of adverse events include allergic skin reactions, orthostatic hypotension, hypomania, seizures, and behavioral agitation.

In our review of TCA efficacy, we reported a significant side-effect profile in over half of all children treated with imipramine or desipramine (Sommers-Flanagan & Sommers-Flanagan, 1996b). Overall, approximately 20% to 33% of treated subjects developed side effects that were so severe that they were forced to discontinue imipramine or desipramine (DMI) treatment.

TCA side effects are particularly disturbing in prepubertal children. For example, there have been reports of TCA-induced hypomania, wherein the child displays inability to concentrate or to sleep and complains of restless energy or feelings of being "hyper." In addition, DMI has been implicated recently in the sudden deaths of four prepubertal children (Kashani, Hodges, & Shekim, 1980; Popper & Elliot, 1990; Walsh, Giardina, Sloan, Greenhill, & Goldfein, 1994). Although DMI use has not been established as the causal factor in these children's deaths, there is ample evidence available attesting to the potentially cardiotoxic effects of DMI in young people (Walsh et al., 1994).

Although SSRIs originally were believed to have a less problematic side effect profile than do TCAs, this may not be the case (Nelson, 1994). For example, prominent side effects produced by fluoxetine include hypomania or restlessness, insomnia or sleep disturbance, general irritability or social disinhibition, and gastrointestinal distress; these symptoms generally afflict 20% to 45% of children/adolescents who are prescribed Prozac (Sommers-Flanagan & Sommers-Flanagan, 1996b). Additionally, one study indicated that emergence of self-destructive impulses occurred in over 14% of children and adolescents being treated with Prozac for obsessive–compulsive disorder (King et al., 1991). Overall, there is little scientific evidence available to inform therapists and physicians regarding the long-term effects of SSRIs on the developing brain (Jacobs, 1994; Riddle et al., 1990–1991). Of course, the main point here is that professionals should exercise caution and vigilance when using antidepressant medications with young clients.

Given their problematic side effects and lack of established effi-cacy, it should come as no surprise that we cannot recommend rou-tine antidepressant treatment for child/adolescent depression (see Table 8.3). Instead, it is our position that parents of young clients with depressive symptoms should initially seek counseling or psy-chotherapy for their children. Although scientific support for nonpharmacologic treatment is also lacking, such procedures are considerably less risky (Mufson, Moreau, Weissman, & Klerman, 1993; Wilkes et al., 1994).

Table 8.3. Checklist For Referring Young Clients For Medications

The following list is designed to aid nonphysician mental health provid-ers in determining when they should refer young clients to a physician for potential pharmacologic treatment. Pharmacologic treatment should be considered if any one of the following factors is present:

_____ 1. A youth is exhibiting psychiatric symptoms (e.g., depres-sion, anxiety, aggression) despite the absence of clear environmental determinants, such as family conflict, di-vorce, etc.

_____ 2. The psychiatric symptoms have strong physiologic com-ponents (e.g., sleep disturbance, somatic complaints, appetite changes and associated weight loss or gain).

_____ 3. There has been a lack of treatment response after 8 to 12 sessions of psychotherapy, family therapy, or cogni-tive-behavioral therapy.

_____ 4. The parents or child are opposed to psychological treat-ment or are strongly in favor of medication treatment.

_____ 5. There is a clear genetic history of positive response to a particular medication for a particular disorder.

_____ 6. There are concerns about the child's general physical health and, to the best of your knowledge, the child has not had a recent physical examination.

Anxiety disorders. Two specific medications, Anafranil (clomipramine) and Prozac (fluoxetine) have shown promise in the treatment of child/adolescent obsessive–compulsive disorder (OCD). Consequently, medication intervention is routine in cases of severe OCD (Rapoport, Swedo, & Leonard, 1992). However, when OCD symptoms are mild to moderate, specific cognitive-behavioral interventions have also shown promise (March, Mulle, & Herbel, 1994).

Other than in the treatment of OCD, pharmacologic agents have not proven effective in treating anxiety disorders. Of course, despite the lack of controlled studies attesting to medication effectiveness with anxiety disorders, some practitioners advocate using antidepressants or benzodiazepines for treating severe anxiety or as an adjunctive treatment for mild to moderate anxiety (Kronenberger & Meyer, 1996). While it is likely that benzodiazepines (e.g., Xanax, Valium, Serax, Librium, etc.) may be useful as a short-term intervention for debilitating anxiety associated with panic disorder or school phobia, this entire class of medications is generally contraindicated due to addictive qualities. Finally, although TCAs have demonstrated efficacy in treating panic disorder and agoraphobia in adults, controlled studies with young clients are lacking (Kronenberger & Meyer, 1996).

Conduct disorders and/or oppositional defiant disorder. Children with CD and/or ODD constitute a particularly difficult-to-treat population. Specifically, as described intermittently in this book, these young clients most often engage in behaviors that are quite annoying to adults and others, but they generally do not identify themselves as having a problem. Like therapists, physicians have had little success in consistently treating CD and ODD. Consequently, a number of different pharmacologic agents have been used in the treatment of CD and ODD.

The primary guideline for determining which medication should be prescribed for young people with CD or ODD emphasizes comorbid symptomatology (Cohen et al., 1993). Specifically, if CD or ODD clients exhibit concurrent depressive symptoms, an antidepressant medication is usually prescribed. If concurrent symptoms include attentional problems, a psychostimulant is prescribed.

If concurrent symptoms are primarily aggression or explosiveness, lithium, neuroleptics, or anticonvulsants may be prescribed. Overall, there is no systematic data demonstrating the effectiveness of any medication or medication combination in the treatment of CD and/or ODD.

Medication Myths and Realities

The preceding review indicates that there are few reliable medication treatments available for children and adolescents suffering from specific psychiatric disorders. It appears that psychiatric or psychopharmacologic treatment of young clients continues to be a clinical art, rather than a medical science. Of course, many young clients respond favorably to medication treatment and many physicians practice their clinical work rigorously and professionally. We believe that it is important for child and adolescent therapists to have a balanced view regarding the contributions of medications to child/adolescent treatment. At this point in time it is inappropriate to view medications as either salvation for young clients or an evil and dangerous effort to control our youth. The true role of medications in the treatment of difficult young clients lies somewhere in the middle of these two extreme positions.

The following paragraphs review some of the most common myths associated with medication treatment.

Myth: psychoactive medications are given to patients to correct a "chemical imbalance." Fact: There is no scientific evidence supporting a specific type of "chemical imbalance" which can be directly alleviated using a specific medication. As a psychiatrist colleague once informed us, if one person can speak French and another person cannot, these people have brains that are chemically different from one another. Thus, one of these two people might be considered to have a "chemical imbalance" with respect to the other (J. Cannell, personal communication, May 14, 1994).

Myth: ADHD is a biogenetic disorder which requires medication treatment. Fact: Although there are biogenetic components of ADHD, environmental circumstances can have a powerful effect on the manifestation of ADHD symptoms (Barkley, 1990; Gordon, 1991). Further, as noted in this chapter, standards of medical practice indicate that nonpharmacologic approaches should be used initially, with medications added only if other interventions are insufficient.

Myth: antidepressant medications are highly effective in alleviating depressive symptoms in young people. Fact: Although antidepressants such as imipramine, desipramine, fluoxetine, and sertraline can have an extremely positive effect for some young people, none of these medications ever has been shown through scientific studies to alleviate depressive symptoms to a greater extent than do placebos. Some professionals have identified these medications as "ineffective" or "experimental" procedures with regard to reducing depressive symptoms among youth (Rosenberg et al., 1994; Sommers-Flanagan & Sommers-Flanagan, 1996b).

Myth: Ritalin is a highly dangerous and addictive drug. Fact: Ritalin has been fairly well-researched and is considered very medically useful. In the words of Rosenberg and colleagues (1994):

> ...in the field of child psychiatry, and in psychiatry in general, the use of stimulants is not considered controversial. These medications are solid, first-line, bread-and-butter type medications with a remarkably benign side-effect profile. The disorder that they are most commonly used to treat, ADHD, is one with marked functional impairment, long-term morbidity, and enormous consequences for the child and family. (pp. 19–20)

MEDICATION REFERRAL GUIDELINES

Sometimes, whether and when young clients should be referred for medication treatment can be confusing to counselors and parents. Currently, we utilize the guidelines in Table 8.3 when deciding whether to recommend medication evaluation and/or treatment for young clients. Although these guidelines are far from foolproof and will require modification as additional research on the efficacy of various pharmacologic and nonpharmacologic treatments becomes available, they provide a practical model for making decisions regarding medical referral.

CONCLUDING COMMENTS

As discussed in previous chapters, young clients, due to their natural resistance to counseling or psychotherapy, may evoke frustration in their parents and, eventually, in their counselor. When parents are unable to change their child's symptoms, they sometimes become frustrated and turn to professionals for assistance. Subsequently, if the child does not respond to professional counseling or psychotherapy, the counselor or parent may recommend alternative treatments for the child. In most cases, if counseling or psychotherapy is ineffective the counselor may recommend pharmacologic evaluation and the child may initiate medication treatment.

This chapter emphasized how important it is for counselors, social workers, and psychologists to have at least minimal knowledge regarding pharmacologic treatment alternatives. Additionally, this chapter took note of the fact that there is little evidence supporting pharmacologic treatment as a primary intervention for most child/adolescent mental and behavioral disorders. If nonphysician mental health professionals are ill-informed or too biased to effectively discuss medications, or if they are uncomfortable discussing treatment alternatives, they should either work with a physician or refer clients to another professional who can discuss medication treatment alternatives with clients. Overall, our review of pharmacologic treatments for difficult young clients suggests that nonphysician mental health providers should *not* be reluctant to recommend utilizing nonpharmacologic treatments before initiating a medication trial.

9

Ethical Endings

Meg knew all at once that Mrs. Whatsit, Mrs. Who, and Mrs. Which must be near, because all through her she felt a flooding of joy and of love that was even greater and deeper than the joy and love which were already there.

She stopped laughing and listened, and Charles listened, too. "Hush."

Then there was a whirring, and Mrs. Whatsit, Mrs. Who, and Mrs. Which were standing in front of them, and the joy and love were so tangible that Meg felt that if she only knew where to reach she could touch it with her bare hands.

Mrs. Whatsit said breathlessly, "Oh, my darlings, I'm sorry we don't have time to say good-bye to you properly. You see, we have to—"

But they never learned what it was that Mrs. Whatsit, Mrs. Who, and Mrs. Which had to do, for there was a gust of wind, and they were gone. (from L'Engle, A Wrinkle in Time, 1962, pp. 210–211)

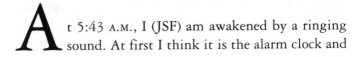

t 5:43 A.M., I (JSF) am awakened by a ringing sound. At first I think it is the alarm clock and

I fumble blindly, trying to make the sound stop. Finally, I realize that it is the telephone. Gathering my awareness, I answer, trying my best to sound awake and relaxed. It is a distraught father. His 16-year-old son was located yesterday after having run away to another state. Although his son made it back on the Greyhound bus at 5:15 A.M., the boy ran away again when the father began taking him to a local shelter for displaced youth. The fact that he asks me if I have ideas about where his son may have gone suggests that he is desperate. I have only seen the boy for one therapy session, but I have spoken to the father a half dozen times in the past 3 days. The police are of little support. For good reason, the father is confused and scared and calling me for advice and support. Obviously, there is little I can do. Feeling the need to provide something, I suggest that he check riverside parks and the boy's girlfriend's house. He says he will call me with updates as the day passes. I think to myself that our scheduled family therapy meeting today at 1:00 P.M. is likely to be canceled. In fact, this may be termination.

Even with relatively well-adjusted children and families, termination can be difficult. Termination is often associated with deep family issues and personal issues having to do with leaving, being left, saying good-bye, and/or acknowledging that something is over; it often triggers mildly regressive or maladaptive behaviors in well-adjusted individuals and families. And of course, this isn't a book about treating well-adjusted children and families who come to therapy for minor assistance.

With challenging youth and their often less well-adjusted families, therapy engagement is inconsistent and termination is unpredictable. As discussed previously, it can be very difficult to establish a trusting, collaborative relationship with difficult young clients, partly because they seem to cultivate distant and defiant relationships with adults. Similar to beginning relationships with difficult young clients, termination with this type of client is also challenging.

When working with difficult young people, termination can occur without warning for a number of reasons. Sometimes, as in the preceding case, the client disappears, only to reappear, then disappear, and then perhaps, reappear again. Other times, parental impatience and/or impulsivity drives termination; it is not uncommon for parents of challenging young clients to expect immediate change, and when such change does not occur they blame therapy and/or the therapist and abruptly discontinue treatment.

Alternatively, some parents feel threatened when their child begins to build a strong positive relationship with a therapist, or they may react negatively when their child begins to exhibit less dysfunctional and more adaptive behavior. In such cases, there may be strong systemic resistance to change and therefore the family insists that therapy end. There are also financially based terminations; in many states, Medicaid and insurance funding is capped and parents' ability to pay is limited.

Despite our preceding statements regarding potential difficulties leading to therapy termination with difficult young clients, therapists should avoid adopting negative attitudes toward termination with this population. After experiencing numerous disappointing terminations, it is tempting to generalize such disappointment to most endings with most difficult young clients. However, on occasion, there is steady and positive relationship development, consistent parental support for therapy, clear cognitive, behavioral, and affective progress, and ample opportunity to discuss termination and plan for termination before it occurs. Speaking realistically, however, optimal terminations with difficult young clients are the exception, rather than the norm. In other words, we encourage therapists who work with this difficult population to stay positive but realistic.

In this chapter we describe and discuss a variety of termination situations and a range of emotional reactions therapists and clients may have during therapy and termination. Additionally, we explore guidelines for attaining the elusive optimal termination process. Finally, we discuss methods for potentially salvaging atypical termination situations.

THERAPIST EMOTIONAL REACTIONS TO THERAPY AND TERMINATION WITH DIFFICULT CLIENTS

It is common for therapists to have emotional reactions to therapy and termination with clients who have been hard to work with.

Primary emotional reactions include but are not limited to anxiety and relief, fear, anger, and disappointment/sadness.

Anxiety and Relief

Sometimes, with particularly difficult young clients, therapists may feel a clear sense of relief upon termination. Further, it is not unusual for therapists to hope for termination and to terminate prematurely or inappropriately with young clients who behave with hostility, defiance, and/or disinterest toward therapy and the therapist.

Relief is also a common reaction when extremely aggressive or gang-affiliated young clients miss appointments or terminate therapy. Generally, this sensation of relief is a signal of anxiety or discomfort reduction. In other words, when therapists are afraid of particular clients they consistently experience high levels of anxiety during the course of therapy, and similarly they experience high levels of relief after therapy has ended.

In most cases we believe that it is acceptable and normal for therapists to experience low levels of anxiety/tension when conducting therapy with difficult young clients who have opposed therapy. Similarly, we believe that some measure of relief when clients miss appointments, or when termination occurs, is normal; these are common reactions to working with difficult clients. However, therapists should examine or scrutinize closely higher levels of anxiety and relief, either during consultation or supervision. Anxiety and relief are important signals pertaining to therapists' perceptions of competence, efficacy, and safety. Additionally, such feelings may constitute important countertransference signs that the therapist can use to facilitate therapy or the therapist's personal awareness and growth (Beitman, 1983).

Fear

A frequent emotional reaction to working with challenging young clients is fear; there are many valid reasons for this reaction. Initially, we may fear that these young people will never truly become engaged in therapy and may therefore end up terminating even before therapy can be helpful. After difficult young clients become engaged in therapy, our fears shift; we are no longer fearful of premature termination. Instead we begin fearing that termination will never occur. Finally, in many cases, we fear that these disturbed young people may hurt someone or themselves during therapy or after therapy has ended.

On a basic and personal level, therapists may simply feel afraid of aggressive or gang-affiliated young clients. This fear initially may not be associated with termination, but as termination approaches the fear may affect therapist behavior. For example, because of growing anxiety, a therapist may choose to end therapy prematurely. Alternatively, some therapists may display counterphobic responses to working with dangerous and scary young clients; that is, they minimize or deny their anxiety and inappropriately continue with therapy despite lack of progress.

Fearful reactions to clients warrant close attention and scrutiny. For example, Jake, a 17-year-old, was referred for therapy by his probation officer. Previously, Jake had been arrested for burglary, intimidation, and assault. Despite the fact that therapy attendance was a requirement of his probation, Jake was completely uncooperative with therapy. He attended three sessions but refused to speak to his therapist for the majority of each of the three sessions. Due to lack of cooperation, Jake's therapist needed to consider termination, but he felt fear associated with the prospect of discussing this with Juan because of Jake's history of aggression.

In this case, it is important for the therapist to address his fear about telling Jake about termination. This is important because his fear may be a signal of danger. Our recommendation in this type of case is that the therapist have a joint meeting with Jake and his probation officer to discuss the future of therapy and requirements of cooperation. If the therapist is fearful of Jake, it may be inappropriate for individual therapy to continue.

Disappointment/Sadness

Therapy with difficult young people can be extremely disappointing. Obviously, part of this disappointment stems from the fact that the client may not make progress. In such cases, disappointment is natural and may evolve into sadness and even despair. Eventually, when there is repeated disappointment from unsuccessful work with difficult young clients, therapists may begin to believe that they are ineffective and/or inadequate. Given the naturally depressing quality of repeated negative treatment outcomes, it is not surprising that some therapists who work with difficult young clients may experience depressive symptoms and question whether they should be in the mental health field.

In our experience, disappointment, sadness, and depression generally may occur in several forms. First, disappointment develops from lack of treatment progress. This is especially true in cases in which difficult young clients appear to have some degree of potential for improving their lives. Unfortunately, many of these clients are unable to take advantage of their positive personal qualities; they continue to act out impulsively, to underachieve academically, to exhibit poor peer relationships, and to involve themselves in illegal activities. Often, these young clients are experiencing depressive symptoms and they also are disappointed about their lack of progress. Consequently, therapists may experience parallel process or contagion depressive symptoms (i.e., therapists experience depressive symptoms associated with underachievement, similar to those of the client).

Second, many young clients have accumulated very harsh personal experiences, including but not limited to physical abuse, parental rejection, repeated academic difficulty or failure, and peer harassment/rejection. However, instead of reflecting on their emotionally painful experiences and verbalizing associated feelings, challenging young people almost invariably engage in externalizing behaviors. That is, they act out their depressive symptoms by stimulation-seeking, self-destructive behaviors (e.g., unsafe sex, drug use), and aggression. In such cases, because the client is not expressing sadness directly, a therapist may begin functioning as an emotional conduit and consequently feel and express sadness *for* their client.

Third, sadness is a common response to termination with young clients. If therapist and client have established a positive relationship, feelings of missing the client are natural. In cases in which the therapist has worked hard to establish a close interpersonal relationship with a young client who is usually interpersonally distant, ending the relationship can evoke sadness within both therapist and client. Further, when therapist and client have established a close relationship, they may have impulses to continue in a relationship after therapy termination.

We take a clear stance regarding forming other types of relationships with current or former young clients. Most ethical codes guide counselors away from dual relationships, noting the potential confusion and harm that may result for clients (American Counseling Association, 1995; American Psychological Association, 1992; American School Counselor Association, 1992). With difficult youth, one can never be sure which termination might actually be a final termination. It is not uncommon to terminate with clients, have them move away or be sent away for months or even years, and then have them resurface needing more therapy. Our first and highest calling is the welfare of our clients *as clients*, not as friends, foster children, members of a team we coach, a choir we lead, or a club we advise. Therefore, we strongly recommend guarding the counseling relationship as primary and not giving in to the temptation to form other relationships with the youth.

Case example. Dina was an overweight, angry, belligerent young woman who had repeatedly run away from home and acted out in other destructive ways. She began therapy while still at home, but was soon transferred to a local youth home where she stabilized and began to thrive in the much more structured environment. After 8 months of therapy, it was clear that she was ready to terminate. However, she had become a very rewarding client, and it was hard for her therapist to say good bye. While Dina was proud of her progress and her graduation from therapy, she too was struggling with termination. She found out her therapist was also a private tennis coach and begged the group home staff to reward her good behavior with tennis lessons taught by her old therapist. The therapist was very tempted. She argued with herself. Her relationship with Dina as counselor was over, wasn't it? The therapist was a good tennis coach, and she was excited that Dina wanted to engage in physical exercise, but the therapist's colleagues gently helped her to say no. She explained to Dina that there were many good tennis coaches in town and that someday, Dina may need to check in with her again for counseling. She helped Dina see that she made the decision out of caring and respect for Dina and for the therapy relationship. Both Dina and her therapist benefited from keeping therapy boundaries in place.

Anger/Resentment

Some resistant young clients provoke anger in their therapists throughout therapy and at termination. Anger may arise when clients insult the therapist, deliberately light up cigarettes in the office and blow smoke at the therapist, destroy therapist's property, or try to physically intimidate the therapist. We have had all of these situations occur, and depending upon the particulars of the situation we have sometimes experienced strong anger (e.g., after a client knocked a picture off the wall) or strong fear (e.g., when a client threatened to wait for one of us outside the office in a dark parking lot).

It is obviously important for therapists to refrain from acting on their anger toward young clients. To act on one's anger is to risk recapitulation of dysfunctional or traumatic family dynamics (not to mention risks of engaging in unethical or illegal behaviors). In some of our workshops we have joked about identifying when it is clinically appropriate to swear at our young delinquent clients. Of course, just as we would teach aggressive young clients the difference between having aggressive impulses and engaging in aggressive behaviors, we teach ourselves that while swearing at clients is *never* appropriate, it is perfectly acceptable to *feel like* swearing at our clients on occasion.

When therapists experience feelings of relief, anger, fear, or sadness upon termination or in response to client behavior, it sometimes has more to do with the therapist's personal history and emotional style than with the client's behavior. On the other hand, some client behaviors would evoke such reactions in almost anyone. Whichever is the case, if therapists experience strong feelings of relief, anger, fear, or sadness toward a client during therapy or upon termination, they should explore these feelings in supervision or with a consultant or consultation group. In most cases, strong emotional reactions within therapists are worth close personal and professional scrutiny.

IDEAL THERAPY AND IDEAL TERMINATION

Termination appropriately occurs when the client has attained the therapeutic goals. Further, in the ideal scenario, parents, child, and therapist mutually identify and agree upon therapy goals. During therapy, all parties monitor progress and consistently give clients feedback regarding their personal progress and how such progress relates to upcoming termination. Of course, the problem with linking termination with therapy goals is that a single course of therapy is often not sufficient to achieve all treatment goals. Even when goals are carefully articulated, termination may occur prior to complete problem resolution or goal attainment.

The influence of managed care and other benefit packages with specific benefit limits necessitates that therapist and clients discuss a different ideal therapy and ideal termination scenario (Fox, 1995; Steenbarger, 1992, 1994; Stern, 1993). Specifically, in some cases managed care organizations dictate to professionals and clients exactly how many therapy sessions can occur between therapist and client. Consequently, therapy is time-limited and ends when therapist and client have used an allotted number of therapy sessions, regardless of problem resolution or goal attainment. If this is the case, it is incumbent upon the counselor to work as carefully and realistically within this framework as possible, using the time to address problems that have the best chances of change during the time allocated. In other cases, the managed care specialty manager may work with the counselor to develop a coherent brief treatment plan with goals that are compatible with the referral problem(s).

In either case, therapists and clients can openly discuss and anticipate termination because it will not occur at some mysterious and unknown future time. As mentioned previously, with some openly resistant young clients termination may serve as motivation, and time-limited approaches help clients who do not want to be in therapy see light at the end of the therapy tunnel. Time-limited therapy may assist in developing a treatment contract with young clients who are uncomfortable with interpersonal intimacy. Such clients are often relieved that therapy will not require too much of their time, because less time translates into less interpersonal closeness.

Whether termination is linked to therapy goals or whether it is linked to the number of therapy sessions may be irrelevant with regard to the quality of termination. This is because when therapists closely and efficiently monitor *either* treatment goals *or* number of sessions, termination issues will emerge and therapist and client can discuss them appropriately as the end of therapy approaches. Also, regardless of termination issues that may or may not emerge, there are common themes and topics that therapist and client should process as a part of termination. We include a termination content checklist in Table 9.1.

Unfortunately, when working with difficult young clients, often there is not time for therapists to facilitate an optimal termination process. Consequently, below we review some less-than-optimal therapy termination scenarios.

LESS-THAN-OPTIMAL TERMINATION SCENARIOS

We have identified several less-than-optimal treatment scenario categories. These include "termination deja vu," therapist-initiated terminations, parent-initiated terminations, and sudden terminations.

Termination Deja Vu

Some clients repeatedly initiate and terminate therapy. This repetitive relationship may prompt therapists to think, "Haven't I been through this before? Is this termination again?" We must happily report that termination deja vu is one of our "preferred" less-than-optimal termination experiences with difficult young clients. We prefer this scenario because, generally speaking, if clients (and cli-

Table 9.1. Termination Content Checklist

_____ 1. At the outset of therapy and throughout therapy, the therapist identifies progress toward termination (e.g., "Before our meeting today, I noticed we have 4 more sessions left," or "You are doing so well at home, at school, and with your friends... let's talk about how much longer you will need to come for counseling").

_____ 2. The therapist reminisces about early sessions or the first time therapist and client met. For example: "I remember something you said when we first met, you said: 'there's no way in hell I'm gonna talk with you about anything important.' Remember that? I have it right here in my notes. You were sure excited about coming for counseling."

_____ 3. The therapist identifies positive behavior, attitude, and/or emotional changes. This is part of the process of providing feedback regarding problem resolution and goal attainment: "I've noticed something about you that has changed. It used to be that you wouldn't let adults get chummy with you. And you wouldn't accept compliments from adults. Now, from what you and your parents have told me and from how you respond to me in here, it's obvious that you give adults a chance. You aren't always nasty to an adult every time you see one. I think that's a sign of you feeling better and better about yourself."

_____ 4. Acknowledge that the relationship is ending with therapy termination: "Next session will be our last session. I guess there's a chance we might see each other some time, at the mall or somewhere. If we see each other, I hope it's okay for us to say hello. But I want you to know that I'll wait for you to say hello first. And of course, I won't say anything about you having been in counseling."

_____ 5. Identify a positive personal attribute that you noticed during therapy. This should be a personal characteristic

(continued)

Table 9.1. Termination Content Checklist (Cont.)

separate from goals the client may have attained: "From the beginning of counseling I always enjoyed your sense of humor. You are really creative and really funny, but you can be serious too. Thanks for letting me see both those sides. It took courage for you to seriously tell me how you really feel about your mom."

_____ 6. If there is unfinished business (and there always will be) provide encouragement for continued work and personal growth: "Of course, your life isn't perfect, but I have confidence that you will keep working on communicating well with your sister and those other things we've been talking about."

_____ 7. Provide opportunities for feedback to you: "I'd like to hear from you. What did you think was most helpful about coming to therapy? What did you think was least helpful?"

_____ 8. Let the client know that he or she may return for counseling in the future: "I hope you know that you can come back for a meeting sometime in the future if you want to or need to."

_____ 9. Make a statement about your hope for the client's positive future: "I'll be thinking of you and hoping that things work out for the best. Of course, like I said in the beginning, I am hoping you get what you want out of life, just as long as it's legal and healthy for you."

_____ 10. As needed, listen to and discuss client wishes about continuing therapy forever or client wishes about transforming their relationship with you from one of therapist–client to that of parent–child or friend: "Like you've known all along, counseling is kind of weird. It's not like we're mom and daughter or aunt and niece. And even though I like you and feel close to you, it isn't really the same as being friends" (further discussion and processing of feelings follows).

ents' parents) choose to return to therapy, they probably had at least a minimally positive and beneficial experience the first time around.

After an initial termination, difficult young people frequently return for additional therapy or booster sessions. This usually occurs when, during the initial therapy trial, either parents or the child viewed therapy as helpful. Upon return to therapy, most often we hear statements from parents such as, "We don't know how you helped Susan last time, but we've been having trouble again and figured it was time for Susan to come back for a few visits," or "Stephen said there were some things he'd like to talk with you about and so that's why we're here," or "Dave got into some trouble again. We told him he had to see someone for counseling. He said you are the only person he would come to see again."

Although there are many exceptions, we ordinarily formulate a repeat therapy experience as a series of time-limited booster sessions. After an initial meeting or two, we establish an agreement with the young client for a specific number of therapy sessions (usually 4 to 10 sessions) designed to address a specific problem or two. Our rationale involves capitalizing on remnants of a previous positive relationship and positive therapy experience. Because less time is needed to reestablish trust and a working alliance, a more problem-focused and solution-oriented approach tends to be effective.

Therapist-Initiated Termination

Hopefully, most therapist-initiated terminations will occur because some specific goals have been attained and, in the therapist's best judgment, additional therapy sessions would likely add little additional therapeutic benefit (Steenbarger, 1994). However, when working with resistant young clients, it is equally likely that therapists may initiate termination when specific goals have not been attained and, in the therapist's best judgment, additional treatment is unlikely to facilitate progress at the present time. In many cases, we recommend evaluating therapeutic progress after about six therapy sessions. Subsequently, if there has been little progress and you expect little progress, we suggest what might be considered a premature therapist-initiated termination. We suggest this premature termination because, in our experience, extending therapy only increases and solidifies client and parental negative attitudes toward therapy (and the therapist). Consequently, our rationale in the following termination scenario is to facilitate therapy by increasing chances of a successful second therapy trial.

Give me a call. The long version of the title of this termination technique is "give me a call when you're ready to begin working on your problems." However, as always, tact is required when communicating this message to clients and their parents.

> I need to be honest with you all. As you know, we haven't made much progress with counseling. My best guess is that it has to do with timing. Sometimes it just isn't the right time for counseling to be effective. And so I'm recommending that we have a last session or two and then end counseling for now. But I want you to know, when the time is right, I would be happy to work some more with Andy. I am optimistic that there will be a time when you (Andy) and the whole family will be really ready for counseling. And I think you folks will be the ones who know when the right time for counseling comes. When it is the right time, call me and we can schedule an appointment. Or, if the time comes and you decide that maybe I'm not the right person for you to work with, you can still call and I'll be glad to give you the names of some other excellent therapists with whom you could work.

Most therapists will realize that the preceding comments about timing are really comments about motivation. In many cases, young clients are not motivated for therapy, but if they begin experiencing greater distress at some point in the future they might agree to return for therapy. If we suspect that this is the case, then we emphasize to young clients "give me a call" and "I'll be looking forward to hearing from you." Additionally, if we believe that a motivational deficit is within the young client him- or herself, then we emphasize that the youth (and not the parent) should call for counseling when ready.

Parent- and Client-Initiated Termination

Parents and resistant young clients are notorious for terminating therapy at all the wrong times. Most likely, parents initiate termination because they are dissatisfied with the pace, process, or current outcome of therapy. Unfortunately, many parents have little clue regarding signs and signals of potentially positive therapy outcomes. Parents are naturally impatient regarding their children's therapy progress and are sometimes insensitive to small signs of progress.

As suggested at the beginning of this chapter, perhaps it is especially aggravating or frustrating when parents terminate therapy precisely when substantial progress has begun. This occurs with parents and families when they really are not invested in having positive change occur in their family. They may be threatened when their child begins to establish a close and positive relationship with another adult. Ideally, therapists can reduce this motivation for termination by including parents in the therapy process and by working hard on improving parent–child relations.

Once parents (or clients) decide that therapy should end, there is really no point in arguing about when and if this should occur; doing so will only increase negative attitudes clients may have toward therapy. Instead, therapists should try their best to be empathic with parents' feelings about therapy and should try to maintain some positive connection between the parents and potential future therapy. In fact, in our experience, we find that parents are more likely to have their children continue in therapy or return to therapy if we give them an opportunity to criticize therapy. It is much more productive for therapists to empathize with parents' therapy frustrations than it is to argue with them about their feelings. Parents can be relieved to hear therapists make statements like: "This is such a hard problem, I wish therapy was working quicker," or "I get frustrated too, when therapy doesn't work as fast as I'd like," or "These are the times when I wish I had a magic wand or some powerful technique that would just get rid of all the problems and bad feelings in your family."

When parents or clients terminate therapy prematurely and inappropriately, therapists may have an impulse to place what we call an emotional curse on the individual or family. An emotional curse is a statement to clients or parents predicting negative outcome due to premature termination. For example, "You really need to work on anger and how it is expressed in your family. If you don't get the therapy you need I can foresee health problems, perhaps escalating physical conflicts, and other major problems."

Obviously, the purpose of this curse is neither positive nor health-promoting. It is a threatening and vindictive statement based primarily on therapist disappointment and anger. Expressing these feelings to clients, especially in the form of a curse, is inappropriate. In contrast, as described below, we recommend using positive and hopeful statements with clients who terminate from therapy prematurely. After all, therapy is simply one of many paths available to individuals and families who have problems and who want to learn, grow, and improve their lives.

Sudden Termination

Sudden terminations are characterized by unfinished business. Most frequently, termination occurs suddenly because a young client becomes unavailable for treatment. This may be due to a number of reasons, including parent-initiated termination. For the purposes of this discussion, sudden terminations are defined as those situations wherein *the client* has made him- or herself unavailable for therapy. This most commonly occurs when the young client acts out impulsively in some manner, causing or requiring a major change in living status. For example, we have experienced sudden termination when young clients are incarcerated (due to an illegal act), are transferred to a different foster home or into a residential living situation, run away to their noncustodial parent, move in with some relatives from a different city (often after a runaway or acting-out incident), or vehemently refuse to attend therapy.

When sudden terminations occur, there is usually little or no opportunity for a final therapy session between therapist and client. In such cases we recommend therapists use either a closure conversation or a termination letter to briefly address termination issues.

Closure conversations. Obviously, if a final session is impossible or impractical, we recommend an effort by the therapist at having a closure conversation. The purpose of a closure conversation is to model a semblance of appropriate termination for young clients who may never have experienced a smooth or appropriate ending to a relationship. We have had closure conversations over the telephone and in jail cells or detention centers.

Closure conversations generally follow the termination model we reviewed previously. It is especially important to acknowledge the relationship ending or the need to say goodbye, to identify one of the client's positive personal attributes that you noticed or appreciated during therapy, to encourage the client to make the most of his or her new personal situation, to indicate that he or she may return for counseling in the future if he or she so desires, and to express hope for a positive outcome and/or a positive life.

Termination letters. If a closure conversation is not possible, then our last resort for dealing with termination is a termination letter. Again, the purpose of a termination letter is to model appropriate communication regarding a relationship ending. We include a sample termination letter in Box 9.1.

Sometimes, there is opportunity for neither a closure conversation nor a termination letter with young clients. Abrupt relationship beginnings and endings are often the norm for disruptive children and adolescents. In such cases, therapists are left to deal with their unresolved termination feelings in whatever manner they believe is most healthy and adaptive. We believe that consultation groups are particularly useful for processing therapist feelings associated with sudden terminations. On the other hand, in some cases, if young clients were seen for only a session or two and little relationship or rapport was established, there may be little need for therapists to discuss their emotional reactions with others or to attempt a closure conversation or termination letter.

Box 9.1. Sample Termination Letter

Dear Shalini:

I am sorry you had to leave so suddenly and move to Mountain View School. I wish we could have at least had a last meeting, so we could talk about your future and say goodbye. Even though we didn't have a chance for a meeting, I hope you know that I'll be thinking of you and wishing you well in your new living situation.

If you ever end up back in Missoula, and want to come back for counseling, give me a call and set up an appointment. Even if you don't want or need counseling, you can always call my office and update me on how you're doing and what's happening in your life. If you want, sometime you can even write me a short letter to let me know how you're doing.

Although our sessions together were not always fun, I enjoyed having the opportunity to get to know you. And I wish you the best in the future.

Sincerely,

Rita S-F

IS IT FINALLY OVER?

As noted above, sometimes therapy with difficult young clients ends suddenly and other times it seems never-ending. We have decided to incorporate both of these concepts into the ending of this book. First, training in working with difficult, challenging young clients is never-ending. This book provides only technical assistance in providing such treatment. Additional reading, training, and supervision is necessary—basically forever. Second, rather than affectionately or sentimentally rehashing any of what has been discussed in this or other chapters, we choose to end this book in a manner similar to how many of our young clients end therapy. Bye.

REFERENCES

Achenbach, T. M. (1991a). *Manual for the Child Behavior Checklist and 1991 Profile.* Burlington, VT: University of Vermont Press.

Achenbach, T. M. (1991b). *Manual for the Youth Self-Report and 1991 Profile.* Burlington, VT: University of Vermont Press.

Adler, A. (1969). *The practice and theory of individual psychology.* Paterson, NJ: Littlefield.

Ainsworth, M. D. S. (1979). Infant–mother attachment. *American Psychologist, 34,* 932–937.

Ainsworth, M. D. S. (1989). Attachments beyond infancy. *American Psychologist, 44,* 709–716.

Alexander, F., & French, K. (1946). *Psychoanalytic psychotherapy: Practical applications.* New York: Guilford Press.

American Counseling Association. (1995). *Code of ethics and standards of practice.* Alexandria, VA: Author.

American Psychiatric Association. (1994). *Diagnostic and statistical manual of mental disorders* (4th ed.). Washington, DC: Author.

American Psychological Association. (1992). Ethical principles of psychologists and code of conduct. *American Psychologist, 47,* 1597–1611.

American School Counselor Association. (1992). *Ethical standards for school counselors.* Alexandria, VA: Author.

Anastopoulos, A. D., Barkley, R. A., & Sheldon, T. L. (1996). Family based treatment: Psychosocial intervention for children and adolescents with attention deficit hyperactivity disorder. In E. D. Hibbs & P. S. Jensen (Eds.), *Psychosocial treatments for child and adolescent disorders* (pp. 267–284). Washington, DC: American Psychological Association.

Andrews, J. A., & Lewinsohn, P. M. (1992). Suicidal attempts among older adolescents: Prevalence and co-occurrence with psychiatric disorders. *Journal of the American Academy of Child and Adolescent Psychiatry, 31,* 655–662.

Archer, R. (1992). *MMPI-A: Assessing adolescent psychopathology.* Hillsdale, NJ: Erlbaum.

Axline, V. M. (1964). *Dibs: In search of self.* New York: Ballantine.

Baillargeon, R. (1987). Object permanence in 3.5- and 4.5-month-old infants. *Developmental Psychology, 23,* 655–664.

Bandura, A., Ross, D., & Ross, S. (1963). Imitation of film-mediated aggressive models. *Journal of Abnormal and Social Psychology, 66,* 3–11.

Banerjee, S., Srivastav, A., & Palan, B. M. (1993). Hypnosis and self-hypnosis in the management of nocturnal enuresis: A comparative study with imipramine therapy. *American Journal of Clinical Hypnosis, 36,* 113–119.

Banks, L. R. (1980). *The Indian in the cupboard.* New York: Avon.

Barkley, R. A. (1990). *Attention-deficit hyperactivity disorder: A handbook for diagnosis and treatment.* New York: Guilford Press.

Bartholomew, K. (1990). Avoidance of intimacy: An attachment perspective. *Journal of Social and Personal Relationships, 7,* 147–178.

Baumeister, R. F., & Scher, S. J. (1988). Self-defeating behavior patterns among normal individuals: Review and analysis of common self-destructive tendencies. *Psychological Bulletin, 104,* 3–22.

Beck, A. T. (1976). *Cognitive therapy and the emotional disorders.* New York: International Universities Press.

Beck, A. T. (1986). Hopelessness as a predictor of eventual suicide. In J. J. Mann & M. Stanley (Eds.), *Psychobiology of suicidal behavior* (pp. 90–96). New York: Academy of Sciences.

Beck, A. T., Brown, G., & Steer, R. A. (1989). Prediction of eventual suicide in psychiatric inpatients by clinical ratings of hopelessness. *Journal of Consulting and Clinical Psychology, 57,* 309–310.

Beck, A. T., Rush, A. J., Shaw, B. F., & Emery, G. (1979). *Cognitive therapy of depression.* New York: Guilford Press.

Beck, A. T., & Steer, R. A. (1993). *Manual for the Beck Hopelessness Scale.* San Antonio, TX: Psychological Corporation.

Beitman, B. D. (1983). Categories of countertransference. *Journal of Operational Psychiatry, 14,* 82–90.

Belsher, G., & Wilkes, T. C. R. (1994). Ten key principles of adolescent cognitive therapy. In T. C. R. Wilkes, G. Belsher, A. J. Rush, & E. Frank (Eds.), *Cognitive therapy for depressed adolescents* (pp. 36–54). New York: Guilford Press.

Benjamin, A. (1981). *The helping interview* (3rd ed.). Boston: Houghton Mifflin.

Berman, A. L., & Jobes, D. A. (1991). *Adolescent suicide: Assessment and intervention.* Washington, DC: American Psychological Association.

Bettleheim, B. (1977). *The uses of enchantment: The meaning and importance of fairy tales.* New York: Vintage Books.

Bienert, H., & Schneider, B. H. (1993). Deficit-specific social skills training with peer-nominated aggressive–disruptive and sensitive–isolated preadolescents. *Journal of Applied Developmental Psychology,24,* 287–299.

Bornstein, P. H., & Bornstein, M. T. (1986). *Marital therapy: A behavioral–communications approach.* New York: Pergamon Press.

Bowlby, J. (1977). The making and breaking of affectional bonds. *British Journal of Psychiatry, 130,* 201–210.

Bowlby, J. (1988). *A secure base.* New York: Basic Books.

Bradford, E., & Lyddon, W. J. (1994). Assessing adolescent and adult attachment: An update. *Journal of Counseling and Development, 73,* 215–219.

Brandell, J. R. (1984). Stories and storytelling in child psychotherapy. *Psychotherapy, 21,* 54–62.

Braun, L. A., Coplon, J. K., & Sonnenschein, P. C. (1984). *Helping parents in groups: A leader's handbook.* Boston: Wheelock College.

Brazelton, T. B. (1989). *Toddlers and parents.* New York: Delacorte Press.

Breggin, P. R., & Breggin, G. R. (1994). *Talking back to Prozac.* New York: St. Martins Press.

Brems, C. (1993). *A comprehensive guide to child psychotherapy.* Boston: Allyn & Bacon.

Brent, D. A. (1995). Risk factors for adolescent suicide and suicidal behavior: Mental and substance abuse disorders, family environmental factors, and life stress. *Suicide and Life-Threatening Behavior, 25,* 52–63.

Brent, D. A., Perper, J. A., Moritz, G., Baugher, M., Roth, C., Balach, L., & Schweers, J. (1993). Stressful life events, psychopathology, and adolescent suicide: A case-control study. *Suicide and Life-Threatening Behavior, 23,* 179–187.

Brofenbrenner, U. (1977). Toward an experimental ecology of human development. *American Psychologist, 32,* 513–531.

Brofenbrenner, U. (1979). *The ecology of human development.* Cambridge, MA: Harvard University Press.

Brofenbrenner, U. (1986). Ecology of the family as a context for human development: Research perspectives. *Developmental Psychology, 22,* 723–742.

Burns, D. (1989). *The feeling good handbook.* New York: Morrow.

Butcher, J. N., Williams, C. L., Graham, J. R., Archer, R. P., Tellegen, A., Ben-Porath, J. S., & Kaemmer, B. (1992). *MMPI-A: Manual for administration, scoring and interpretation.* Minneapolis: University of Minnesota Press.

Campbell, J. D., Manksch, H. O., Neikirk, H. H., & Hosakawa, M. C. (1990). Collaborative practice and provider styles of delivering health care. *Social Science and Medicine, 30,* 1359–1365.

Canino, I. A., & Spurlock, J. (1994). *Culturally diverse children and adolescents: Assessment, diagnosis, and treatment.* New York: Guilford Press.

Capuzzi, D. (1994). *Suicide prevention in the schools: Guidelines for middle and high school settings.* Alexandria, VA: American Counseling Association.

Carlson, G. A., & Garber, J. (1986). Developmental issues in the classification of depression in children. In M. Rutter, C. E. Izard, & P. B. Read (Eds.), *Depression in young people: Developmental and clinical perspectives* (pp. 399–434). New York: Guilford Press.

Caron, A. (1993). *Strong mothers, strong sons.* New York: Guilford Press.

Carver, C. S., & Scheier, M. F. (1981). *Attention and self-regulation: A control-theory approach to human behavior.* New York: Springer-Verlag.

Church, E. (1994). The role of autonomy in adolescent psychotherapy. *Psychotherapy, 31,* 101–108.

Cleary, B. (1975). *Ramona the brave.* New York: Dell.

Cohen, P., Cohen, J., Kasn, S., Velez, C. N., Hartmark, C., Johnson, J., Rojas, M., Brook, J., & Streuning, E. L. (1993). An epidemiological study of disorders in late childhood and adolescence: I. Age- and gender-specific prevalence. *Journal of Child Psychology and Psychiatry, 34,* 851–867.

Curry, J., & Craighead, W. E. (1990). Attributional style in clinical depression and conduct disordered adolescents. *Journal of Consulting and Clinical Psychology, 58,* 109–115.

Dahl, R. (1988). *Matilda.* New York: Puffin.

Davidson, M. W., Wagner, W. G., & Range, L. M. (1995). Clinicians' attitudes toward no-suicide agreements. *Suicide and Life-Threatening Behavior, 25,* 410–414.

Davis, J. (1986). Storytelling: Using the child as consultant. *Elementary School Guidance and Counseling, 21,* 89–92.

Deaux, K. (1993). Commentary: Sorry, wrong number: A reply to Gentile's call. *Psychological Science, 4,* 125–126.

Deci, E. L., & Ryan, R. M. (1980). The empirical exploration of intrinsic motivational processes. *Advances in Experimental Social Psychology, 13,* 40–82.

Diamond, G., & Liddle, H. A. (1996). Resolving a therapeutic impasse between parents and adolescents in multidimensional family therapy. *Journal of Consulting and Clinical Psychology, 64,* 481–488.

Dodge, K. A., & Frame, C. L. (1983). Social cognitive biases and deficits in aggressive boys. *Child Development, 53,* 620–635.

Dodge, K. A., & Somberg, D. R. (1987). Hostile attributional biases among aggressive boys are exacerbated under conditions of threat to the self. *Child Development, 58,* 213–224.

Donovan, J. M., Steinberg, S. M., & Sabin, J. E. (1994). Managed mental health care: An academic seminar. *Psychotherapy, 31,* 201–207.

Drye, R. D., Goulding, R. L., & Goulding, M. E. (1973). No-suicide decisions: Patient monitoring of suicidal risk. *American Journal of Psychiatry, 130,* 171–174.

Dupre, D., Miller, N., Gold, M., & Rospenda, K. (1995). Initiation and progression of alcohol, marijuana, and cocaine use among adolescent abusers. *American Journal on Addictions, 4,* 43–48.

Eagen, T. (1994, January 30). A Washington city full of Prozac. *New York Times,* p. 16.

Edwards, D. J. A. (1996). Case study research: The cornerstone of theory and practice. In M. A. Reinecke, F. M. Dattilio, & A. Freeman (Eds.), *Cognitive therapy with children and adolescents: A casebook for clinical practice.* New York: Guilford Press.

Ekman, P. (1989). *Why kids lie: How parents can encourage truthfulness.* New York: Penguin Books.

Elkind, D. (1984). *All grown up and no place to go: Teenagers in crisis.* Reading, MA: Addison-Wesley.

Ellis, A. (1988). *How to stubbornly refuse to make yourself miserable about anything, yes, anything!* New York: Carol Publishing.

Erickson, M. H., & Rossi, E. L. (1980). The indirect forms of suggestion. In E. L. Rossi (Ed.), *The collected papers of Milton H. Erickson on hypnosis: Vol. 1. The nature of hypnosis and suggestion* (pp. 452–477). New York: Irvington.

Erikson, E. (1968). *Identity: Youth and crisis.* New York: Norton.

Erickson, J. R. (1984). *The adventures of Hank the cowdog.* Houston, TX: Maverick Books.

Feindler, E. L., & Ecton, R. B. (1986). *Adolescent anger control: Cognitive behavioral strategies.* Elmsford, NY: Pergamon Press.

Fisher, R. L., & Fisher, S. (1996). Antidepressants for children: Is scientific support necessary? *Journal of Nervous and Mental Disease, 184,* 99–102.

Fisher, S., & Greenberg, R. P. (Eds.). (1989). *The limits of biological treatments for psychological distress.* Hillsdale, NJ: Erlbaum.

Fong, M. L., & Cox, B. G. (1983). Trust as an underlying dynamic in the counseling process: How clients test trust. *Personnel and Guidance Journal, 62,* 163–166.

Forgas, J. P. (1991). Affect and social perception: Research evidence and an integrative theory. In W. Stroebe & M. Newstone (Eds.), *European review of social psychology* (pp. 183–223). New York: Wiley.

Fox, R. E. (1995). The rape of psychotherapy. *Professional Psychology, 26,* 147–155.

Frank, J. D. (1979). The present status of outcome studies. *Journal of Consulting and Clinical Psychology, 47,* 310–316.

Fridrich, A. H., & Flannery, D. J. (1995). The effects of ethnicity and acculturation on early adolescent delinquency. *Journal of Child and Family Studies, 4,* 69–87.

Furnham, A. (1989). Personality and the acceptance of diagnostic feedback. *Personality and Individual Differences, 10,* 1121–1133.

Gardner, G. G. (1974). Parents: Obstacles or allies in child hypnotherapy? *The American Journal of Clinical Hypnosis, 17,* 44–49.

Gardner, G. G., & Olness, K. (1981). *Hypnosis and hypnotherapy with children.* New York: Grune & Stratton.

Gardner, R. A. (1971). *Therapeutic storytelling with children: The mutual storytelling technique.* New York: Jason Aronson.

Garland, A. F., & Zigler, E. (1993). Adolescent suicide prevention: Current research and social policy implications. *American Psychologist, 48,* 169–182.

Garrison, C. A., Jackson, K. L., Addy, C. L., McKeown, R. E., & Waller, J. L. (1991). Suicidal behaviors in young adolescents. *American Journal of Epidemiology, 133,* 1005–1014.

Garstang, W. (1922). The theory of recapitulation: A critical restatement of the biogenetic law. *Journal of the Linnaean Society, Zoology, 35,* 81–101.

Gaylin, N. L. (1989). Ipsative measures: In search of paradigmatic change and a science of subjectivity. *Person-Centered Review, 4,* 429–445.

George, M. S. (1994). Introduction: The emerging neuroanatomy of depression. *Psychiatric Annals, 24,* 635–636.

Gibson, P. (1994). Gay male and lesbian youth suicide. In M. R. Feinleib (Ed.), *Report of the secretary's task force on youth suicide: Vol. 3. Prevention and interventions in youth suicide* (pp. 110–142). Rockville, MD: U.S. Department of Health and Human Services.

Ginott, H. (1969). *Between parent and teenager.* New York: Avon.

Gittleman-Klein, R. (1987). Pharmacotherapy of childhood hyperactivity: An update. In H. Y. Meltzer (Ed.), *Psychopharmacology: The third generation of progress* (pp. 1215–1224). New York: Raven Press.

Goldman, L. (1972). Tests and counseling: A better way. *Measurement and Evaluation in Guidance, 15,* 70–73.

Goldstein, A. P. (1988). *The Prepare curriculum: Teaching prosocial competencies.* Chicago, IL: Research Press.

Goldstein, A. P., Glick, B., Reiner, S., Zimmerman, D., & Coultry, T. M. (1987). *Aggression replacement training: A comprehensive intervention for aggressive youth.* Champaign, IL: Research Press.

Gordon, M. (1991). *ADHD/Hyperactivity: A manual for parents and teachers.* Dewitt, NY: GSI Publications.

Gorin, S. S. (1993). The prediction of child psychotherapy outcome: Factors specific to treatment. *Psychotherapy, 30,* 152–158.

Gottman, J. M. (1979). *Marital interactions: Experimental investigations.* San Diego, CA: Academic Press.

Gottman, J. M., & Krokoff, L. J. (1989). Marital interaction and satisfaction: A longitudinal view. *Journal of Consulting and Clinical Psychology, 57,* 47–52.

Greenhill, L. L. (1992). Pharmacologic treatment of attention deficit hyperactivity disorder. *Psychiatric Clinics of North America, 15,* 1–27.

Greenson, R. R. (1967). *The technique and practice of psychoanalysis* (Vol. 1). New York: International Universities Press.

Gustafson, K. E., McNamara, J. R., & Jensen, J. A. (1994). Parents' informed consent decisions regarding psychotherapy for their children: Consideration of therapeutic risks and benefits. *Professional Psychology: Research and Practice, 25,* 16–22.

Haeckel, E. (1874). *Anthropogenie.* Berlin: Georg Reimer.

Hancock, L. (1996, March 18). Mother's little helper. *Newsweek, 127,* 50–56.

Handelsman, M. M., & Glavin, M. D. (1988). Facilitating informed consent for outpatient psychotherapy: A suggested written format. *Professional Psychology: Research and Practice, 19,* 223–225.

Harrington, R. (1993). *Depressive disorder in childhood and adolescence.* Chichester, U.K.: Wiley.

Hazan, C., & Shaver, P. R. (1987). Romantic love conceptualized as an attachment process. *Journal of Personality and Social Psychology, 59,* 270–280.

Henggeler, S. W., Melton, G. B., & Smith, L. A. (1992). Family preservation using multisystemic therapy: An effective alternative to incarcerating serious juvenile offenders. *Journal of Consulting and Clinical Psychology, 60,* 953–961.

Hibbs, E. D., & Jensen, P. S. (1996). *Psychosocial treatments for child and adolescent disorders.* Washington, DC: American Psychological Association.

Holmes, C. B., & Wiederhold, J. (1982). Depression and figure size on the Draw-A-Person test. *Perceptual and Motor Skills, 55,* 825–826.

Holmgren, V. S. (1996). *Elementary school counseling: An expanding role.* Boston: Allyn & Bacon.

Houser, R., Daniels, J., D'Andrea, M., & Konstam, V. (1993). A systematic behaviorally based technique for resolving conflicts between adolescents and their single parents. *Child and Family Behavior Therapy, 15,* 17–31.

Huston, A. C., Donnerstein, E., Fairchild, Feshbach, N. D., Katz, P. A., Murray, J. P., Rubinstein, E. A., Wilcox, B. L., & Zuckerman, D. (1992). *Big world, small screen: The role of television in American society.* Lincoln, NE: University of Nebraska Press.

Isen, A. M. (1987). Positive affect, cognitive processes, and social behavior. In L. Berkowitz (Ed.), *Advances in experimental social psychology* (Vol. 20, pp. 203–253). New York: Academic Press.

Ivey, A. E. (1986). *Developmental therapy: Theory into practice.* San Francisco: Jossey-Bass.

Ivey, A. E. (1991). *Developmental strategies for helpers.* Pacific Grove, CA: Brooks/Cole.

Jacobs, B. L. (1994). Serotonin, motor activity, and depression-related disorders. *American Scientist, 82,* 456–463.

Jacobson, L. K., Rabinowitz, I., Popper, M. S., Solomon, R. J., Sokol, M. S., & Pfeffer, C. R. (1994). Interviewing prepubertal children about suicidal ideation and behavior. *Journal of the Academy of Child and Adolescent Psychiatry, 33,* 439–452.

Joffe, R. T., Offord, D. R., & Boyle, M. H. (1988). Ontario child health study: Suicidal behavior in youth ages 12–16 years. *American Journal of Psychiatry, 145,* 1420–1423.

Kaplan, S. L., Simms, R. M., & Busner, J. (1994). Prescribing practices of outpatient child psychiatrists. *Journal of the Academy of Child and Adolescent Psychiatry, 33,* 35–40.

Kashani, J. H., Goddard, P., & Reid, J. C. (1989). Correlates of suicide ideation in a community sample of children and adolescents. *Journal of the Academy of Child and Adolescent Psychiatry, 28,* 912–917.

Kashani, J. H., Hodges, K. K., & Shekim, W. O. (1980). Hypomanic reaction to amitriptyline in a depressed child. *Psychosomatics, 21,* 867–872.

Kashani, J. H., Reid, J., & Rosenberg, T. (1989). Levels of hopelessness in children and adolescents: A developmental perspective. *Journal of Consulting and Clinical Psychology, 57,* 496–499.

Kazdin, A. E. (1988). Child psychotherapy: Developing effective treatments. New York: Pergamon Press.

Kazdin, A. E. (1995). *Conduct disorder in childhood and adolescence* (2nd ed.). Thousand Oaks, CA: Sage.

Kazdin, A. E. (1996). Problem solving and parent management in treating aggressive and antisocial behavior. In E. D. Hibbs & P. S. Jensen (Eds.), *Psychosocial treatments for child and adolescent disorders* (pp. 377–408). Washington, DC: American Psychological Association.

Kernberg, P. F., & Chazan, S. E. (1991). *Children with conduct disorders.* New York: Basic Books.

Kestenbaum, C. J. (1985). The creative process in child psychotherapy. *American Journal of Psychotherapy, 39,* 479–489.

Kimmel, E. A. (1989). *Charlie drives the stage.* New York: Holiday House.

King, R. A., Riddle, R. A., Chappell, P., Hardin, M. T., Anderson, G. M., Lombroso, P., & Scahill, L. (1991). Emergence of self-destructive phenomena in children and adolescents during fluoxetine treatment. *Journal of the American Academy of Child and Adolescent Psychiatry, 30,* 179–186.

Kleepsies, P. M. (1993). Stress of patient suicidal behavior: Implications for interns and training programs in psychology. *Professional Psychology, 24,* 477–482.

Kohen, D. P., & Olness, K. (1984). The use of relaxation–mental imagery (self-hypnosis) in the management of 505 pediatric behavioral encounters. *Journal of Developmental and Behavioral Pediatrics, 5,* 21–25.

Koppitz, E. M. (1968). *Psychological evaluation of children's human figure drawings.* New York: Grune & Stratton.

Kovacs, M., & Paulaukas, S. L. (1984). Developmental stage and the expression of depressive disorders in children: An empirical analysis. *New Directions for Child Development, 26,* 59–80.

Kramer, P. D. (1993). *Listening to Prozac.* New York: Viking.

Kronenberger, W. G., & Meyer, R. G. (1996). *The child clinician's handbook.* Boston: Allyn & Bacon.

Ladd, G. W. (1984). Social skill training with children: Issues in research and practice. *Clinical Psychology Review, 4,* 307–337.

Lambert, M. J. (1989). The individual therapist's contribution to psychotherapy process and outcome. *Clinical Psychology Review, 9,* 469–485.

Lankton, C. H., & Lankton, S. R. (1989). *Tales of enchantment: Goal-oriented metaphors for adults and children in therapy.* New York: Brunner/Mazel.

Lawson, D. (1987). Using therapeutic stories in the counseling process. *Elementary School Guidance and Counseling, 22,* 134–142.

Lempers, J. D., Flavell, E. R., & Flavell, J. H. (1977). The development in very young of tacit knowledge concerning visual perception. *Genetic Psychology Monographs, 95,* 3–53.

L'Engle, M. (1962). *A wrinkle in time.* New York: Dell.

Lepper, M. R., Greene, D., & Nisbett, R. E. (1973). Undermining children's intrinsic interest with extrinsic reward: A test of the "overjustification" hypothesis. *Journal of Personality and Social Psychology, 28,* 129–137.

Lerner, R. M. (1990). Plasticity, person–context relations and cognitive training in the aged years: A developmental contextual perspective. *Developmental Psychology, 26,* 911–915.

Lewinsohn, P. M., Rohde, P., & Seeley, J. R. (1994). Psychosocial risk factors for future adolescent suicide attempts. *Journal of Consulting and Clinical Psychology, 62,* 297–305.

Lickliter, R., & Berry, T. D. (1990). The phylogeny fallacy: Developmental psychology's misapplication of evolutionary theory. *Developmental Review, 10,* 348–364.

Littrell, J., & Ashford, J. B. (1995). Is it proper for psychologists to discuss medications with clients? *Professional Psychology: Research and Practice, 26,* 238–244.

Lively, P. (1989). Moon tiger. New York: Harper & Row.

Locke, E. A., Shaw, K. N., Saari, L. M., & Latham, G. P. (1981). Goal setting and task performance: 1969–1980. *Psychological Bulletin, 90,* 125–152.

Loeber, R., Lahey, B., & Thomas, C. (1991). Diagnostic conundrum of oppositional defiant disorder and conduct disorder. *Journal of Abnormal Psychology, 100,* 379–390.

Loftus, E. F. (1992). When a lie becomes memory's truth: Memory distortion after exposure to misinformation. *Current Directions in Psychological Science, 1,* 121–123.

Long, P., Forehand, R., Wierson, M., & Morgan, A. (1994). Does parent training with young noncompliant children have long-term effects? *Behaviour Research and Therapy, 32,* 101–107.

Luborsky, L. (1984). *Psychoanalytic psychotherapy: A manual of supportive/expressive techniques.* New York: Basic Books.

MacDonald, B. (1947). *Mrs. Piggle-Wiggle.* New York: Scholastic.

MacDonald, B. (1957). *Hello, Mrs. Piggle-Wiggle.* New York: Scholastic.

Machover, K. (1949). *Personality projection in the drawings of the human figure.* Springfield, IL: Thomas.

Mahler, M. (1972). On the first three subphases of the separation–individuation process. *International Journal of Psychoanalysis, 53,* 333–338.

Mahoney, M. J. (1990, November). Developmental psychotherapy. Workshop presented at the 24th annual meeting of the Association for the Advancement of Behavior Therapy, San Francisco.

Mahoney, M. J. (1991). *Human change processes.* New York: Basic Books.

March, J. S., Mulle, K., & Herbel, B. (1994). Behavioral psychotherapy for children and adolescents with obsessive–compulsive disorder: An open trial of a new protocol-driven treatment package. *Journal of the American Academy of Child and Adolescent Psychiatry, 33,* 333–341.

Maris, R. W., Berman, A. L., Maltsberger, J. T., & Yufit, R. I. (1992). Assessment and prediction of suicide. New York: Guilford Press.

Martin, S. (1995, September). APA to pursue prescription privileges. *APA Monitor,* p. 6.

McGee, R., Feehan, M., Williams, S., Partridge, F., Silva, P. A., & Kelly, C. P. (1990). DSM-III disorders in a large sample of adolescents. *Journal of the American Academy of Child and Adolescent Psychiatry, 29,* 611–619.

Meeks, J. E. (1980). *The fragile alliance* (2nd ed.). New York: Robert E. Krieger.

Mehan, P. J., Lamb, J. A., Saltzman, L. E., & O'Carroll, P. W. (1992). Attempted suicide among young adults: Progress toward a meaningful estimate of prevalence. *American Journal of Psychiatry, 149,* 41–44.

Meier, S. T., & Davis, S. (1996). *The elements of counseling* (3rd ed.). Pacific Grove, CA: Brooks/Cole.

Miller, M. (1985). *Information Center: Training workshop manual.* San Diego, CA: The Information Center.

Miller, T. (1995). *Investigating early adolescents' reluctance to see the school counselor.* Unpublished doctoral dissertation, University of Montana, Missoula.

Minuchin, S., & Fishman, H. (1981). *Family therapy techniques.* Cambridge: Harvard University Press.

Mishne, J. (1986). *Clinical work with adolescents.* New York: Free Press.

Muehrer, P. (1995). Suicide and sexual orientation: A critical summary of recent research and directions for future research. *Suicide and Life-Threatening Behavior, 25,* 72–81.

Mufson, L., Moreau, D., Weissman, M. M., & Klerman, G. L. (1993). *Interpersonal psychotherapy for depressed adolescents.* New York: Guilford Press.

Neisser, U. (1991). A case of misapplied nostalgia. *American Psychologist, 46,* 34–36.

Nelson, J. C. (1994). Are the SSRIs really better tolerated than the TCAs for treatment of major depression? *Psychiatric Annals, 24,* 628–631.

Newman, C. F. (1994). Understanding client resistance: Methods for enhancing motivation to change. *Cognitive and Behavioral Practice, 1,* 47–69.

Novaco, R. W. (1979). The cognitive regulation of anger and stress. In P. C. Kendall & S. D. Hollon (Eds.), *Cognitive– behavioral interventions: Theory, research and procedures.* New York: Academic Press.

Olness, K., & Gardner, G. G. (1988). *Hypnosis and hypnotherapy with children* (2nd ed.). Orlando, FL: Harcourt Brace Jovanovich.

Orbach, I., Lotem-Peleg, M., & Kedem, P. (1995). Attitudes toward the body in suicidal, depressed, and normal adolescents. *Suicide and Life-Threatening Behavior, 25,* 211–221.

Olweus, D. (1979). Stability of aggressive reaction patterns in males: A review. *Psychological Bulletin, 86,* 852–875.

Patterson, C. H. (1996). Multicultural counseling: From diversity to universality. *Journal of Counseling and Development, 74,* 227–231.

Patterson, G. R. (1982). *Coercive family process.* Eugene, OR: Castalia.

Patterson, G. R., Reid, J. B., & Dishion, T. J. (1992). *Antisocial boys.* Eugene, OR: Castalia.

Pedersen, P. B. (1990). The multicultural perspective as a fourth force in counseling. *Journal of Mental Health Counseling, 12,* 93–95.

Pedersen, P. B. (1991). Multiculturalism as a generic approach to counseling. *Journal of Counseling and Development, 70,* 6–12.

Pedersen, P. B., & Ivey, A. E. (1993). *Culture-centered counseling and interviewing skills: A practical guide.* Westport, CT: Praeger.

Peterson, A. C., Compas, B. E., Brooks-Gunn, J., Stemmler, M., Ey, S., & Grant, K. E. (1993). Depression in adolescence. *American Psychologist, 48,* 155–168.

Peterson, J. V., & Nisenholz, B. (1987). *Orientation to counseling.* Boston: Allyn & Bacon.

Pfeffer, C. R., Klerman, G. L., Hurt, S. W., Lesser, M., Peskin, J. R., & Siefker, C. A. (1991). Suicidal children grow up: Demographic and clinical risk factors for adolescent suicide attempts. *Journal of the American Academy of Child and Adolescent Psychiatry, 30,* 609–616.

Piaget, J. (1965). *The moral judgment of the child.* New York: Free Press. (Original work published 1932)

Piaget, J. (1975). *The child's conception of the world.* Totowa, NJ: Littlefield, Adams. (Original work published 1929)

Pipher, M. (1994). *Reviving Ophelia: Saving the selves of adolescent girls.* New York: G. P. Putman's Sons.

Plotkin, R. (1981). When rights collide: Parents, children, and consent to treatment. *Journal of Pediatric Psychology, 6,* 121–130.

Popper, C. W., & Elliot, G. R. (1990). Sudden death and tricyclic antidepressants: Clinical considerations for children. *Journal of Child and Adolescent Psychopharmacology, 1,* 125–132.

Puig-Antich, J., Perel, J., Lupatkin, W., Chambers, W. J., Tabrizi, M. A., King, J., Goetz, R., Davies, M., & Stiller, R. L. (1987). Imipramine in prepubertal major depressive disorders. *Archives of General Psychiatry, 44,* 81–89.

Quay, H. C. (1966). Personality patterns in preadolescent delinquent boys. *Educational Psychological Measurement, 16,* 99–110.

Quay, H. C. (1986). The behavioral reward and inhibition systems in childhood behavior disorder. In L. M. Bloomingdale (Ed.), *Attention deficit disorder* (Vol. 3). New York: Spectrum.

Quay, H. C. (1987). Patterns of delinquent behavior. In H. C. Quay (Ed.), *Handbook of juvenile delinquency* (pp. 118–138). New York: Wiley.

Rapoport, J. L., Swedo, S. E., & Leonard, H. L. (1992). Childhood obsessive compulsive disorder. *Journal of Clinical Psychiatry, 53,* 6–11.

Raymond, D. D., Dowrick, P. W., & Kleinke, C. L. (1993). Affective responses to seeing oneself for the first time on unedited videotape. *Counseling Psychology Quarterly, 6,* 193–200.

Reynolds, C. R. (1978). A quick scoring guide to the interpretation of children's Kinetic Family Drawings (KFD). *Psychology in the Schools, 15,* 489-492.

Ricci, I. (1980). *Mom's house, dad's house: Making shared custody work.* New York: MacMillan.

Riddle, M. A., King, R. A., Hardin, M. T., Scahill, L., Ort, S. I., Chappell, P., Rasmusson, A., & Leckman, J. F. (1990–1991). Behavioral side effects of fluoxetine in children and adolescents. *Journal of Child and Adolescent Psychopharmacology, 1,* 193–198.

Robins, L. N. (1991). Conduct disorder. *Journal of Child Psychology and Psychiatry, 32,* 193–212.

Rogers, C. R. (1957). The necessary and sufficient conditions of therapeutic personality change. *Journal of Consulting Psychology, 21,* 95–103.

Rogers, C. R., & Meador, B. (1984). Client-centered therapy. In R. Corsini & D. Wedding (Eds.), *Current psychotherapies* (pp. 89–126). New York: Peacock.

Rohde, P., Lewinsohn, P. M., & Seeley, J. R. (1991). Comorbidity of unipolar depression: 2. Comorbidity with other mental disorders in adolescents and adults. *Journal of Abnormal Psychology, 100,* 214–222.

Rosenberg, D. R., Holttum, J., & Gershon, S. (1994). *Textbook of pharmacotherapy for child and adolescent psychiatric disorders.* New York: Brunner/Mazel.

Rotheram, M. J., & Phinney, J. S. (1986). Introduction: Definitions and perspectives in the study of children's ethnic socialization. In J. S. Phinney & M. J. Rotheram (Eds.), *Children's ethnic socialization: Pluralism and development* (pp. 10–28). Newbury Park, CA: Sage.

Rotheram-Borus, M. J., Piacentini, J., Miller, S., Sutherland, M., Graae, F., & Castro-Blanco, D. (1994). Brief cognitive–behavioral treatment for adolescent suicide attempters and their families. *Journal of the American Academy of Child and Adolescent Psychiatry, 33,* 508–517.

Rutter, M. (1979). Protective factors in children's responses to stress and disadvantage. In M. W. Kent and J. E. Rolf (Eds.), *Primary prevention of psychopathology: Vol. 3. Social competence in children* (pp. 49–74). Hanover, NH: University Press of New England.

Rutter, M., & Giller, H. (1983). *Juvenile delinquency.* New York: Guilford Press.

Rutter, M., & Rutter, M. (1993). *Developing minds.* New York: Basic Books.

Ryan, N. D. (1990). Pharmacotherapy of adolescent major depression: Beyond TCAs. *Psychopharmacology Bulletin, 26,* 75–79.

Ryan, N. D., Meyer, V., Dachille, S., Mazzie, D., & Puig-Antich, J. (1988). Lithium antidepressant augmentation in TCA-refractory depression in adolescents. *Journal of the American Academy of Child and Adolescent Psychiatry, 27,* 371–376.

Ryan, N. D., Puig-Antich, J., Ambrosini, P., Rabinovich H., Robinson, D., Nelson, B., Iyengar, S., & Twomey, J. (1987). The clinical picture of major depression in children and adolescents. *Archives of General Psychiatry, 44,* 854–861.

Ryan, R. M. (1983). Control and information in the intrapersonal sphere: An extension of cognitive evaluation theory. *Journal of Personality and Social Psychology, 43,* 450–461.

Safran, J. D. (1993). Breaches in the therapeutic alliance: An arena for negotiating authentic relatedness. *Psychotherapy, 30,* 11–24.

Sanua, V. D. (1995). "Prescription privileges" vs. psychologists' authority: Psychologists do better without drugs. *The Humanistic Psychologist, 23,* 187–212.

Satir, V. (1972). *Peoplemaking.* Palo Alto, CA: Science and Behavior books.

Schaeffer, C. E., & Briesmeister, J. M. (1989). *Handbook of parent training.* New York: Wiley.

Selekman, M. D. (1993). *Pathways to change: Brief therapy solutions with difficult adolescents.* New York: Guilford Press.

Semrud-Clikeman, M. (1995). *Child and adolescent therapy.* Boston: Allyn & Bacon.

Shaffer, D., Fisher, P., Hicks, R. H., Parides, M., & Gould, M. (1995). Sexual orientation in adolescents who commit suicide. *Suicide and Life-Threatening Behavior, 25,* 64–71.

Shafii, M., Carrigan, S., Whittinghill, J. R., & Derrick, A. M. (1985). Psychological autopsy of completed suicide in children and adolescents. *American Journal of Psychiatry, 142,* 1061–1064.

Shirk, S., & Harter, S. (1996). Treatment of low self-esteem. In M. A. Reineke, F. M. Dattilio, & A. Freeman (Eds.), *Cognitive therapy with children and adolescents: A casebook for clinical practice* (pp. 175–198). New York: Guilford Press.

Shure, M. B. (1992). *I can problem solve: An interpersonal cognitive problem-solving program.* Champaign, IL: Research Press.

Sidman, M. (1989). *Coercion and its fallout.* Boston: Authors Cooperative, Inc.

Silva, R. R., Munoz, D. M., & Alpert, M. (1996). Carbamazepine use on children and adolescents with features of attention-deficit hyperactivity disorder: A meta-analysis. *Journal of the American Academy of Child and Adolescent Psychiatry, 35,* 352–358.

Sims, J., Dana, R., & Bolton, B. (1983). The validity of the Draw-A-Person as an anxiety measure. *Journal of Personality Assessment, 47,* 250–257.

Smith, D., & Dumont, F. (1995). A cautionary study: Unwarranted interpretations of the Draw-A-Person Test. *Professional Psychology, 26,* 298–303.

Sommers-Flanagan, J. (1995, September 28). Correcting your child's chemical imbalance? *The Missoula Independent,* p. 5.

Sommers-Flanagan, J., & Sommers-Flanagan, R. (1993). *Foundations of therapeutic interviewing.* Boston: Allyn & Bacon.

Sommers-Flanagan, J., & Sommers-Flanagan, R. (1995a). Intake interviewing with suicidal patients: A systematic approach. *Professional Psychology, 26,* 41–47.

Sommers-Flanagan, J., & Sommers-Flanagan, R. (1995b). Psychotherapeutic techniques with treatment-resistant adolescents. *Psychotherapy, 32,* 131–140.

Sommers-Flanagan, J., & Sommers-Flanagan, R. (1995c). Rapid emotional change strategies: Enhancing youth responsiveness to cognitive-behavioral therapy. *Child and Family Behavior Therapy, 17,* 11–22.

Sommers-Flanagan, J., & Sommers-Flanagan, R. (1996a). Counseling difficult adolescents. *Directions in Clinical and Counseling Psychology, 6,* 1–16.

Sommers-Flanagan, J., & Sommers-Flanagan, R. (1996b). The efficacy of antidepressant medications with depressed youth: What psychologists should know. *Professional Psychology, 31,* 145–153.

Sommers-Flanagan, J., & Sommers-Flanagan, R. (1996c). The wizard of Oz metaphor in hypnosis with treatment-resistant children. *American Journal of Clinical Hypnosis, 39,* 105–114.

Sommers-Flanagan, J., & Sommers-Flanagan, R. (in press). Problems and solutions associated with assessment and diagnosis of conduct disorder. *Journal of Counseling and Development.*

Sommers-Flanagan, R., Sommers-Flanagan, J., & Davis, B. (1993). What's new on Music Television? *Sex Roles, 28,* 745–753.

Spencer, T., Biederman, J., Wilens, T., Harding, M., O'Donnell, D., & Griffin, S. (1996). Pharmacotherapy of attention-deficit hyperactivity disorder across the life-cycle. *Journal of the American Academy of Child and Adolescent Psychiatry, 35,* 409–432.

Spiegal, S. (1989). *An interpersonal approach to child therapy.* New York: Columbia University.

Spivack, G., & Shure, M. B. (1982). The cognition of social adjustment: Interpersonal cognitive problem solving thinking. In B. B. Lahey & A. E. Kazdin (Eds.), *Advances in clinical child psychology* (Vol. 5, pp. 323–372). New York: Plenum Press.

Spivack, G., Platt, J. J., & Shure, M. B. (1976). *The problem-solving approach to adjustment.* San Francisco: Jossey-Bass.

Steenbarger, B. (1992). Toward science-practice integration in brief counseling and therapy. *The Counseling Psychologist, 20,* 403–430.

Steenbarger, B. (1994). Duration and outcome in psychotherapy: An integrative review. *Professional Psychology: Research and Practice, 25,* 111–119.

Steinberg, L., & Levine, A. (1990). *You and your adolescent: A parent's guide to ages 10–20.* New York: Harper Perennial.

Stern, S. (1993). Managed care, brief therapy, and therapeutic integrity. *Psychotherapy, 30,* 162–175.

Strober, M., Freeman, R., Rigali, J., Schmidt, S., & Diamond, R. (1992). The pharmacotherapy of depressive illness in adolescence: II. Effects of lithium augmentation in nonresponders to imipramine. *Journal of the American Academy of Child and Adolescent Psychiatry, 31,* 16–20.

Strupp, H. H., & Binder, J. L. (1984). *Psychotherapy in a new key: A guide to time-limited dynamic psychotherapy.* New York: Basic Books.

Sue, D. W. (1991). A model for cultural diversity training. *Journal of Counseling and Development, 70,* 99–105.

Szapocznik, J., Kurtines, W., Santisteban, D. A., & Rio, A. T. (1990). Interplay of advances between theory, research, and application in treatment interventions aimed at behavior problem children and adolescents. *Journal of Consulting and Clinical Psychology, 58,* 696–703.

Tannen, D. (1990). *You just don't understand.* New York: Ballantine Books.

Tavris, C. (1989). *Anger: The misunderstood emotion* (rev. ed.). New York: Touchstone Books.

Tavris, C. (1992). *The mismeasure of women.* New York: Simon & Schuster.

Tharinger, D. J., & Stark, K. (1990). A qualitative versus quantitative approach to evaluating the Draw-A-Person and Kinetic Family drawing: A study of mood- and anxiety-disordered children. *Psychological Assessment, 2,* 365–375.

Thompson, C. L., & Rudolph, L. B. (1992). *Counseling children* (4th ed.). Pacific Grove, CA: Brooks/Cole.

Thoreau, H. D. (1962). *Walden and other writings.* New York: Bantam.

Tisdelle, D. A., & St. Lawrence, J. S. (1988). Adolescent interpersonal problem-solving skill training: Social validation and generalization. *Behavior Therapy, 19,* 171–182.

Vygotsky, L. S. (1987). Thinking and speech. In R. W. Rieber, A. S. Carton (Eds.), & N. Minick (Trans.), *The collected works of L. S. Vygotsky: Vol 1. Problems of general psychology* (pp. 37–285). New York: Plenum. (Original work published 1934)

Wallas, L. (1985). *Stories for the third ear: Using hypnotic fables in psychotherapy.* New York: Norton.

Walsh, B. T., Giardina, E. V., Sloan, R. P., Greenhill, L., & Goldfein, J. (1994). Effects of desipramine on autonomic control of the heart. *Journal of the Academy of Child and Adolescent Psychiatry, 33,* 191–197.

Watkins, J. G. (1987). *Hypnotherapeutic techniques.* New York: Irvington.

Webster-Stratton, C. H. (1996). Early intervention with videotape modeling: Programs with oppositional defiant disorder or conduct disorder. In E. D. Hibbs & P. S. Jensen (Eds.), *Psychosocial treatments for child and adolescent disorders* (pp. 435–474). Washington, DC: American Psychological Association.

Weinberg, W. A., Rutman, J., Sullivan, L., Penick, E. C., & Dietz, S. G. (1973). Depression in children referred to an educational diagnostic center: Diagnosis and treatment. *Journal of Pediatrics, 83,* 1065–1072.

Weiner, I. B. (1975). *Principles of psychotherapy.* New York: Wiley.

Weiner, I. B. (1992). *Psychological disturbance in adolescence* (2nd ed.). New York: Wiley.

Weisz, J. R., Donenberg, D. L., Han, B. B., & Weiss, B. (in press). Bridging the gap between lab and clinic in child and adolescent psychotherapy. *Journal of Consulting and Clinical Psychology.*

Wells, K., & Forehand, R. (1985). Conduct and oppositional disorders. In P. Bornstein & A. E. Kazdin (Eds.), *Handbook of clinical behavior therapy with children* (pp. 218–265). Homewood, IL: Dorsey Press.

Wester, W. C., & O'Grady, D. J. (1991). *Clinical hypnosis with children.* New York: Brunner/Mazel.

Whiting, B. B., & Whiting, J. W. (1975). *Children of six cultures: A psycho-cultural analysis.* Cambridge, MA: Harvard University Press.

Wilkes, T. C. R., Belsher, G., Rush, A. J., & Frank, E. (1994). *Cognitive therapy with depressed adolescents.* New York: Guilford Press.

Williams, L. (1995). This sweet old world. [Recorded by Emmy Lou Harris]. On *Wrecking Ball* [CD]. New York: Warner Tamerlane Publishing, BMI.

Willock, B. (1986). Narcissistic vulnerability in the hyper-aggressive child: The disregarded (unloved, uncared-for) self. *Psychoanalytic Psychology, 3,* 59–80.

Willock, B. (1987). The devalued (unloved, repugnant) self: A second facet of narcissistic vulnerability in the aggressive, conduct-disordered child. *Psychoanalytic Psychology, 4,* 219–240.

Wilson, K. G., Stelzer, J., Bergman, J. N., Kral, M. J., Inayatullah, M., & Elliott, C. A. (1995). Problem-solving, stress, and coping and adolescent suicide attempts. *Suicide and Life-Threatening Behavior, 25,* 241–252.

Wohl, J. (1989). Cross-cultural psychotherapy. In P. B. Pedersen, K. G. Draguns, W. J. Lonner, & J. E. Trimble (Eds.), *Counseling across cultures* (pp. 79–113). Honolulu, HI: University of Hawaii Press.

Wollersheim, J. P. (1974). The assessment of suicide potential via interview methods. *Psychotherapy, 11,* 222–225.

Wolpe, J. (1958). *Psychotherapy by reciprocal inhibition.* Stanford, CA: Stanford University Press.

Wright, J. H., & Davis, D. (1994). The therapeutic relationship in cognitive-behavioral therapy: Patient perceptions and therapist responses. *Cognitive and Behavioral Practice, 1,* 25–46.

Wyatt, R. C., & Livson, N. (1994). The not so great divide? Psychologist and psychiatrists take stands on the medical and psychosocial models of mental illness. *Professional Psychology: Research and Practice, 25,* 120–131.

Zarb, J. M. (1992). *Cognitive-behavioral assessment and therapy with adolescents.* New York: Brunner/Mazel.

INDEX